SEPARATED BRETHREN

We must get to know the outlook of our separated brethren. Study is absolutely required for this, and it should be pursued in fidelity to truth and with a spirit of good will. Catholics, who already have a proper grounding, need to acquire a more adequate understanding of the respective doctrines of our separated brethren, their history, their spiritual and liturgical life, their religious psychology and cultural background.

The Decree on Ecumenism of the Second Vatican Council

SEPARATED BRETHREN

A Survey of Protestant, Anglican, Orthodox,
Old Catholic, and Other Denominations
in the United States

(*Revised and Enlarged*)

by WILLIAM J. WHALEN

Our Sunday Visitor, Inc.
Noll Plaza, Huntington, Indiana 46750

Nihil Obstat:

REV. LAWRENCE GOLLNER
Censor Librorum

Imprimatur:

✠**LEO A. PURSLEY, D.D.**
Bishop of Fort Wayne-South Bend

ISBN 0-87973-841-3
Library of Congress Catalog Card Number: 70-177998
Printed and bound in the U.S.A. by Our Sunday Visitor, Inc.
Noll Plaza, Huntington, Indiana 46750

CONTENTS

PREFACE

THIS VOLUME is intended to offer American Catholic readers a survey of Protestant, Anglican, Eastern Orthodox, and Old Catholic churches and sects in the United States. Additional chapters have been included on the Jews, Mormons, Christian Scientists, Baha'is, Muslims, Buddhists, and other religious groups.

Since 1958 when the first edition of *Separated Brethren* was published, the Catholic world has witnessed the far reaching impact of the Second Vatican Council and the Church's growing involvement in the ecumenical movement. These changes have been reflected in the thorough revision of each denominational description.

The two introductory chapters present an overview of American religious life and the basic theological differences between Catholicism and Protestantism. This was done to avoid restating fundamental Protestant principles such as the sole sufficiency of the Bible in subsequent chapters on particular denominations. Those who wish to use this book as a handbook for reference will want to keep this in mind. The chapters on denominations outline the history, doctrine, ritual, organization, and traditions of each group.

Footnotes have been kept to a minimum. *Separated Brethren* was written for the parish priest, Newman chaplain, reli-

7

gious, and layman. References to further reading are given at the end of most of the sections.

In completing the research for the writing and revision of this book over a period of some 15 years I relied heavily on personal interviews, official church publications, correspondence, published studies, and observation. If space permitted and I were not afraid of inadvertently omitting someone's name, I would like to acknowledge my indebtedness to the scores of ministers, church officials, and laity who generously gave of their time to enable me to get a current picture of the life of their denominations.

I would especially like to thank my wife who read the manuscript chapter by chapter, offered innumerable suggestions, and maintained those conditions of domestic tranquility conducive to writing.

Some of the material on the Pentecostals, Unitarian Universalists, Old Catholics, and Baha'is originally appeared in *U.S. Catholic* magazine and I would like to thank Robert E. Burns, executive editor, for permission to reproduce this in book form.

Thanks are due to the following copyright owners for permission to use quotations: *Life*, Newman Press, Sheed and Ward, *Time*, Herder and Herder, and the Watchtower Bible and Tract Society, Inc. Statistics were generally drawn from the 1970 edition of the *Yearbook of American Churches* published by the National Council of Churches of Christ.

Lafayette, Indiana   W.J.W.
August 1971

Chapter I

AMERICA'S RELIGIOUS PANORAMA
125 Million Belong to U.S. Churches and Synagogues

SHORTLY after the discovery of America, the unity of Western Christendom was shattered by the Protestant Reformation. That bond of common faith which had cemented the brotherhood of European Christians for a millennium was broken and altar was set against altar. Christians remained brothers in the grace of baptism and in loyalty to the person of Jesus Christ but they became separated brethren.

After the dust of the Reformation and the Counter-Reformation had settled, Protestantism consolidated its position in northern Germany, Scandinavia, Holland, Scotland, and England. Colonists and missionaries from these areas would carry the new religion to other continents. Meanwhile the Spaniards, Poles, Italians, French, Portuguese, Austrians, Hungarians, southern Germans, Irish, and other nationalities held fast to the ancient faith.

The apologetic exigencies of the times prompted controversialists in both Christian camps to emphasize the separation more than the brotherhood. They segregated and stressed points of doctrine on which Protestant and Catholic disagreed. For the Catholic the possibility of converting the Muslim was remote; the obstinate Jew clung to his religious beliefs in the shelter of the ghetto; the Protestant was the obvious target for theological debate and polemics.

Earlier the Great Eastern Schism had split Eastern and Western Christians. Most of the Greeks and Slavs were in schism. Efforts at the Council of Lyons in 1274 and the Council of Florence in 1439 failed to effect a permanent reconciliation. Theological differences between East and West, however, were slight compared with those engendered by the wholesale innovations of the Protestant reformers. Moreover, the Eastern Orthodox retained a valid episcopacy, priesthood, Mass, and seven sacraments which Protestantism lacks.

Protestantism soon split into four main branches which persist to this day. The followers of Martin Luther disagreed with the Zwinglians and Calvinists on the Real Presence and other doctrinal issues. In England elements of Catholicism and Protestantism combined to form the Anglican communion. Finally, the left wing of the Reformation, the sects, developed into the various Baptist, Congregational, Mennonite, Disciples of Christ, Churches of Christ, Holiness, and Adventist bodies. The four branches, then, are Lutheranism, Calvinism (Presbyterian and Reformed), Anglicanism, and Independent or Radical.

Through historical and geographical circumstances the fourth branch, variously known as Independent, Radical, Nonconformist, and Free church, gained ascendancy in the United States. The despised sects won the battle of the American frontier. World Protestantism has been dominated by the other three wings, but the success of the radical wing in this country exerts a growing influence. Every second American Protestant is a Baptist or Methodist although worldwide there are far more Lutherans than Baptists, Methodists, Congregationalists, and Disciples of Christ combined.

Estimates vary on the number of Christians in the world, but a reasonable set of figures would indicate 580 million Catholics, 218 million Protestants, and 125 million Eastern Orthodox. Several million other Christians belong to the Lesser Eastern Churches. The Orthodox estimate must be accepted with reservations since at least 50,000,000 Orthodox are supposed to be living behind the Iron Curtain where accurate religious statistics are unavailable.

More Americans are church members than ever before in our national history. The theocratic influence of the Protestant churches in colonial times obscures the fact that only one person in ten was a church member. This percentage was only 16 per cent of the population a century ago but today it has risen to 63 per cent. Protestantism, more or less static in Europe, now claims the allegiance of 35 per cent of the total U.S. population compared to 27 per cent in the late 1920s. When poll takers ask for religious "preference" they find that many more register a "preference" for Protestantism even though they are not on the church register.

What is significant in the growth of Protestantism in recent decades is that this growth has taken place outside of what is called "co-operative Protestantism." Generally "co-operative Protestantism" includes those denominations represented in the National and World Council of Churches: Methodists, northern Baptists, most Lutherans, Episcopalians, Presbyterians, Disciples, Negro Baptists, etc. Between 1949 and 1965 the nonco-operative Southern Baptists increased almost 65 per cent, the co-operative American Baptist Convention increased only 1 per cent; the nonco-operative Missouri Synod Lutherans increased 76 per cent, the co-operative Disciples of Christ increased only 7 per cent; the nonco-operative Christian Reformed Church grew by 92 per cent and the co-operative Methodists barely kept up with the national increase with 19 per cent. The really amazing membership gains have been made by the Southern Baptists, Jehovah's Witnesses, Missouri Synod Lutherans, Mormons, Nazarenes, Christian Reformed, Seventh-day Adventists, and Pentecostals.

While the sects emerged from the suppressed left wing of the Reformation, the Protestant churches emerged from the right wing. The two terms, church and sect, are not precise. In general, however, the church refuses to cut the ties with the past, tends to seek state support and protection, considers all members of the nation in its constituency, baptizes infants, demands subscription to creeds and confessions, and adopts an episcopal or presbyterian form of government.

The sect denies what the church affirms. It usually latches on to one doctrine such as adventism or perfectionism, rejects infant baptism and often insists on immersion, advocates complete separation of church and state, prefers a congregational polity, appeals mainly to the poor and uneducated, establishes personal conversion as the chief condition of church membership, enforces a Puritan morality, urges tithing as the divine method of fund raising, and dispenses with art and fixed ritual in worship.

A sect may become a church. As its members rise in social status the sect often modifies its original stand. Methodism, for example, began as a sect within Anglicanism even though it never rejected infant baptism and retained an episcopacy in America. Today Methodism reveals all the characteristics of a church. Disaffected Methodists who preferred the milieu of the ' sect tended to drift into Holiness and Pentecostal sects. We can observe the evolution of some sects into churches in our own day: the Church of the Nazarene has almost completed the transformation. Many sects peter out after the death of the leader or else remain numerically insignificant.

No other nation has witnessed the proliferation of Christian churches and sects which we find in the United States. European nations are likely to have one dominant Christian religion — Lutheranism, for instance, in Sweden or Catholicism in Spain— or two major denominations as in Germany and Holland. Estimates place the number of churches and sects in the United States at 265.

Every European religious tradition has been transplanted to American soil. Yankee inventiveness sometimes extended into ecclesiastical realms and added further divisions and varieties. Historical circumstances in the young nation combined with the Protestant principles of private interpretation of the scriptures and the denial of religious authority furthered the fragmentation.

When Lutheran immigrants came to the New World they brought their own pastors, languages, and church traditions. As a result the Germans, Swedes, Norwegians, Danes, Finns, and Slovaks organized separate and independent synods. Immigrants from Eastern Europe—the Albanians, Greeks, Russians, Bulgarians, Romanians, Serbs, Syrians, and Ukrainians—set up their own Orthodox denominations with close ties with the autocephalous mother churches in Europe and Asia.

The Civil War and the issue of slavery further split many Protestant denominations into northern and southern branches.

The Methodists reunited in 1939 but other such schisms persist: the American (northern) Baptists and the Southern Baptists, the northern United Presbyterian Church in the U. S. A. and the southern Presbyterian Church in the U. S.

The conservative Churches of Christ broke away from the Disciples of Christ on a question of worship—they could not find scriptural justification for the use of a pipe organ in church. A serious schism was precipitated among the Mennonites by the problem of whether one man should wash and wipe the believer's feet in the foot washing ceremony or whether one man should wash and another wipe. Mennonites also separated over the use of new fangled buttons instead of hooks-and-eyes.

Booker T. Washington once remarked that if you find a Negro who is not a Methodist or Baptist someone has been tampering with his religion. Practically all Negro Christians are Methodists and Baptists and most of them are members of independent Negro denominations. Perhaps 500,000 blacks belong to racially mixed Protestant churches and most of these are found in the United Methodist Church. There are about 800,000 Roman Catholics who are black.

Nine out of ten Protestant Negroes worship in segregated denominations such as the African Methodist Episcopal Church, the African Methodist Episcopal Church Zion, the Christian Methodist Episcopal Church, and the two National Baptist Conventions. Many smaller denominations are composed entirely of Negro Christians.

Theological controversies produced Unitarianism, the Christian Reformed Church, and the fundamentalist Evangelical Presbyterian and Orthodox Presbyterian Churches. Dozens of fundamentalist and holiness sects have arisen as a protest against the modernism of the older denominations or as the personal vehicle of a popular preacher such as Aimee Semple McPherson.

A number of churches and sects are home grown, including the Seventh-day Adventist, Christian Science, Church of the Nazarene, Disciples of Christ, Jehovah's Witnesses, Mormon, Polish National Catholic, Spiritualist, and Unity School of Christianity. The Adventists and Witnesses now find the bulk of their membership outside continental United States and the Mormons are also engaged in an aggressive foreign missionary program.

This amazing array of churches, sects, and cults should not mislead the student of the American religious scene. After all the denominations have been tallied the fact remains that nine out of ten American Protestants belong to one of the six great denominational families: Baptist and Disciples, Methodist, Lutheran, Episcopalian, Presbyterian and Reformed, and the United Church of Christ. Even counting separate denominations we find that 90 per cent of the Protestants in this country belong to the 20 largest denominations.

Since its founding the U. S. has moved from a situation in which most of the states favored established Protestant churches to one of religious pluralism. At the time the Declaration of Independence was signed Roman Catholics numbered only some 25,000 of the several million people in the new nation. Now Catholics constitute the largest single denomination in the U. S. (about 48 million) and one out of every four Americans identifies himself as a Catholic. Other religious traditions have taken their place in a society once characterized as pan-Protestant: 5½ million Jews, 4 million Eastern Orthodox, 2 million Latter-day Saints, and many others who identify themselves as secular humanists, Buddhists, Muslims, etc.

On the local level the average Protestant can attend a Methodist church one Sunday, a Baptist the next, a Presbyterian church after that and find himself more or less at home. So long as he stays within the predominant Puritan-Independent tradition he can switch denominational affiliation with a minimum of accommodation and inconvenience. On the other hand, a monthly cycle of Christian Science, Anglo-Catholic, Southern Baptist, and Quaker worship would be conducive to acute schizophrenia. For the Protestant the choice of church affiliation may be based on family background, the personality and preaching ability of the minister, adequacy of the physical plant, proximity to home, social advantages, Sunday School, Youth programs, or preference for one type of church polity over another.

Three types of church government predominate: congregational, presbyterial, and episcopal. We might mention that in practice the episcopal form is never so autocratic nor the congregational so independent as the labels suggest. Some of the most highly organized denominations in the country, such as the Seventh-day Adventist and Missouri Synod Lutheran, operate under a congregational or consistorial system. In at least a third of the Protestant denominations the congregation is theoretically supreme and recognizes no authority beyond itself. Besides the two churches just mentioned the Baptists, Disciples of Christ, Churches of Christ, Quakers, Unitarians, and many Holiness groups are congregational in polity. The congregational-type church hires and fires the minister whose position then depends on maintaining the good will of his parishioners. The congregation likewise holds title to all property, manages church finances, elects its own officers, and perhaps formulates its creedal statement.

The Episcopalians, Eastern Orthodox, and Methodists maintain an episcopal form of church government. In most cases the bishops are elected rather than appointed as in the Catholic Church.

The presbyterial system dispenses with bishops but exercises a measure of control over the local congregations by means of representative presbyteries. Clerical and lay delegates cast equal votes and no individual holds an ecclesiastical office superior to another. Besides the Presbyterians themselves other Protestants who are governed by this polity are those in the Reformed and Christian Reformed Churches, and the Assemblies of God. Smaller groups such as the Salvation Army and the Volunteers of America follow a military organization adapted to religious life.

The average Protestant congregation is small with fewer than 350 members (compared to more than 1800 in the average Catholic parish). These parishioners may reside in any part of the city since they are not assigned to a specific church as in the Catholic parochial arrangement. Members usually make an annual pledge to support the church and its benevolences.

Architecturally the familiar Protestant church is a semi-circular auditorium. A pulpit, organ, or altar may occupy the chief focal point in the chancel. A liturgical revival in Protestantism is introducing the cross, central altar, vestments for minister and choir, stained glass, sculpture, and ecclesiastical furniture common in Catholic churches. Episcopalian and Lutheran churches have always employed art and music to greater advantage than churches in the Puritan heritage.

The 10:30 or 11 o'clock service is usually the main Sunday worship service although larger churches may offer duplicate services at other hours. An usher escorts the worshipers to the pews. The typical nonliturgical Protestant worship service lasts about an hour and consists of the invocation, Lord's Prayer, hymn, responsive reading, anthem, scripture lesson, anthem, pastoral prayer, offering, hymns, sermon, closing prayer, and benediction. The sequence of these elements may vary according to the denomination or the wishes of the minister or congregation. Music is provided by both the trained choir and the congregation as a whole. Liturgical churches follow the Christian year and a fixed ritual resembling the Catholic Mass.

Communion is observed monthly or quarterly except by the Episcopalians and Disciples of Christ who celebrate the Lord's Supper every week. Communion is distributed under both kinds; all denominations use bread but some use wine, some grape juice, and one (Mormon) water.

At an earlier hour the children will be listening to Bible stories, singing hymns, drawing or playing games in the Sunday School. More than 44 million children are enrolled in these part-time religious schools since fewer than 360,000 attend Lutheran, Christian Reformed, and Seventh-day Adventist full-time parochial grade and high schools. Volunteer lay people conduct the 286,000 Sunday Schools which attempt to provide at least a minimum of religious instruction. The larger city churches may employ a trained director of education to supervise the educational program for the various age groups.

The old-fashioned midweek prayer meeting has fallen into disuse except in the South and certain rural areas. Many of the sects sponsor annual revival services either in the church building or in a tent or rented hall. Church facilities may be used during the week for meetings, choir rehearsals, suppers, Boy Scout activities, dances, dramatics, study clubs and the like. During the summer months union services are sometimes scheduled to accommodate depleted congregations and allow pastors to take a vacation. Similar union programs among various churches have been arranged for the Lenten season, Reformation Sunday, Thanksgiving, and other special events.

An increasing number of Protestant ministers are entering their profession with the benefit of college and seminary training. Some Baptist, Methodist, and Holiness clergy are still ordained with little or no education beyond high school or with no regular seminary training. On the other hand, the Lutherans, Episcopalians, Presbyterians, and Congregationalists have always insisted on high educational standards for their clergy.

About 4 per cent of the Protestant ministry in this country are ordained women ministers. Two thirds of these 6000 women serve in the United Methodist Church, the Church of God, International Church of the Foursquare Gospel, and the Volunteers of America. Other denominations which now ordain women include the Presbyterian, United Church of Christ, Disciples of Christ, Quaker, and Church of the Nazarene. Relatively few women have become pastors of city churches; they generally serve rural parishes or assist as associate pastors.

Few comprehensive studies have been undertaken on the social classes in American Protestantism. Those which have been published indicate that there are more lower class Episcopalians and more upper class Baptists than popularly thought. Nevertheless, many denominations are more or less classbound. The Episcopalian, Presbyterian, Congregational, and Unitarian Churches appeal to the wealthy and privileged; the Baptist, Assemblies of God, and fundamentalist churches find their chief support among the common people in the South and in rural America.

Despite the election and brief presidency of John F. Kennedy the ruling power in the U.S. remains as it has since the founding of the nation firmly in the hands of white Anglo-Saxon Protestants. As such social analysts as Domhoff, Baltzell, and Lundberg amply demonstrate the WASP establishment furnishes the leaders who sit on the major corporation boards, control the private foundations, run the elite universities, decide the national candidates of both political parties, and ultimately make the major decisions of American society. Few Roman Catholics, Jews, blacks, Mexican-Americans, Orientals, Indians, or Protestants from non-Anglo-Saxon background (*e.g.*, Lutherans) ever enter the ruling class. The members of this class can be identified by their independent wealth, attendance at private prep schools and elite universities, listing in the various social registers, membership in exclusive clubs, etc.

Protestants support home missions to Negroes, Indians, Orientals, Puerto Ricans, and Mexican-Americans, but most of their missionary efforts are directed to foreign lands. For centuries after the Reformation the Catholic Church carried the burden of Christian missions alone. This Catholic head start in the mission fields is illustrated by the fact that today 130,000,000 Catholics reside in mission territories compared to 25,000,000 Protestants. American Protestantism maintains 6000 mission centers in 100 nations and provides two thirds of the support and half the personnel of world Protestantism's missionary program. Since the Chinese missions have been abandoned, Protestant missionaries have turned their attention to Latin America.

Protestantism's success in Latin America has been phenomenal. It has been estimated that more Catholics have become Protestants in 20th century Latin America than in all of Europe during the Reformation. In 1914 there were only 100,000 Protestants in Latin America; the 10 million member mark was passed in 1960. More converts enter Pentecostal churches than all the other mainline Protestant churches combined.

The remarkable improvement in relations between Catholics and Protestants during the past decade is one of the rare examples of genuine reconciliation in the U.S. In a nation divided between hawks and doves, blacks and whites, liberals and conservatives this religious reconciliation is a hopeful sign. The Cold War waged by rival Christian groups for more than four centuries has ended and the major Christian churches have set their sights on eventual reunion no matter how long this may take.

The very first statement of the Decree on Ecumenism is "The restoration of unity among all Christians is one of the principal concerns of the Second Vatican Council." Christians of many different traditions are finally listening to one another, praying with one another, respecting one another. Many years ago Cardinal Mercier of Belgium wrote: "To unite, we must love one another; to love one another, it is necessary to know one another; to know one another, we must meet one another." In the following chapters the author invites the reader to meet those whose beliefs and practices may be different from his own but which deserve serious study and sympathetic understanding.

Chapter II

BASIC DIFFERENCES BETWEEN CATHOLICISM AND PROTESTANTISM
Theological Disagreements Divide Western Christians

COMPARED to the chasm between atheist and theist, between Christian and non-Christian, the differences which separate Catholic and Protestant Christians may seem relatively slight. A Christian world which saw Christendom divided into two neat camps in Western Europe developed rival apologetics which emphasized the theological points of disagreement. Today in what some have labeled the post-Christian era we find Western man offering his allegiance to dozens of religions and *ersatz* religions: Communism, nationalism, scientism, secularism, hedonism, sentimentalism, cultism. The *Weltanschauung* of these devotees contrasted with the Christian philosophy of life puts the twentieth-century picture into sharper focus and reveals the Christian camp as a besieged outpost in an aggressively hostile world.

To minimize the real differences between the Catholic and the Protestant interpretations of the gospel would be dishonest. But to fail to recognize the bonds of unity between separated brethren is also dishonest and shortsighted. Of course, we are speaking of those who believe in a personal God, the divinity of Christ, and other central Christian dogmas. Despite the profound differences between them, the Catholic and the Protestant Christian in the modern world are more often allies than antagonists.

Catholic and Protestant share a spiritual outlook which looks beyond material things to spiritual values, which reminds man to live for eternity as well as for time. They share a belief in God and a loyalty to the person of Jesus Christ. They accept the same Ten Commandments as a rule of conduct, acknowledge that fallen man unaided cannot attain his own salvation but needs a Savior, honor and read essentially the same Bible, recite the same Apostles' and Nicene creeds, pray the same Lord's Prayer. According to Catholic teaching both are admitted to the life of grace through the sacrament of baptism which may be administered by priest, minister, layman, or even Jew or Moslem. Bride and groom, whether baptized Catholics or Protestants, bestow the sacrament of matrimony on each other which brings the necessary graces to their Christian homes and makes their marriage a truly sacramental union. The feasts of Christmas and Easter, the writings of the Fathers of the Church, devotional literature and hymns form a common heritage for Catholic and Protestant Christians.

The Decree on Ecumenism of the Second Vatican Council insisted "that all who have been justified by faith in baptism are incorporated into Christ; they therefore have a right to be called Christians, and with good reason are accepted as brothers by the children of the Catholic Church" (Chapter I, Section 3).

While insisting that membership in the Catholic Church is the ordinary channel of God's grace, Catholic theologians acknowledge that God is free to bestow His grace on whom He will. The Jansenist proposition that "outside the Church there is no grace" was long ago condemned by Rome even though the grace which non-Catholics receive comes to them somehow in virtue of the Catholic Church.

Referring to churches and communions separated from the Catholic Church, the Decree on Ecumenism affirmed that they "have been by no means deprived of significance and importance in the mystery of salvation. For the Spirit of Christ has not refrained from using them as means of salvation which derive their efficacy from the very fullness of grace and truth entrusted to the Catholic Church" (I, 3).

As we examine the basic differences between Catholicism and Protestantism we should keep in mind the distinction between fundamental and accidental differences. The latter are products of church discipline, historical development, and cultural adaptations which may be amended and changed as the Church sees fit. Fundamental differences touch the core of the Christian faith, dogmas which God has revealed to mankind through His Son.

We can logically classify mankind into two groups: those who believe that man was once better than he is today and those who believe that he was once worse. Christians believe that man was once better but forfeited his favored position through disobedience to God in the Fall. Social evolutionists deny the Fall and maintain that despite occasional temporary setbacks man is getting better and better.

Although Catholics and Protestants attach great importance to the Fall, they disagree on the consequences of that Fall. We discover the first basic difference between the two Christian theologies in the view of man's nature after the Fall. Catholics believe that through the Fall man's natural and religious endowments were weakened. The first transgression by man's first parents lost for them and for their descendants those supernatural and preternatural gifts which were theirs in the Garden of Eden. These gifts included supernatural grace, potential bodily immortality, integrity, impassability. Were it not for the promise of a Redeemer and the sacrifice of the Son of God on the cross man would have been utterly unable to attain his supernatural end, the vision of God. But Catholics hold that these gifts were not due man but were free gifts of God which God withdrew; man, stripped of these gifts, remained man and his nature, though his will was weakened and his intellect darkened, remained intact.

To use a necessarily inadequate example, the Fall was as though someone took back the million dollars which he had given to another person who had previously only fifty cents in his pocket. Without the million dollars the second person realized he had suffered a great loss but he was still solvent. His situation has not changed to bankruptcy, his nature remained intact.

Luther, however, concluded that man's nature was totally corrupted by the Fall. This cardinal principle of Protestantism led logically to most of the other theological innovations. Man's nature is totally depraved and inclined only to evil, declared the German friar. Man is a sinner in whatever he does and all his actions are disgusting to God.

How can such a worthless creature be justified, be made pleasing to God? In an age when religion had become for all too many the mechanical performance of external devotions and Nominalism had undercut the orthodox positions of Thomism, Luther proclaimed his discovery of the truth that justification was by faith alone. Salvation is a free gift of God which man cannot merit. All is grace, pure grace.

Soon justification by faith became associated with three other principles not inherent in the original doctrine nor acceptable to the Church. These were the denial of free will, the doctrine of extrinsic justification, and the denunciation of all good works. Luther denied that man could co-operate with the actual graces God bestowed before justification. The Church, on the other hand, traditionally taught that man could reject God's graces through the exercise of his free will. By extrinsic justification the German Reformer taught that the act of justification is something entirely outside of man. Man remains a sinner, totally depraved, but God, so to speak, looks the other way. God covers man's sins with a cloak but the sins remain. Justification never touches the inherently sinful nature of man.

Catholicism has always denied that good works without justification would avail to man's salvation. After justification, however, the good works which a man performs, ethical or ceremonial, earn merit. Luther flatly denied the idea of merit and urged his followers to perform good works only as fruits or evidence of their justification. But no matter what they do, even in their loving God, they sin. The Church upheld the value of good works after justification in the firm belief that faith without works is dead.

It is one thing to deny Luther's positions on free will, extrinsic justification, and good works, but it is something else to suggest that man can merit his own justification by good works. He must co-operate with the actual graces he receives, do penance, seek the truth, but he cannot thereby earn his justification.

A serious complication has clouded theological argumentation since the Reformation. When the Reformers spoke of faith, they did not mean what the Church has always meant by the term. The Church defines faith as an intellectual assent given on the authority of another. For example, if a railroad conductor informs you that the next stop is Chicago and you accept his word, you have faith in him. If the Son of God declares that marriage is indissoluble or that baptism is necessary to salvation, you accept these statements because you have faith in Him. He has not proved these statements by mathematics or laboratory experiments but, because He is who He is, you accept them. Faith, then, is an assent to God's revelation. But to the founders of Protestantism faith became a supreme act of confidence that God had spared you from hell and covered up your sins. Faith became an act of the will and the emotions for the Protestant but remains primarily an act of the intellect for the Catholic.

Early in his career Luther saw that the Roman Catholic Church would never accept his theological views. On the other hand, he soon witnessed Protestant extremists, the Anabaptists, denying any authority in religion or appealing to weird visions and revelations. Unable to appeal to the Roman Church for authority and unwilling to allow the fanatics to overthrow all religious authority, Luther claimed the supreme religious authority to be found not in a man or institution but a book, the Bible. Protestantism dethroned the Church and set up the Bible as the sole rule of faith. Only what the Apostles had committed to writing would be binding on Christians; that oral tradition handed down through the Church from apostolic times was denied. Eventually Protestantism became the religion of the book par excellence.

Catholic controversialists could point out that Christ was a preacher not a writer, that the first Christians never saw a complete Bible, that the Church herself compiled the New Testament and fixed the canon, that the rejection of oral tradition was purely arbitrary, that the Bible itself claimed no supreme authority, and that prior to the invention of printing most of mankind had no access to the Bible even if they could read. But the new religion erected the Bible as the sole rule of faith while vilifying the Church which had compiled, translated, and preserved the Bible through the ages.

Not only was the Bible the sole rule of faith, the source of all that was needed for salvation, but the individual Christian now had the right, the duty, to interpret the Bible for himself. The spectacle of hundreds of churches and sects in this country alone gives testimony to the fruits of this disastrous principle of private interpretation. Of course, the masses of the Protestant faithful never exercised this right and duty in the face of a state-supported orthodoxy. Someone has estimated that there are at least 300 distinct interpretations of four words in the New Testament: "This is my body."

Catholics believe that the Church under the ever present guidance of the Holy Spirit is the proper interpreter of scripture. No matter how flattering to the man in the street, the invitation to become his own Bible scholar has always been illusory. Anyone with the slightest acquaintance with the Bible soon admits that a knowledge of languages, theology, history, and archaeology is a prerequisite to mastery of scripture. Apparently Luther believed that once the layman was encouraged to read the Bible, fortified by the principles of the Reformation, he would come to the same interpretations as his fellow Christians. Religious history since the Reformation disproves this theory. Most Protestant communions sooner or later imposed on their constituencies official interpretations of the Bible which only the most intrepid would dispute.

Searching their Bibles, Protestants came across numerous references to the Church. They knew that the Church of Rome had not adopted Luther's views. Evidently, then, the church must be an invisible rather than a visible body. The members of this invisible church would be known only to God; the head of this invisible church was not the pope, whom Luther branded the anti-Christ, but Christ Himself. Violent opposition to the See of Peter has animated Protestantism for four centuries. Catholics believe in One, Holy, Catholic, and Apostolic Church, founded by Christ, whose visible head is the Vicar of Christ, the successor to St. Peter, the Holy Father, the Bishop of Rome. This visible Church composed of saints and sinners has been the Mother of an estimated 5 billion souls since its founding in Jerusalem.

Most Protestants refuse to recognize the Church as a divine institution with authority to teach; they see the Church as a fellowship of believers in Jesus Christ with access to the Word of God in the scriptures. Roman Catholics and Eastern Orthodox hold that the message of salvation comes to the individual through the Church which enjoys protection against error which no individual Christian can claim.

The traditional Christian sacraments were included in the Reformer's denunciation of good works. Luther reasoned, however, that two sacraments, baptism and the Lord's Supper, were specifically enjoined by Christ and would be observed out of obedience to His will. Penance, confirmation, holy orders, matrimony, and extreme unction were denied any sacramental meaning but were retained as ceremonies of the church.

A simplified worship service patterned after the Catholic Mass but eliminating the idea of sacrifice was introduced. Not sacrifice but the preaching of the Word of God became the central feature of Protestant worship. Without a visible church, a Mass, and five of the seven sacraments, there was little need for a priesthood. Rather, all Christians were declared priests whose only ordination was baptism. Nevertheless some men (and eventually some women) were specially trained for the ministry, ordained in a rite of the church, and given a measure of authority over the congregation. To a great degree this doctrine of the priesthood of all believers suffered the same fate as private interpretation of the scriptures and was compromised by organizational necessities. Catholics believe that all men participate in some way in the royal priesthood of Christ as members of His Mystical Body but that some men are set apart and ordained for sacrifice.

Predestination preoccupied the Reformed branch of Protestantism for several centuries. Catholics flatly deny that absolute or double predestination which teaches that God has elected some to salvation and damned others to hell. This doctrine, so stated, leaves no room for man's free will and has been all but disowned by modern Protestants, even those who fall in the Calvinist tradition.

Protestants deny the doctrine of transubstantiation but differ among themselves on belief in the Real Presence. Lutherans, for example, claim to believe in the Real Presence but propose that the bread and wine and the body and blood of Christ co-exist in the elements; they disclaim the term "consubstantiation" to describe this theory. Calvinists speak of receiving Christ in a spiritual and heavenly manner. Even after the prayer of consecration the bread and wine remain bread and wine. The Methodists, Baptists, Disciples and Mennonites consider the Lord's Supper a simple memorial service. Anglicans encompass a variety of views from transubstantiation to memorial service, and the Quakers and Salvationists have no communion service.

Other Protestant positions were derived from the basic principles of total depravity, justification by faith alone, the Bible as the sole rule of faith, private interpretation of the scriptures, and the priesthood of all believers. The existence of purgatory was denied; after death the soul was assigned to either heaven or hell. Prayers for the dead were useless and unscriptural. Devotion to Mary as the Mother of God and intercession of the saints were abandoned although Luther kept alive a tender devotion to the Blessed Virgin until his death. The Reformer continued the practice of private confession all during his lifetime but this too died out in the non-Anglican branches of Protestantism although it has been revived in German Lutheranism in recent years.

A former Lutheran minister now a Catholic priest, Fr. Louis Bouyer, writes in his challenging book, *The Spirit and Forms of Protestantism:*

"It should be quite evident that the principles of Protestantism, in their positive sense—that most consonant with the spirit of the Reformation—are not only valid and acceptable, but must be held to be true and necessary *in virtue of Catholic tradition itself,* in virtue of what makes up the authority of the Church both of today and of all time. Salvation as the pure gift of God in Christ, communicated by faith alone, in the sense that no other way can be thought of apart from faith or even along with faith; justification by faith in its subjective aspect, which means that there is no real religion where it is not living and personal; the absolute sovereignty of God, more particularly of his Word as contained in the inspired writings—all these principles are the heart of Protestantism as a reforming movement. Yet, if we go to the root of them all, to what the Reformers considered most essential, to what is retained by living Protestantism, today and always, we are bound to say that they are all corroborated by Catholic tradition, and maintained absolutely by what is authoritative, in the present, for all Catholics."[1]

While insisting on an understanding of the basic principles of the Reformation and suggesting the harmony between these positive religious insights and Catholic truth, we must bear in mind that we cannot base current judgments of American Protestantism on classical statements. Many classical positions receive lip service at best and concern Protestant seminarians and theologians far more than the man in the pew. The laymen may choose not to dwell on the doctrine of total depravity, abdicate his right to private interpretation of the scriptures by subscribing to detailed creeds and confessions, submit to a clerical system which practically negates the priesthood of all believers concept, and still consider himself a genuine Protestant.

Perhaps the majority of Protestants in the United States can be classified as activist evangelicals, neither theological liberals nor fundamentalists. They probably hold most of the traditional Protestant principles which we have discussed without hesitating to modify any particular position. A thorough theological examination would doubtless also reveal considerable unorthodoxy among lay Catholics who also consider themselves in good standing.

After emphasizing that baptism "constitutes the sacramental bond of unity existing among all who through it are reborn" the Fathers of Vatican II examined the Protestant expression of Christianity:

"The Christian way of life of these brethren is nourished by faith in Christ. It is strengthened by the grace of baptism and the hearing of the Word of God. This way of life expresses itself in private prayer, in meditation of the Scriptures, in the life of a Christian family, and in the worship of the community gathered together to praise God." (III,22,23)

[1]Westminster, Md., Newman Press, 1956, p. 137.

Chapter III

THE LUTHERANS
'The Just Man Lives by Faith'

A GERMAN Augustinian friar touched off the explosion which shattered the unity of Western Christendom in the sixteenth century. Except for the Eastern schism of 1054 and the minor defections of the Waldensians and Moravians, this unity had remained intact for almost 1500 years after the death of Christ.

Soon after the initial revolt and the spread of its doctrinal teachings, the Protestant movement split into several camps which remain divided to this day. The followers of Martin Luther consolidated their position in northern Germany and Scandinavia while the Reformed or Calvinists captured Scotland and Holland, parts of Switzerland, and for a while threatened to win France and England.

Today Lutheranism with 75 million adherents is by far the largest component in world Protestantism. This fact is sometimes obscured by the strength of the Baptist and Methodist denominations concentrated in the United States. Many of these Lutherans, especially in the Scandinavian countries, must be classed as inactive or nominal, as must millions of Catholics in France, Italy, Spain, and South America.

To understand Protestantism we must understand Lutheranism; to understand Lutheranism we must know Luther. In order to do this we must try to project ourselves into his age. Catholics occasionally point out what some Protestants seem willing to admit: the Reformation would have been an impossibility in the twentieth century. The conditions in the Church which cried out for reform no longer exist. The refusal to see Luther in the context of his own era magnifies the enormity of his rebellion since Catholics see so little justification for the dismemberment of Christendom.

The modern Church has been singularly blessed by a succession of saintly, capable, and devoted pontiffs. But Alexander VI who is generally conceded to be the worst pope in history occupied the papal throne in Luther's youth.

Not long before Luther's birth three rival popes claimed the allegiance of the faithful, each excommunicating the other and his followers. The bishop of Rome had resided not in Rome but in Avignon in France for 65 years. To support the luxuries of the papal court new schemes for taxes and revenues had to be devised. The successors of St. Peter installed their children and relatives in the highest church offices, sold ecclesiastical positions to the highest bidders, and lived more like Chinese war lords than spiritual leaders.

Not all the abuses were confined to the papacy. The parish clergy, a huge clerical proletariat in Germany, had lost all ideals of celibacy which had been made mandatory on Latin clergy in the eleventh century. They exacted such large sums for their services that the sacrament of extreme unction was commonly called the rich man's sacrament, too expensive for the dying poor. The upper clergy was composed largely of the sons of royalty for whom lucrative church offices had been purchased. Monasteries grew lax and wealthy and the monks earned the contempt of the people. Among the laity infidelity, illegitimacy, and superstition were rife. The educated classes turned to the pagan writers of Greece and Rome rather than to the Bible or the Church Fathers and fed on a wisdom of hedonism and sensuality.

We must not overstate the case. The age also produced its saints and devout Christians. Not all priests and monks were untrue to their vows. A few bishops called for reform of the manifold scandals. But after all these allowances are made we must admit that the Church of Christ had fallen on evil days.

Into this situation was born a baby boy named Martin Luther after St. Martin on whose feast day he was baptized. The boy knew poverty in his youth but his father's fortunes improved and he was able to study at three prep schools. At 18 he transferred to the University of Erfurt to study, not theology, but law. He won his master's degree in 1505.

At this point the course of Luther's life changed dramatically. While riding in a storm he was hurled to the ground by a bolt of lightning and in terror he cried, "St. Anne, help me. I will become a monk." Evidently the reputation of the monastery he chose was such that a young man would consider it a logical refuge if he wished to consecrate his life entirely to God. Luther joined the strict Hermits of St. Augustine.

No one doubts that Luther determined to be a good religious. In fact, his self-imposed penances went far beyond the rules of the order. Professed in 1506, he was ordained a year later and only then began his study of theology. No religious order today would accept a candidate who sought entrance because of a vow made in fear of his life and certainly no one would be ordained two years after entering as a novice and without theological preparation.

Father Martin was barely able to complete his first Mass as he contemplated the miracle he was about to perform. Subject to extreme states of depression and melancholia, the young friar was obviously a victim of scrupulosity. He would spend as much as six hours in the confessional attempting to recall all his sins. What if he had forgotten to confess some sin? What if he had violated some rule of his order and had forgotten about it? His weary but wise confessor finally told him, "Man, God is not angry with you. You are angry with God. Don't you know that God commands you to hope?" Luther continued to be haunted by the thought that he might lose his soul and efforts by his religious superiors to assuage his fears were useless.

He visited Rome briefly on official business for his order and returned with a lowered estimate of Italian Catholicism. From Erfurt he was transferred to the young university at Wittenberg where he received a doctor of theology degree in 1512. Frederick the Wise had founded this university only 11 years before in a village of about 2500 population. Luther became a professor of scripture and began an intensive study of the Bible.

His theological system was taking shape. He was already teaching that through the Fall man's nature was radically corrupted. In essence man is a sinner, inclined only to evil, a possession of the devil. "Sin is not only a specific wrongdoing but also the basic condition of our fallen existence," decided Luther. All man can do is make a complete act of trust in God who confers forgiveness on him through the merits of Christ.

Luther tormented himself with the question, "Where can I find a merciful God?" How could he be assured that he would be saved? While preparing his scripture lectures he came upon a passage in Romans which he called the "door to paradise." He read, "The just man lives by faith." Here was the answer to his anxiety.

Luther used his conception of justification by faith as the key to interpret the rest of the Bible. It remains the basis of the experiential Protestant theology of consolation. St. James wrote that "Faith without good works is dead"; the Reformer dismissed this epistle as a "straw epistle."

When God gave mankind the Ten Commandments He knew they could not be observed. They were given to humble man, to break his willful spirit and bring him to a complete act of faith in God's goodness and mercy. For the sake of His Son, Jesus Christ, God casts a cloak over man's sins and man, still a sinner, is justified.

Since every action of man is sinful, good works are sinful and of no avail for salvation even after man is justified. Perhaps Luther knew the traditional Catholic position that good works performed by man in the state of original sin are of no merit. He now denied the merit of any and all good works for justification.

Since Luther considered good works useless to salvation, we may not assume that he encouraged moral laxity. The just man will gladly perform good works and avoid evil for the glory of God. That not all Luther's followers reasoned in the same manner cannot be blamed on the Reformer.

The barefoot friar of Wittenberg developed his doctrinal position while busily engaged in a variety of other tasks. In a letter to a friend written in 1517 he wrote:

"I really ought to have two secretaries or chancellors. I do hardly anything all day but write letters. . . . I am at the same time preacher to the monastery, have to preach in the refectory, and am even expected to preach daily in the parish church. I am regent of the house of studies and vicar, that is to say prior eleven times over; I have to provide for delivery of the fish from Lietzkau pond and to manage the litigation of the Herzberg friars at Torgau; I am lecturing on Paul, compiling lectures on the Psalter, and, as I said before, writing letters most of the time. . . . It is seldom that I have time for recitation of the Divine Office or to celebrate Mass, and then, too, I have my peculiar temptations from the flesh, the world, and the devil."

The sale of indulgences was the occasion of Luther's open protest but quite incidental to his theological creation. No one denies that scandalous abuses of all sorts had crept into the granting of indulgences. Luther's own patron, Frederick, boasted a collection of relics said to include a strand of Jesus' beard, a nail from the crucifixion, a piece of the swaddling clothes, and a twig from Moses' burning bush. Those of the faithful who venerate all these relics and made a contribution could amass a total indulgence of 1,909,202 years and 270 days.

Pope Julius II granted a new indulgence in order to obtain funds for the building of St. Peter's in Rome. The preaching of such an indulgence resembled a modern parish mission although the salesmen claimed to guarantee results even though the recipients were not in the state of grace. Frederick forbade the preaching of this indulgence in his province since it would compete with his own collection. But many Wittenbergers crossed the nearby border to obtain its extravagant promises from a Dominican priest by the name of Tetzel. Tetzel employed all the devices of the modern huckster in promoting this indulgence. A representative of the Fugger's banking house sat next to the coffer to collect his share of the proceeds as promised by the playboy archbishop of Mainz.

Luther nailed a list of 95 theses on indulgences to the church door in Wittenberg which was the usual manner in which scholars invited debate. About these theses Luther would insist: "In all we wanted to say, we have said nothing that is not in agree-

ment with the Catholic Church and the teachers of the Church."
The debate never took place but the theses were widely circu-
lated throughout Germany.

Soon Luther was driven to more radical positions and he
launched attacks on papal authority, infallibility, confession, invocation of the saints. He presented himself as the champion of
the German people, groaning under the demands of Rome.

At one stage the Reformer may have hoped that his new
theology would find acceptance by the Church. Indeed, as we
have seen in the preceding chapter, the positive principles of the
Reformation are in complete harmony with the teachings of the
Church. The Church was forced to condemn the negative principles of extrinsic justification, the wholesale condemnation of
good works, absolute predestination, a personal religion which
dispensed with the Church itself, and the denial of the role of
tradition. Luther sought authority in a council rather than in the
pope but he finally settled for the authority of the Bible. We
have seen that he ridiculed the Epistle of St. James since it contradicted his pet theory. When he realized that the doctrine of
purgatory and prayers for the dead were implied in the Second
Book of Maccabees, he threw out that book. The Book of Esther
he called a "superfluity of heathen naughtiness" and he relegated the Apocalypse (the Protestant Book of Revelation) to the
appendix. He nevertheless insisted that the Bible was the complete and infallible Word of God.

Among those who joined Luther at Wittenberg were two
fellow professors: Carlstad and Melanchthon. Luther had refused to go to Rome at the pope's orders to answer charges of
heresy but Carlstad was challenged to a debate by Dr. John
Eck at Leipzig. Luther's voluminous writings were receiving wide
circulation through the relatively new medium of the printing
press and he grew bolder and denounced the pope as the anti-
Christ. While he lost the support of some humanists such as
Erasmus he won a number of dissatisfied priests, monks, nuns,
and lay people to his cause.

Three influential tracts went to the printer in 1520. In these
tracts, *The Babylonian Captivity, The Freedom of the Christian
Man,* and the *Address to the German Nobility,* Luther trimmed

the number of sacraments from seven to three (he later eliminated confession as a sacrament).

His revolutionary theology was formally condemned by the
faculties of the Universities of Paris, Louvain, and Cologne.
When the papal bull threatening excommunication and citing
41 errors finally reached Luther from Rome in 1520 he tossed it
on the fire while admiring students sang the *Te Deum*. He was
summoned before the civil Diet of Worms by the Emperor
Charles V and asked to admit the authorship of his heretical
books. Closing his defense the defiant friar declared: "Unless
I am convicted by Scripture and plain reason—I do not accept
the authority of popes and councils for they have contradicted
each other—my conscience is captive to the Word of God. I
cannot and will not recant anything, for to go against conscience
is neither right nor safe. God, help me. Amen." Assuming his sin-
cerity, his stand on the supremacy of conscience was, of course,
strictly orthodox and St. Thomas Aquinas points out that anyone
convinced that the Church is in error is bound to leave it.

At Worms Luther stood convicted of heresy but the emperor
promised him safe conduct back to his home in Wittenberg.
The followers of Luther refused to accept the decision of what
they called a rump court. En route a band of masked men kidnaped Luther and delivered him into protective custody at the
castle at Wartburg. Frederick arranged this maneuver to forestall
possible treachery since Luther was now an outlaw in the rest of
Germany by order of the emperor. During his year in the Wartburg Luther completed his translation of the New Testament
into German. We should note, however, that before 1518 there
had been 14 translations into High German and four into Low
German.

Back at Wittenberg his two colleagues assumed the leadership of the snowballing Reformation. Priests, monks, and nuns
began to marry; German replaced Latin in the liturgy; images
were smashed; Masses for the dead were forbidden. When Luther
returned home in the disguise of a bearded knight he upbraided
Carlstad for his violence and iconoclasm but otherwise ap-
plauded the changes.

When three laymen from neighboring Zwickau visited Wittenberg and began to denounce infant baptism, Luther was horrified. He repudiated any connection with these anarchistic Anabaptists while they, in turn, chided the Lutherans as compromisers. Since Luther maintained the necessity of faith for the reception of a sacrament, he was hard pressed to present a convincing case for infant baptism.

The general disparagement of authority and the radical doctrine of the priesthood of all believers inflamed the German peasants and inspired the bloody peasant revolt of 1524-25. Rather than becoming their leader Luther penned the vicious tract, *Against the Murderous and Thieving Hordes of Peasants.* In this tract he advised, "Let everyone who can, smite, slay and stab secretly or openly, remembering that nothing can be more poisonous, hurtful or devilish than a rebel. It is just as when one must kill a mad dog; if you don't strike him, he will strike you, and the whole land with you." More than 5000 peasants were slain in the hopeless uprising. Luther, the peasant, turned his attention to the princes while the betrayed peasants listened with greater interest to the left-wing Anabaptists.

The marriage of parish priests was one thing but that of monks was quite another. Seeing his Augustinian brethren in Wittenberg taking wives Luther exclaimed, "Good heavens! Will our Wittenbergers give wives to monks? They won't give one to me." But they did. Nine Cistercian nuns arrived at the cloister in search of husbands and Luther acted as matchmaker. After two years one ex-nun remained unmarried, Katherine von Bora. Urged to practice what he preached and to give his father a grandson, Luther finally married the former nun and established his household in the Augustinian monastery. Six children were born to the union and the male succession continued until 1759.

Turning from the peasants for his support, Luther came to rely more and more on the German princes as "emergency bishops." Lutherans early disassociated themselves from secular affairs and have traditionally allowed the prince, emperor, president, or dictator to manage state affairs with a minimum of church interference or ethical judgment. The Reformation gave the princes an opportunity to seize coveted church property and to escape the inconveniences of an international Church.

The Diet of Spires in 1529 reaffirmed the verdict of Worms and insisted on liberty for Catholics in Lutheran areas but limited the further spread of the new religion in Germany. The Lutherans protested and this gave rise to the term "Protestant." They had formerly preferred the term "Evangelical" and eventually came to be known as Lutherans despite Luther's wishes: "I beg that my name be passed over in silence, and that men will call themselves not Lutherans but Christians. What is Luther? My teaching is not mine. . . . How does it happen that I . . . have the children of Christ called after my unholy name? Let us root out party names and call ourselves Christians, for it is Christ's gospel we have."

Unlike the Reformed leader, Calvin, Luther left no systematic statement of his theology. His co-worker Melanchthon performed this task and represented Lutheranism at the Diet of Augsburg in 1530 called by the emperor to restore religious unity. Melanchthon prepared a conciliatory confession which softened the more abusive criticism of the ancient church and went so far as to suggest that the adoption of vernacular in the liturgy would solve most of the differences. This Augsburg confession remains the most authoritative Lutheran doctrinal statement. It also branded the Zwinglians and Anabaptists as heretics.

Plagued by insomnia and constipation Luther nevertheless turned his tremendous energies to institutionalizing the Reformation movement. He translated the Old Testament and prepared his Larger and Smaller Catechisms. He composed several dozen hymns including "A Mighty Fortress Is Our God," the battle hymn of Protestantism. His revised liturgy emphasized preaching and congregational singing as integral parts of the Eucharist.

Toward the end of his life Luther found himself carried along by the revolution he had triggered. One of his young supporters, Philip of Hesse, tired of his wife and appealed to Luther to approve a divorce. This Luther refused but he suggested that the prince take a second wife as in Old Testament days. Wife No. 2 was to be kept secret but her mother objected and the Reformer then advised recourse to a lie. Luther's conduct during the peasants' revolt and his countenancing of bigamy are seldom defended by even his staunchest admirers.

Many results of his Reformation distressed him. He saw moral standards sink below those of former times and he lamented: "Avarice, usury, debauchery, drunkenness, blasphemy, lying and cheating are far more prevalent now than they were under the Papacy. This state of morals brings general discredit on the Gospel, and its preachers, as the people say, if this Gospel were true, the persons professing it would be more pious."

As the years went by the Reformer grew intolerant of any who might venture to disagree with him. "He who does not believe my doctrine is sure to be damned," he announced. Toward the end of his life he penned two unfortunate attacks on the Jews and the papacy, illustrated with lewd cartoons. Referring to the Jews he recommended, "That their synagogues be burned, their houses broken down and destroyed, and their rabbis forbidden to teach under pain of death." Martin Luther died on February 18, 1546, in Eisleben, a village in Thuringia where he was born on November 10, 1482.

Luther had not intended to found another church. In 1519 he would write to Pope Leo X: "Before God and all his creatures, I bear testimony that I neither did desire, nor do desire to touch or by intrigue undermine the authority of the Roman church and that of your holiness." He never considered himself outside the fold of the historic Catholic Church.

Centuries later the German priest Karl Adam would offer this appraisal of Luther:

"Yes, it was night. Had Martin Luther then arisen with his marvelous gifts of mind and heart, his warm penetration of the essence of Christianity, his passionate defiance of all unholiness and ungodliness, the elemental fury of his religious experience, his surging, soul-shattering power of speech, and not least that heroism in the face of death with which he defied the powers of the world—had he brought all these magnificent qualities to the removal of the abuses of the time and the cleansing of God's garden from weeds, had he remained a faithful member of his Church, humble and simple, sincere and pure, then indeed we should today be his grateful debtors. He would be forever our great Reformer, our true man of God, our teacher and leader, comparable to Thomas Aquinas and Francis of Assisi. He would have been the greatest saint of our people, the refounder of the Church in Germany, a second St. Boniface."[1]

Another Catholic scholar, Willem Hendrick van de Pol, writes: "The integrity of his character and personality, the purity of his intentions, the unselfishness of his actions, the genuineness and depth of his piety and his extraordinary gifts of mind and heart are beyond any doubt of suspicion."[2]

The Catholic convert Friedrich Leopold Graf von Stolberg wrote, "The Reformation proceeded originally from a pure intention. I will never raise a stone against Luther in whom I honor not only one of the greatest minds that ever lived but also the profound religiosity which never forsook him." Martin Luther was and is a Catholic priest for eternity; he wore the habit of a friar for 19 years, including three years after his excommunication. Had he not been captivated by the Nominalist philosophy of William of Occam he might have discerned that the Pelagian influence in the Church of his day was what should have been uprooted. Had Luther imbibed his philosophy from St. Thomas Aquinas instead of from the Nominalists he might have filled the role of the Great Reformer and Saint of the German people which Karl Adam depicted.

Where the Swiss Reformers attempted to dispense with everything not specifically commanded or authorized by the Bible, Luther preserved whatever was not specifically forbidden by scripture. The Lutheran Church retains more of the liturgy, church year, vestments, and church architecture than other continental Protestant churches. He halted the destruction of works of art which had been instigated by Carlstad.

Lutheranism soon hardened into a rigid orthodoxy which made the Protestant right of private interpretation inoperative. Conformity or excommunication was the choice after 1580. This orthodoxy went far beyond Luther in rejecting ancient practices such as confession and the veneration of Mary.

[1] Karl Adam, *One and Holy* (New York, Sheed and Ward, 1951), p. 25.

[2] W. H. Van de Pol, *World Protestantism*, (New York, Herder and Herder, 1964), p. 33.

Pietism arose as a reaction to Lutheran orthodoxy in the late 17th century and gave full vent to emotionalism and subjectivism. The University at Halle sponsored a pietistic movement which encouraged Bible study, hymn singing, and religious literature. Dogma took a back seat and as a consequence the Protestant world was wholly unprepared for the assaults of the Enlightenment after 1770.

The Lutherans in America have often been considered religious isolationists by their fellow Protestants. For many years, they clung to the German and Scandinavian languages; contributed little to the propagation of the social gospel, liberal theology, prohibition efforts, and the ecumenical movement; often educated their children in their own parochial schools. Their continental background gave them a more relaxed attitude toward beer drinking, smoking, dancing, and Sunday blue laws. A greater degree of co-operation between Lutherans and non-Lutheran Protestants can be observed today although such groups as the Missouri and Wisconsin Synod Lutherans usually stand aloof from many ecumenical movements.

American Lutheranism constitutes the third largest religious family in U.S. Protestantism. The three largest Lutheran bodies enroll more than 95 per cent of the nation's nearly 9 million Lutherans. About 3,135,000 belong to the mildly liberal *Lutheran Church in America,* 2,786,000 to the *Lutheran Church—Missouri Synod,* and 2,560,000 to the *American Lutheran Church.* The only other large body is the 358,000-member ultraconservative *Wisconsin Synod.* In general, Lutherans are scarce in New England and the South and strongest in the Middle West with large constituencies in Minnesota, Pennsylvania, Wisconsin, Illinois, and Michigan.

The first stable colony of Lutherans in this country was composed of Swedish immigrants in Delaware in 1638 but most of the descendants of these Swedes eventually became Episcopalians.

Henry Melchior Muhlenberg is known as the great patriarch of American Lutheranism since it was through his 45 years labor that the scattered German parishes were organized on a permanent basis. Of his 11 children all the men became ministers and most of the women married ministers. One son became a general and served under Washington.

A wave of conservative German Lutherans in the 1840's initiated the confessional revival in American Lutheranism. The breach between conservative and liberals and between north and south was not healed until 1917. The amalgam, the United Lutheran Church in America, heir of colonial Lutheranism, became the largest Lutheran body in the country, the most liberal branch of a conservative theological family, and a member of both the National and World Councils of Churches.

Four Lutheran Churches merged in 1962 to create the Lutheran Church in America. They included the United Lutheran Church in America, the Augustana Synod and the small American Evangelical Lutheran Church (Danish) and the Finnish Evangelical Lutheran Church (Suomi Synod).

Several boatloads of "Old Lutherans" from Luther's own province of Saxony landed near St. Louis in 1839. These ultra-conservative Lutherans fought the proposed union with the Reformed in their homeland and also waged war against all forms of rationalism. In this country they soon drove their pastor from the community for alleged immorality and for assuming the powers of a bishop. Fortunately for the group a brilliant organizer, C. F. W. Walther, assumed leadership and can be called the real father of the Lutheran Church-Missouri Synod. The synod was formally organized in Chicago in 1849. Today the Missouri Synod is a nationwide church with its largest membership in Illinois.

The Missouri Synod Lutherans built their own parochial school system from kindergarten to university. They operate 1400 grade and high schools, Valparaiso University in Indiana, and one of the largest Protestant seminaries in the nation, Concordia in St. Louis. They demand strict adherence to the Lutheran confessions. In recent years they have emerged from isolation and have pioneered in aggressive radio, TV, advertising, and church public relations programs. They sponsor "This Is the Life" series on television, and the "Lutheran Hour" on radio. The Missouri Synod Lutherans are also known for their outstanding work among the deaf and mentally ill. The Missourians maintain 1135 home and 729 foreign mission congregations and have doubled their membership in the past 25 years.

The American Lutheran Church was formed in 1930 in a union of three German Lutheran branches, the Ohio, Buffalo, and Iowa Synods which had begun between 1818 and 1854. When it merged with two other Lutheran bodies in 1960 Lutherans of German, Danish, and Norwegian backgrounds were united in one Church.

The Wisconsin Synod shares most Missouri Synod positions but also bans membership in the Boy Scouts and the Lutheran Men of America. From 1872 on the Missouri and Wisconsin Synods co-operated in the Lutheran Synodical Conference of North America which included Norwegian, Slovak, and Negro bodies. In 1963 the Wisconsin Synod criticized the Missourians as too liberal and severed its relations with Missouri. It had previously made clear its disapproval of Missouri's common confession of faith with the American Lutheran Church. The small body of Norwegians who affiliated with the Synodical Conference had already withdrawn because of Missouri's alleged laxity.

Lutheran pastors receive the benefit of a thorough, classical theological education. A candidate for the Missouri Synod ministry, for example, often begins his studies after completing grade school. He attends one of 11 prep schools to take six years of pretheological training through junior college. He then completes two more years of college, two years of theology, one year as a vicar in some larger parish or college student foundation, and a final year of theology before ordination. The course includes Latin, Greek, Hebrew, and German.

Both the LCA and the American Lutheran Church have agreed to accept women candidates for ordination but the Missouri and Wisconsin Synods balk at this step. Women have been ordained in Lutheran churches in Sweden, Denmark, and Slovakia.

Lutheran deaconesses undergo special training, staff foreign missions, hospitals, parish offices, and welfare homes. They take installation vows and sometimes wear no distinctive garb but usually serve for life. Synods such as Missouri and Wisconsin operate training colleges for parochial school teachers. The immediate aim of the Missouri synod is 50 percent of its children in parochial schools.

All Lutheran churches have regulations against membership in lodges but only the Missouri and Wisconsin Synods enforce these regulations strictly. Some older LCA ministers are themselves high ranking Masons but LCA ministers are now forbidden to join a lodge. Synodical conference churches carry on active campaigns against secret societies and continually warn their members against affiliation.

Some synods have come out flatly in favor of birth control while other synods leave this matter up to the individual. Divorce with remarriage is allowed for such reasons as adultery and desertion because of "hardness of hearts." The LCA permits Lutheran pastors to witness a marriage of any divorced person who shows "repentance."

Lutheran worship is liturgical to a greater degree than that of most Protestants. They observe the church year, wear vestments, follow a set ritual. Their order of worship closely resembles the Catholic Mass from which it was adapted. The Common Service consists of silent prayer, hymn, confession of sin, declaration of grace, introit, Kyrie Eleison, gloria, collect, epistle and gospel, creed, hymn, sermon, general prayer, announcements, offering, hymn, the Our Father, and benediction.

The Lord's Supper is observed every Sunday by an increasing number of congregations. Others hold a communion service at least once a month. The preface, sanctus, communion prayer, words of institution, and *agnus dei* are used in the Order of Holy Communion on these occasions.

Music has always played a prominent part in Lutheran worship and someone has estimated that there are at least 100,000 Lutheran hymns. Their hymnology is enriched by the compositions of Bach, a devout Lutheran.

Either a crucifix or a plain cross will be found on the Lutheran altar which occupies the central position in the chancel. Candles, the Bible, and flowers are often found on the altar, and the altar hangings and vestments follow a color cycle which calls for white for Christmas, red for Reformation Sunday (Sunday nearest October 31), violet for Ash Wednesday, etc. Most ministers wear a cassock, surplice, and stole and some use the historic chasuble. During the day some pastors wear a clerical collar and dark suit but most wear ordinary business clothes. They prefer to be addressed as "Pastor" rather than as "Reverend" or "Mr."

European Lutheran churches follow an episcopal polity but those in America have preferred a congregational system which allows the local church to own property, call pastors, and elect church officers but which preserves doctrinal unity.

Surveying the Protestant panorama, Catholics will see that their Lutheran brethren have retained more of the central Christian doctrines than other Protestants. Modernism made little headway in Lutheran ranks. Relations between Catholics and Protestants in Germany, the homeland of the Reformation, have never been more cordial since the sixteenth century.

Encouraging signs of better feeling between Lutherans and Catholics in the U. S. have been seen in recent years. Lutheran ministers and Catholic priests are engaging in theological dialogue. Lutheran choirs have sung in Catholic churches and Catholics may be found singing Luther's powerful "A Mighty Fortress Is Our God" at Mass. Creative Lutheran theologians such as George Lindbeck, Martin E. Marty, and Jaroslav Pelikan have shown a profound understanding of Catholicism.

Professor Pelikan of the Yale University Divinity School faculty recently commented: "We (Lutherans) are theologically specific and theologically concerned. We are not concerned with positive thinking, with hustle-bustle for its own sake. The interesting thing is that while historical differences remain, Lutherans have begun to recognize that they are closer to Roman Catholics in many ways than they are to other Protestants."

A convention of the Lutheran Student Association of America in 1967 called for the organic reunion of the Lutheran and Roman Catholic chuches. The student resolution declared "the Lutheran tradition is not one of a separate church so much as an emergency movement within the pale of Roman Catholicism."

In 1970 a group of 25 distinguished Lutheran and Catholic theologians who had engaged in dialogue for some years called for a mutual recognition of ministry and Eucharist. The Roman

Catholic participants declared "The Lutheran communities with which we have been in dialogue are truly Christian churches, possessing the elements of holiness and truth that mark them as organs of grace and salvation. . . . We have found serious defects in the arguments customarily used against the validity of the Eucharistic ministry of the Lutheran churches. Accordingly we ask . . . that the Roman Catholic Church recognize the validity of the Lutheran ministry and the presence of the body and blood of Christ in the Eucharistic celebrations of the Lutheran churches."

Further Reading

Bainton, Roland, *Here I Stand* (Nashville, Abingdon, 1950).

Bergendoff, Conrad, *The Church of the Lutheran Reformation* (St. Louis, Concordia, 1967).

Loew, Ralph W., *The Lutheran Way of Life* (Englewood Cliffs, N.J., Prentice-Hall, 1966).

Todd, John M., *Martin Luther* (Westminster, Md., Newman, 1964).

Wentz, S. R., *A Basic History of Lutheranism in America,* rev. ed. (Philadelphia, Muhlenberg Press, 1955).

Chapter IV

THE PRESBYTERIANS
Calvinism Emphasizes the Sovereignty of God

LIKE the Episcopal Church, the Presbyterian Church takes its name from its form of government. Elected elders rather than bishops rule the Presbyterian churches. But the larger church exercises supervision over the congregations through presbyteries or associations of churches in a given area. This representative system strikes a mean between the town meeting democracy of the congregationalists and the autocracy of the episcopalians.

Theologically the Presbyterians also follow the teachings of John Calvin, a French lawyer who systematized non-Lutheran Protestantism in the sixteenth century. Not all Calvinists, for instance the Baptists and Congregationalists, are presbyterian in polity and likewise not all presbyterians, e.g., some Lutherans, are Calvinist in theology. We should keep in mind that presbyterianism refers to a particular representative form of church government while Calvinism refers to a theological emphasis which centered around the absolute sovereignty of God and the helplessness of man and, at least originally, predestination to heaven or hell.

American Presbyterianism is wealthy, sizable, influential, middle and upper class, generally conservative, often fashionable, and largely English, Scotch, and Scotch-Irish. Three denominations, the *United Presbyterian Church in the U.S.A.*, *The Presbyterian Church in the U.S.* (south), and the *Cumberland Presbyterian Church* enroll 98 per cent of the 4,327,000 commu-

46

nicants. Presbyterian or Reformed churches predominate in Scotland, Northern Ireland, and Holland and claim large constituencies in Switzerland, South Africa, Germany, and Hungary. Most French Protestants or Huguenots adhere to a Reformed theology. The world total is about 15,000,000 members of Presbyterian and Reformed Churches.

To trace the development of Presbyterianism we must go back to the early days of the Reformation. While Luther led the revolt in Germany an ex-priest, Ulrich Zwingli, established the new religion in Switzerland. Zwingli began to devour Luther's writings in 1518 and four years later he was denying the value of fasting and clerical celibacy. He petitioned his bishop for a release from the obligations of celibacy and when this was naturally denied he married the widow with whom he had been living. A daughter was born four months after the wedding.

Zwingli soon parted company with the German reformer on the question of the Real Presence of Christ in the Eucharist. This led to the split between Lutheran and Reformed Protestantism which continues to this day. Zwingli held the Lord's Supper to be nothing more than a simple memorial service whereas Luther upheld the Real Presence while denying the doctrine of transubstantiation. The Swiss reformer stripped the churches of all art and music and established a theocracy at Zurich. He was slain in 1531 in a battle against the Catholic cantons.

Jean Cauvin, known to us as John Calvin, was the son of a minor French ecclesiastical official. A year after his father's excommunication Calvin turned from the study of theology to law and in 1533 he embraced the new religious ideas of the Reformation. His reasons for leaving the Catholic Church were never explicitly stated but he became the tireless propagator of the new religion. Fearing persecution he left his native country. At Basle he composed his classic exposition of Reformation doctrine, the *Institutes of the Christian Religion*. He was 27 at the time.

A reformer at Geneva, where he had stopped to spend the night, persuaded him to stay and guide the Protestant community in this Swiss city of about 15,000 population. Calvin agreed and set about establishing what might be termed a religious police state. Modeled after Old Testament theocracies, the Geneva city government employed harsh penalties, espionage, and religious sanctions to enforce a drab and severe religious code. Calvin fulminated against dancing, amusements, luxuries, feast days, indolence, and vestigial Catholic practices. After two years of this regime the citizens rebelled and forced Calvin to leave.

He taught at Strassbourg for three years, married a widow, and finally received a second invitation to come to Geneva. During his exile he had perfected his presbyterian system of representative church government. Older and wiser, Calvin returned and undertook to transform Geneva into a model Protestant community. Thousands of religious rebels from Europe and the British Isles swelled the city's population and returned to their homelands with Calvinistic orientations.

Calvinism furnished the theological foundation for the Huguenots and for the more successful Reformed churches of the Netherlands. John Knox brought Calvinism to Scotland and Scotland has always been the main Presbyterian center. English divines banished by the Catholic Queen Mary found refuge in Geneva and when they returned under Elizabeth they carried their Calvinism with them.

Classical Calvinism based its theology on five points, all of which have been drastically modified by modern Presbyterianism: (1) predestination or election; (2) limited atonement; (3) total depravity; (4) the irresistibility of grace; and (5) perseverance of the saints. In other words, Calvin taught that man's nature since the Fall is totally depraved. God elects some men to salvation and damns others to hell. Christ died only for the elect, who cannot resist God's grace and cannot backslide once they have received this grace of election.

"We assert that by an eternal and immutable counsel, God has once for all determined, both whom He would admit to salvation, and whom He would condemn to destruction," wrote Calvin. Calvinists generally relied on passages from St. Augustine to substantiate their views of absolute or double predestination. They deduced that unbaptized babies were certain to be cast into hell and the American theologian and preacher Jonathan Edwards asserted, "Hell is paved with the skulls of unbaptized children."

The pure Calvinist impulse to reaffirm the absolute sovereignty of God and to expose the idolatry of acting as though God and man existed on the same plane was often misdirected. By 1741 Edwards was presenting the following picture of God the Father to his congregation: "The God that holds you over the pit of hell, much as one holds a spider, or some loathsome insect, over the fire, abhors you and is dreadfully provoked; His wrath towards you burns like fire; He looks upon you as worthy of nothing but to be cast into the fire; He is of purer eyes than to bear to have you in His sight; you are ten thousand times so abominable in His eyes, as the most hateful and venomous serpent is in ours."

The Catholic Church approaches the question of predestination with greater trepidation than Lawyer Calvin. The Council of Trent called predestination "a hidden mystery." Catholicism upholds the truth that salvation is primarily God's work and His grace but that man is not totally depraved. After justification he may offer the merits of good works for his salvation. Man possesses free will, and whether a man is saved or damned he arrives at this state through the exercise of his free will. God condemns no one to hell; man condemns himself to hell by his sins. Calvinism finds itself in the position of implicating God with sin since, if God damns a soul to hell, He must also force that soul to sin to deserve hell.

Whereas Luther claimed to preserve whatever was not specifically forbidden by the Bible, Calvin sought to reject everything which was not positively commanded. He divested the Reformed worship service of all beauty when he discarded vestments, altar, images, paintings, organs, and hymns. God could be praised only by His own words, therefore, Calvin forbade any hymns but the psalms themselves. Today Presbyterians acknowledge Calvinistic excesses and have reintroduced Christian art and symbolism into their architecture, chancels, and liturgies.

Calvin adopted a position on the Eucharist slightly closer to Luther's than was Zwingli's, but like Zwingli he upheld a mystical rather than a substantial Real Presence. The Calvinist receives the bread and wine as a guaranty of the grace flowing into his soul from Christ in heaven.

Calvinism encouraged education, sobriety, thrift, political as well as religious democracy, philanthropy, capitalism, Bible reading, and the somber Sabbath. The Bible became an infallible rule of conduct and the Calvinists accorded relatively greater emphasis to the Old Testament than did other Christians.

Max Weber and R. H. Tawney have suggested the positive relationship between Calvinism and the rise of capitalism. Calvinism stressed the secular vocation, lifted the bans against interest, offered investment opportunities to the many Protestant refugees in Geneva, and pointed out that the elect might well be identified by their material prosperity since God would favor His elect.

In striving to give all possible honor to God Calvin eventually presented a God who arbitrarily damned souls to hell and forced men to sin, who condemned innocent babies to eternal torment, who denied free will to both the elect and the reprobate. His followers today generally regard predestination as a "hidden mystery." The expected reaction against the harsher aspects of Calvinism came from the Dutch theologian Arminius who re-emphasized free will and inspired Wesleyan theology.

Afflicted by headaches and indigestion, Calvin nevertheless kept up an exhausting daily routine. In 1553 he consented to the burning of the Spanish Unitarian, Michael Servetus. Humorless, cold, and ruthlessly logical, he had few close friends but was greatly respected. He died at the age of 54 and shares with Martin Luther the title Father of the Protestant Reformation.

Protestantism never managed to make much headway in Calvin's native France. The politically inspired St. Bartholomew's Day massacre in 1572 involved the slaughter of 30,000 Huguenots. The Edict of Nantes in 1598 granted them freedom of worship but when it was revoked by Louis XIV in 1685 thousands of French Protestants, many of them skilled artisans, fled to other lands.

Among the Huguenot refugees who fled to America were the Duponts whose descendants control a family fortune estimated at several billion dollars. The French Revolution decimated Protestant as well as Catholic churches and today French Protestants number fewer than one million.

The Reformed faith took deep root in the Netherlands and the royal family of Holland and a majority of the people belong to one of the two main Reformed churches. Dutch colonists carried the Reformed Church to North America, South Africa, and the Dutch East Indies.

On the continent about 600,000 Germans hold the Reformed faith in a nation which is largely Lutheran and Catholic; the once powerful Hungarian Reformed Church has sustained losses.

John Knox had been a Catholic priest, Protestant preacher, exile in England, and galley slave in the French navy before reaching Geneva. What he learned from Calvin during three years in that city he taught in his native Scotland, opposing the Catholicism of Mary Queen of Scots and the Anglicanism of the English. He helped dethrone Mary and maneuvered the Scottish parliament into establishing Presbyterianism as the state religion. Periodic attempts were made to overthrow Scottish Presbyterianism and substitute an episcopal system. Charles II sniffed, "Presbyterianism is not a religion for gentlemen." The church suffered a number of schisms over the issues of monarchy and lay patronage but a union of all major branches was effected in 1929 in the Church of Scotland.

Scotch colonists settled confiscated lands in Northern Ireland or Ulster and soon that area of the island was mainly Scotch. These Scotch-Irish took their Presbyterianism with them to the Catholic island. Today Ireland, including the six northern countries, is one fourth Protestant, mainly Presbyterian. Between 1729 and 1809 a steady stream of Scotch-Irish emigrated to America and one such immigrant, the Rev. Francis Makemie, is considered the father of Presbyterianism in this country. The Scotch-Irish influenced the course of American Presbyterianism more than any other nationality.

In England the Church of England was pestered by two groups: the Puritans and the Separatists. Both wished to purify the state church of such popish practices as the sign of the cross, the use of vestments and images, kneeling for prayer, feast days, etc. The Separatists, however, believed that the Anglican church was hopeless; they felt compelled to separate from this church and found another, purer church. The Puritans were convinced that they could remain Anglicans and bring about their reforms from within. Calvinism pervaded both parties and most but not all of the Puritans were also Presbyterians, with a sprinkling of Congregationalists.

Eventually the Puritan party gained power in England and the episcopacy was abolished. "No bishop and no king" was their motto. Parliament called together 151 clergymen and laymen, most of whom were Presbyterians, to formulate a confession of faith. The delegates remained in session for five years at Westminster, threw out the Book of Common Prayer, and prepared the Westminster Confession of 1648, a Directory of Worship, a Form of Government, and a Larger and Shorter Catechism. Fourteen years later the Puritan Commonwealth under Cromwell gave way to the monarchy and the Anglican hierarchy was restored.

The Westminster Confession remains the standard of faith for American, Scottish, and English Presbyterianism but its statement on predestination has been modified from its original form: "By the decree of God, for the manifestation of His glory, some men and angels are predestined unto everlasting life, and others fore-ordained to everlasting death. . . . The rest of mankind, God was pleased . . . to pass by, and to ordain them to dishonor and wrath for their sin, to the praise of His glorious justice."

Presbyterianism in England crumbled in the eighteenth century as a result of government disabilities, Arian and Unitarian heresies, and a poorly trained ministry. Only later Scottish immigration saved Presbyterianism from extinction there and even now the denomination counts only 100,000 adherents in that country.

Puritan ministers brought Presbyterianism to America where they soon followed the Separatists out of the Church of England. Some switched to Congregationalism in the Massachusetts Bay Colony but others remained Presbyterians. Makemie organized the first presbytery, an essential of that form of polity, at Philadelphia in 1706. Disagreement over the place of revivals in the church and interpretations of the Confession led to the New Side-Old Side division which lasted from 1741 to 1758.

Presbyterians were almost 100 per cent behind the colonists in the American Revolution. In fact, the Revolution was known by many in England as the "Presbyterian Rebellion." This attitude was in contrast to that of the Loyalist Methodists and Anglicans.

Of the 55 signers of the Declaration of Independence, 12 were Presbyterians including the only clergyman to sign: the Rev. John Witherspoon. Eventually six Presbyterians would occupy the White House: Presidents Buchanan, Jackson, Benjamin Harrison, Cleveland, Wilson, and Eisenhower. General Eisenhower delayed joining any church until he had retired from active military service and entered politics. His opponent in the 1952 and 1956 elections, Adlai Stevenson, held dual membership in Unitarian and Presbyterian churches.

The two Calvinist denominations, Presbyterian and Congregationalist, entered into a Plan of Union whereby congregations on the western frontier could maintain affiliations with both denominations. Although this Plan usually worked to the advantage of the Presbyterians, an Old School party within Presbyterianism complained of Congregational influence. This led to the schism of 1837 which was not healed until after the Civil War. In 1920 the Welsh Calvinistic Methodists joined what was then known as the northern *Presbyterian Church in the U.S.A.*

Slavery was not the sole reason for the schism of the southern branch, now known as the *Presbyterian Church in the U.S.,* with 961,000 members. The southerners also disliked the liberalism of their northern brothers. They have remained more conservative than the northern church and are concentrated in 16 southern states. Fraternal relations are cultivated between the northern and southern Presbyterian churches and ministers and members freely switch affiliation.

Revivalism led in 1810 to the secession of the Cumberland presbytery which had begun to ordain preachers lacking the proper educational qualifications. The Cumberlanders organized their own church when they were officially dissolved by the Kentucky synod. They preached an Arminian rather than a pure Calvinist doctrine but no greater a departure from Geneva Calvinism than that now held by the northern church. Most of the

Cumberlanders rejoined the parent church in 1906 but 88,000 members are reported by the *Cumberland Presbyterian Church* which refused to enter the reunion. The parallel *Second Cumberland Church* enrolls another 30,000.

The United Presbyterian Church of North America represented an 1858 merger of two strict Scotch Presbyterian churches. Both had withdrawn from the Church of Scotland. Particularly before 1925 this denomination had been known for its espousal of classical Calvinism, opposition to secret societies, exclusive use of the psalms in worship, and closed communion.

Completion of the merger of the northern Presbyterians and the United Presbyterians was announced in 1958. The 3,165,000 member church is known as the *United Presbyterian Church in the U.S.A.* Overtures for a similar merger with the southern branch have encountered opposition and disinterest but an eventual union is anticipated within a decade.

While Episcopalians have fussed over ritualism and Methodists debated the evils of smoking and drinking, Presbyterians have stoked the fires of theological controversy. They stood on the firing line in the leading fundamentalist-modernist battles which shook American Protestantism from 1910 to about 1925.

Two wealthy Presbyterian laymen in Los Angeles published the tracts which outlined the "fundamentals" of the Christian faith. More than 3,000,000 copies of *The Fundamentals*, the articles of war against modernism, the social gospel, and evolutionary theory, were distributed in 1910 and the years following. Presbyterian evangelist, the Rev. Dr. (Westminster college) Billy Sunday, enlivened tent and tabernacle with his colorful denunciations of modernists, saloon keepers, birth controllers, and Socialists.

Dr. Harry Emerson Fosdick, a Baptist, occupied the pulpit of New York's First Presbyterian church. His frankly modernist position and specific denial of the virgin birth prompted the General Assembly to invite him to become a Presbyterian (under its jurisdiction) or give up his position as pastor of a Presbyterian church. He followed the latter course and continued to expound his liberal theological views at Riverside church.

Modernism continued to upset Presbyterian conservatism

long after the main battle ended. A small group of conservatives followed Prof. J. Gresham Machen of Princeton out of the mother church. Machen, one of the ablest advocates of fundamentalism and one of its few real scholars, organized the Presbyterian Church of America but the courts made him adopt another name for his church, the *Orthodox Presbyterian Church*.

Shortly thereafter some of the Machen schismatics disagreed with him on total abstinence and millennialism and set up their own *Bible Presbyterian Church* now known as the *Evangelical Presbyterian Church*. Rev. Carl McIntire, leader of this faction, also bitterly opposed the Federal Council of Churches as modernist and organized his American Council of Churches and later the International Council of Churches.

Presbyterianism has traditionally been strong in the Middle Atlantic states of New York, New Jersey, and Pennsylvania but it also enrolls large memberships in Ohio, Michigan, Indiana, Illinois, Iowa, and California.

Forty-four colleges and universities are related to the northern church and 16 others to the southern church. Presbyterian seminary curricula still include Hebrew and Greek and more theology than most Protestant denominations offer their ministerial candidates. Princeton and McCormick in Chicago are two leading seminaries. It has been estimated that 85 per cent of young Presbyterians of college age are attending college.

The whole number of the elect comprise the invisible church according to Presbyterian thought; the visible church consists of "all those throughout the world that profess the true religion, together with their children, and is the Kingdom of the Lord Jesus Christ." The following description of the visible head of the Roman Catholic Church was revised by the northern Presbyterians in 1903: "There is no other head of the Church but the Lord Jesus Christ. Nor can the pope of Rome in any sense be head thereof; but is that anti-christ, that man of sin, and son of perdition, that exalteth himself, in the Church, against Christ, and all that is called God."

On that matter of predestination and free will today's Presbyterian stands much closer to the original Catholic position than did Calvin. You would have to look to the tiny Presbyterian sects to hear absolute or double predestination preached. The drastic modification of the Westminster Confession is indicated in the 1903 interpretation of the northern church: "Concerning those who perish the doctrine of God's eternal decree is held in harmony with the doctrine that God desires not the death of any sinner, but has provided in Christ a salvation sufficient for all . . . men are fully responsible for their treatment of God's gracious offer . . . his decree hinders no man from accepting that offer . . . no man is condemned except on the ground of his sin."

Presbyterians do not consider baptism necessary for salvation but do urge that infants and adults receive the sacrament. The usual form is sprinkling. The current theory about the fate of unbaptized infants who die in infancy differs from Edwards' grim description of hell's pavement. Presbyterians now assume that death in infancy is a sure sign of election and the soul of the infant will spend eternity not in hell or limbo but in heaven, even though unbaptized.

Each Presbyterian congregation elects about a dozen ruling elders and a teaching elder all of whom are ordained church officials. The teaching elder is the minister but theoretically he holds a position on a par with the other elders. The Session, comprised of the pastor and the ruling elders, is supervised by the presbytery or regional body to which it belongs. At least five Sessions are needed to form a presbytery which is composed of all the ministers and one ruling elder from each church. The presbytery examines and ordains candidates for the ministry, installs and removes ministers, settles doctrinal and disciplinary questions, checks the records of local churches, starts new churches, and the like. Except in the case of national or racial groupings, the presbyteries are plotted on geographical lines.

The Synod performs the same function for the presbyteries which the latter perform for the churches. Most Synods are organized along state lines with at least three presbyteries in each synod. In the northern church, for example, there are 40 synods and in the southern church, 14. The member presbyteries elect an equal number of ministers and ruling elders to the synod which meets once a year.

The General Assembly tops the national Presbyterian structure and includes an equal number of pastors and elders from each presbytery. The powers of the Assembly include the right to suppress heresy and schism, reorganize synods, settle doctrinal and disciplinary controversies, and ratify mergers with other denominations.

Members of Presbyterian churches in the United States need not subscribe to the Westminster Confession or any other creed. Such a declaration of belief is required of ministers, ruling elders, and deacons but even in these cases ingenious interpretations may be devised by modernist sympathizers. If we were to rank Protestant denominations according to theological liberalism, we would probably put the Presbyterians somewhere between the Congregationalists, Disciples, and Methodists, on the one hand, and the Lutherans, Episcopalians, and Baptists on the other.

Controversy surrounds the proposal to adopt a new confession of faith to supplement the Westminster Confession of 1648. The new confession rejects a literal interpretation of the Bible and urges the application of literary and historical scholarship to scripture study. It also disclaims the original Calvinist doctrine of predestination and affirms that salvation occurs when divine love heals the conflicts that separate man from God. Some presbyteries have opposed the new statement but adoption is expected. Some Presbyterians of a fundamentalist persuasion might feel more comfortable in another Reformed church.

Presbyterianism has always made its greatest appeal to activist Anglo-Saxons. Unchurched Americans looking for a church home may decide to affiliate with the Presbyterian church which they see as less nationalistic than the Lutheran, more fashionable than the Baptist, more democratic than the Episcopalian, less blue-nosed than the Methodist, and more traditional than the Disciples.

As we have seen, traditional Calvinist principles carry little weight in twentieth-century Presbyterianism. Predestination, for example, may be the first thought a Catholic observer associates with this church but it has become an historical curiosity for the average Presbyterian layman. The drab and barren Calvinist worship is being enriched by a return to the practices of the ancient church. Here more so than in many denominations we find a huge gulf between the classical formulation and present-day beliefs.

Further Reading

Mackinnon, James, *Calvin and the Reformation* (New York, Russell and Russell, 1962).

McNeill, John T., *The History and Character of Calvinism* (New York, Oxford University Press, 1967).

Wendell, Francois, *Calvin* (New York, Harper & Row, 1963).

Chapter V

THE EPISCOPALIANS

Comprehensive Christianity:
Calvinism and Catholicism

A ROMAN Catholic who happened to visit an "Anglo-Catholic'" church some Sunday morning would find himself in a familiar setting. He would observe the holy water fonts, the confessional booths, the stations of the cross, statues, and the sanctuary lamp. The officiating Episcopalian priest wears the traditional Christian vestments, the alb, stole, cincture, and chasuble or cope. The sermon at this Holy Communion or Mass might concern the seven sacraments, fast and abstinence regulations, or the Real Presence of Christ in the Eucharist. The visitor might easily imagine himself in his own parish church.

But were he to continue his Episcopalian itinerary, he might be puzzled at his next stop. This second Episcopal church, three or 300 miles away, might resemble a typical Protestant chapel in architecture, ecclesiastical furniture, vestment, and liturgy—little different from a Congregational or Methodist church. The minister would be vested in surplice and stole and the main worship service would be Morning Prayer rather than a communion service or Anglican Mass. The congregation might be hearing a sermon on justification by faith alone or the sole sufficiency of the scripture or the two Christian sacraments as opposed to the seven sacraments of the Catholic Church.

A third Episcopal church might resemble the first or second in appearance and liturgy but the sermon would soon disclose a rationalist or modernist slant which would find an equal welcome in Unitarian circles.

Our Catholic visitor would have seen representative parishes of the three main parties in Anglicanism: the High Church or "Anglo-Catholic," the Low or Evangelical, and the broad or Modernist. The Church of England and its American counterpart, the Protestant Episcopal church, embraces a wider spectrum of doctrine and practice than any major Protestant communion.

Claiming to be both Catholic and Protestant, it combines the ritual and polity of Catholicism with a moderately Calvinistic theology. Episcopalians assert that they resist the "additions of Romanism and the subtractions of Protestantism." Episcopal divines do not claim that theirs is the only Catholic Church but that it constitutes one of four branches of the Catholic Church: Roman Catholic, Eastern Orthodox, Anglican, and Old Catholic.

Unlike most Protestant sects, Anglicanism values the apostolic succession, the episcopacy, and the priesthood. Anglicans are happy to acknowledge the authority of the pope as the Bishop of Rome but deny that his authority extends beyond the boundaries of his own diocese. Pope Leo XIII declared Anglican orders invalid in 1896 although the Church has always recognized the validity of Orthodox and Old Catholic orders.

Anglicanism differs from the products of the Continental Reformation in that the motives for the separation of the Church of England from Rome were admittedly political rather than religious. No one suggests that Henry VIII severed the English ties with Rome and set himself up as head of the national church for spiritual reasons. Neither theological disputes nor a demand for the elimination of abuses played a big part in the English revolt.

One consequence of the purely political motivation has been that the Anglican church retains more Catholic beliefs and forms than either the Lutheran or Reformed churches. And since the Oxford Movement of the past century the Church of England has witnessed a revival of Catholic practices which has brought large sections of the establishment closer to Rome than at any time since the reign of Queen Elizabeth.

Forty monks accompanied St. Augustine to Britain on a missionary journey commissioned by Pope Gregory. He found a handful of Christians in Wales and Western England, remnants of the Christian community which had flourished in Roman times, who had been pushed into corners of the island by pagan Angles and Saxons. He became the first Archbishop of Canterbury.

For nearly 1000 years the Church in England recognized the supremacy of the bishop of Rome as did the rest of Western Christendom. For example, Venerable Bede wrote in A.D. 735: "The Pope bears pontifical power over the whole world." In the eleventh century St. Anselm of Canterbury declared, "It is certain that he who does not obey the Roman Pontiff is disobedient to the Apostle Peter, nor is he of that flock given to Peter by God." In 1154 an Englishman, Nicholas Breakspeare, was elected pope.

Episcopalians have good reason to object to Catholic controversialists who attempt to prove that their church was founded by the lustful Henry VIII. The monarch would have been an uncomfortable Episcopalian. A fair theologian himself, Henry penned a volume on the Seven Sacraments and a refutation of Lutheran errors which won him the title from the pope of "Defender of the Faith." English kings still bear this papal title.

Validly married to the Spanish princess Catherine of Aragon, the king became enamored of Anne Boleyn, a lady in waiting. Anxious to marry Anne and provide a male heir for the throne, the king asked for an annulment but the pope hesitated and refused.

His archbishop of Canterbury, Thomas Cranmer, took it upon himself to declare the marriage to Catherine invalid and Henry announced himself to be the sole head of the Church of England in 1534. The Act of Supremacy stated that: "The Bishop of Rome hath not by Scripture any greater authority in England than any other foreign bishop." Sir Thomas More, the Lord Chancellor, among others, was executed for refusing to recognize this spiritual supremacy of the king. All of the English bishops except one, John Fisher, bowed to the king's wishes.

Although he suppressed some 616 monasteries (to get needed funds) and murdered hundreds of bishops, monks, nobles, and women, the king never departed from orthodox Catholic teachings except for the question of papal supremacy. He insisted on communion under one species, auricular confession, clerical celibacy, requiem masses, and belief in transubstantiation. No Catholic wishes to present Henry as a Christian model but he did hold fast to dogmatic positions and he quashed efforts to Protestantize the national church. Cranmer was obliged to pack his secret Lutheran wife and children back to Germany.

Henry VIII removed the English church from obedience to the Roman See but he never tampered with doctrine. Priests continued to offer true Masses and bishops ordained true priests during his rule. For the common man Catholic life continued much as before the administrative quarrel. England was in schism not heresy. Rather than being the first Anglican, Henry was a disobedient and wicked Catholic.

The Protestant party captured the English church during the subsequent seven year reign of the tubercular boy king Edward VI, the son of Henry and wife No. 3, Jane Seymour. Members of the Reformed faith flocked to England from the continent with their novel doctrines of justification by faith alone, two sacraments, the sole sufficiency of the Bible. Priests took wives, the Mass was abolished, and churches were stripped of works of art. Cranmer's Book of Common Prayer cut the sacrificial heart out of the Mass and the revised ordination rite made no mention of the sacrificial powers of the priest.

Matthew Parker, a married cleric with Lutheran sympathies, was consecrated (1559) according to the defective Edwardian ordinal of 1552. Through Parker; all Church of England bishops claim to trace their apostolic succession. The defective form was employed, from the accession of Queen Elizabeth until 1662. By the end of this period all validly consecrated Anglican bishops had died and the apostolic succession was broken.

Queen Mary, the daughter of Henry and Catherine, reigned until 1558 and vowed to return the church to its Catholic heritage. For a period of almost five years from 1554 the English church was reunited with Rome and the Holy Father sent Cardinal Pole as his delegate to consolidate the reunion. The Protestant innovators were exiled and Cranmer was burned at the stake. Mary's efforts to re-establish the ancient faith failed and earned her the title "Bloody Mary" in Protestant history texts.

Elizabeth, the daughter of Henry and Anne, again cut the ties with Rome. She abolished the Mass and reintroduced the oath of supremacy although she called herself the Supreme Governor rather than the Supreme Head of the church. She stabilized what has become known as Anglicanism and could more logically be considered the founder of the Church of England than her notorious father. The Thirty-nine Articles, trimmed from 42, formed the doctrinal standard for the national church, now definitely in the Protestant camp. Queen Elizabeth and all members of the Church of England were excommunicated by Pope Pius V, an action which Cardinal Newman and other Catholic writers have considered a blunder which only bolstered anti-Catholicism in the nation.

Successes over the hated Spanish and the destruction of the Armada, political astuteness, and economic prosperity contributed to the queen's popularity. The new religion shared the credit for the nation's good fortune. As critical of the dissenting Presbyterians and Congregationalists as of the Papists, the queen suppressed all non-Anglicans by force.

Eventually the Puritans, Anglicans who wished to purify their church of lingering popish practices, established a dictatorship under Oliver Cromwell. In the restoration Charles II again made the Anglican church supreme.

The established church lost members to the energetic Baptist, Congregational, Quaker and Presbyterian bodies; in the 18th century the Wesleyan revival led thousands out of the Anglican fold. Today the Church of England reports 27 million baptized members but only 10 million have been confirmed and only 3 million can be found on any parish rolls. The Roman Catholic church also reports about 3 million active members in England.

A century after the start of the Wesleyan movement the Church of England experienced a different sort of revival. The Oxford Movement called for a return to Catholic traditions, a renewed sacramental life, a greater appreciation of the church, the episcopacy, and the priesthood. John Henry Newman and other Oxford men sparked the movement which revitalized Anglicanism and gave birth to the High Church or Anglo-Catholic party. Newman himself submitted to the Catholic Church in 1845, inspired several others to follow him into the Church, and died a cardinal at the age of 89.

British colonists brought Anglicanism to American shores in the Virginia settlement in 1607. Completely dependent on the mother church and the Bishop of London, the American branch had no bishop or diocesan organization for 177 years. Candidates for the priesthood had to risk smallpox and shipwreck to return to England for ordination and the colonials were unable to receive confirmation until after the American Revolution. That an episcopal church without bishops showed little vitality should not be surprising.

At the outbreak of the Revolution most Anglican clergymen fled to England and Canada since they had taken an oath of loyalty to the king. Before the outbreak of hostilities the Church of England had been supported by taxes in seven Southern colonies. In Virginia, for example, the law stipulated an Anglican clergyman's salary at "1,500 pounds of tobacco and 16 barrels of corn." With this financial support gone, its clergy scattered and discredited, and its name closely associated with the recent enemy, the Church of England in the American colonies faced serious postwar problems.

The remaining Anglicans selected Samuel Seabury to be bishop. He spent a year in England seeking consecration but the law forbade consecration of a bishop who was not a British subject. In desperation, Seabury turned to the outlawed Scottish Episcopal Church which granted him consecration in 1784. Three years later the Archbishops of Canterbury and York did consecrate two Americans. A General Convention in Philadelphia in 1789 united the Anglicans in America into the *Protestant Episcopal Church.*

Few immigrants after the Revolution professed the Anglican faith and the church was unable to hold its own on the frontier against the aggressive Methodist and Baptist preachers. By 1830 only 30,000 Protestant Episcopal communicants could be counted and these were clustered on the Atlantic seaboard. During the Civil War the Southern bishops organized a Confederate church but in the calm after the war the two branches were reunited.

As in England the High Church movement introduced more ritual and beauty into the liturgy. The use of incense and the question of vestments enlivened the ritualist controversy with Bishop John Henry Hobart of New York and William Augustus Muhlenberg, a convert from Lutheranism, upholding the High Church position. Between 1825 and 1855 thirty Episcopalian priests entered the Catholic Church.

Phillips Brooks, recognized as the greatest preacher in the Episcopal church, guided the Broad movement from his pulpit in Trinity church, Boston. This party represented modernism and rationalism in the Unitarian stronghold but has remained relatively small compared to the Anglo-Catholic wing.

A group of low churchmen seceded in 1873 to found the *Reformed Episcopal Church,* the only serious schism in Episcopalian history in this country. They abhorred all ritual, and deleted such words as "priest, altar, sacrament, and holy communion" from their revision of the Book of Common Prayer. This church has declined in membership and now numbers fewer than 7,100 members.

The typical Episcopalian minister can be called a Prayer Book clergyman who follows a middle course, avoiding the extremes of Anglo-Catholicism, evangelicalism, and modernism. The Thirty-nine articles, which are relegated to the appendix in the Book of Common Prayer, do not bind either priest or layman. At ordination Episcopal priests must declare: "I do believe the Holy Scriptures of the Old and New Testaments to be the Word of God, and to contain all things necessary to salvation; and I do solemnly engage to conform to the Doctrine, Discipline, and Worship of the Protestant Episcopal Church in the United States of America."

Most Episcopalians would consider that the Apostles' and Nicene creeds reflect their creedal beliefs, but they may attach unorthodox interpretations or reservations to these historic creeds. Anglicans are accustomed to appeal to the teachings of the undivided Church, the Church which existed before the East-West schism in 1054. Despite the ordination declaration the Anglican priest is unlikely to hold the Bible to be the sole rule of faith. He will probably add the tradition of the undivided Church and the use of reason to the Scriptures as rules of faith. Many concur in the Reformed or symbolic interpretation of the Eucharist. Anglicans do not use the term "purgatory" but they believe in a state of purification which they may call the Church Expectant. Some Anglican theologians entertain universalist views and express doubts that God's mercy may be reconciled with an eternal hell.

In contrast to the plainly Protestant positions of most of their Episcopalian brethren, the Anglo-Catholics stress the Catholic heritage. Anglo-Catholicism is aggressive and articulate, which may lead some Roman Catholics to overestimate its strength within the Protestant Episcopal Church. The head of the American Church Union, the chief Anglo-Catholic organization, estimates there are 200,000 Anglo-Catholics out of a total of 3,330,000 Episcopalians but adds that perhaps 1,000,000 more may support specific Anglo-Catholic positions.

A midwestern "biretta belt" of Anglo-Catholicism embraces the dioceses of Fond du Lac, Eau Claire, Milwaukee, Chicago, Quincy, Springfield, and Northern Indiana. The Long Island diocese also figures prominently in the movement and Anglo-Catholic parishes may be found in New York and other Episcopal dioceses. Nashotah House in Wisconsin trains many Anglo-Catholic priests.

Anglo-Catholics emphasize the seven sacraments, the Real Presence, fast and abstinence, auricular confession, prayers and requiem Masses for the dead, retreats, invocation of the saints. They say the rosary, make the sign of the cross, genuflect, address their priests as "Father."

The papalist Confraternity of Unity, with an executive board of 16 Anglican priests, is "composed of members of the Anglican communion who believe that the See of Rome is the Center of Unity for all churches. . . . Members are asked to pray daily for reunion with the Holy Apostolic See."

The Guild of All Souls promotes the celebration of requiem Masses and prayers for the dead. The American chapter of the Living Rosary of Our Lady and St. Dominic encourages Episcopalians to recite the rosary while the Confraternity of the Blessed Sacrament of the Body and Blood of Christ directs the attention of Anglicans to the Real Presence.

Although usually outvoted in the General Convention, the Anglo-Catholics have long urged that the word "Protestant" be dropped from the official title of the church. They have managed to scuttle attempts at merger with the Presbyterians and perennially condemn open communion and open pulpits. They have recently been asking for permission to reserve the communion elements on the altar.

Anglo-Catholicism revived religious orders in Anglicanism after a lapse of 300 years. Eleven Episcopalian orders for men and 14 for women seek to follow the evangelical counsels of poverty, chastity, and obedience. These include the Holy Cross Order, the Society of St. John the Evangelist, and Episcopalian Franciscans, and Benedictines; and the Sisterhoods of St. Mary, the Holy Nativity, St. Margaret, St. Anne, and Poor Clares. Besides the sisters, Episcopalian deaconesses assist rectors in parish work or in any activity entrusted to them by a bishop. Anglican canon law recognizes the religious vocation of those men and women who bind themselves by vows in a religious community. The priests and monks conduct missions and retreats, engage in charitable and parish work, publish magazines and tracts, while the Episcopalian sisters generally operate girls' academies. One such Anglican community, the Society of the Atonement, entered the Catholic Church in a body in 1905 and now numbers more than 500 priests, brothers, and sisters.

With rules closely modeled on those of the Society of Jesus and the Congregation of the Mission (Lazarists), the Society of St. John the Evangelist was the first successful religious order for men in the Church of England. Popularly known as the Cowley Fathers, these Anglican religious came to the United States in 1870, five years after the founding of their community in England. Their spiritual formation centers around the Mass, the Divine Office, confession, and daily meditation.

Anglo-Catholics often find themselves in the awkward position of reinforcing the authority of Episcopal bishops whose views they consider heretical. One Episcopal bishop may encourage, another may tolerate, and another forbid such Anglo-

Catholic practices as the use of incense and holy water in his diocese. The average Episcopalian seems to view the Anglo-Catholics with a mixture of suspicion and amusement. Many of them, of course, are completely unaware of the nature of Anglo-Catholicism and may not even have heard of Anglican religious orders.

Bishops govern the 74 dioceses and 13 mission districts in the United States. They are elected by the clergy and laity of the diocese with the approval of the other bishops and a majority of the standing committees. Compulsory retirement for bishops is set at 72. Every three years the House of Bishops and the House of Deputies convene in the General Convention. The latter House includes clerical and lay delegates.

The worldwide Anglican communion of 40,000,000 Christians comprises a number of independent sister churches such as those of England, Wales, Scotland, Ireland, Canada, Australia and Tasmania, New Zealand, Burma and Ceylon, South Africa, the West Indies, and the United States. Besides these are the semiautonomous churches of China, Japan, East and West Africa, and scattered dioceses and missions. The Anglican church is largely confined to England and to former English colonies.

Every ten years the Archbishop of Canterbury invites all 345 bishops to meet at his residence, Lambeth Palace. The decisions of the Lambeth Conference do not bind independent churches or individual Anglicans. Therefore, some Anglo-Catholics continue to condemn contraception and the remarriage of divorcees after the Conference sanctioned these practices.

The king or queen of England is technically head of the Church of England (he or she automatically becomes head of the Presbyterian Church of Scotland after crossing the border from England). Actually the prime minister appoints the Archbishop of Canterbury and the prime minister may be and has been a Unitarian, Baptist, and Presbyterian, and could conceivably be a Roman Catholic or Jew. Not a Christian monarch but a non-Christian parliament rules the Church of England. When the church presented revisions of the Book of Common Prayer in 1927-28 the House of Commons simply refused to accept the proposed revisions and the churchmen were helpless. The word "obey" was, however, deleted from the wedding ceremony.

The German church historian von Dollinger characterized the Anglican establishment in the following words: "There is no church that is so completely and thoroughly as the Anglican the product and expression of the wants and wishes, the modes of thought and cast of character, not of a certain nationality, but of a fragment of a nation, namely, the rich, fashionable, and cultivated classes. It is the religion of deportment, of gentility, of clerical reserve."

Certainly in the United States the Episcopal church counts a distinguished roster of communicants, among them George Washington, Alexander Hamilton, James Madison, John Marshall, Henry Clay, Patrick Henry, Daniel Webster, Admirals Farragut and Dewey, Robert E. Lee, Washington Irving, James Fenimore Cooper, Francis Scott Key, and Franklin D. Roosevelt.

Here as elsewhere the Episcopal church caters to those in the upper class and this class orientation limits its social ministry. Its settlement houses and home missions attract some of those in the poorer economic status. As in colonial times it finds its chief strength on the Eastern seaboard.

Once labelled "the Republican party at prayer," the Episcopal church has attempted to broaden its appeal in recent years. Many priests and laymen labor in inner city missions among people far removed socially from the society leaders who also attend Episcopalian churches.

Throughout its history in America the Episcopal church has refused to follow the Puritanical path of other Protestant churches and sects. Like the Lutheran church it has declined to join campaigns against liquor, tobacco, gambling, dancing, the theater, and the like.

The Episcopal church has established relatively few colleges for its size: Hobart, Kenyon, St. Augustine, Trinity, and University of the South. However, these are first class institutions. On the other hand, the church supports dozens of academies and prep schools, including some of the best known in the country. Twelve seminaries train Episcopal clergy.

The English background of most of its clergy and laity might be expected but its present clergy lists include such names as

Cherbonnier, Chavez, De Christofaro, Hoffenbacher, Kitagawa, O'Grady, Scarinci, and Wittkofski.

Close relations are cultivated between the Episcopal church and the Polish National Catholic, Eastern Orthodox, and Old Catholic churches. Intercommunion is also observed with the Philippine Independent church (Aglipayan) which traces its orders through Anglicanism, and with the Church of Sweden, a Lutheran body which preserved the episcopacy.

In the past ten years a number of Polish National Catholic and Orthodox bishops have served as co-consecrators in Protestant Episcopal consecrations. A possibility exists that some Episcopalian priests have come to possess valid orders, not from the Anglican succession but from the apostolic succession of these bodies.

A number of Episcopal priests have obtained ordination from non-Anglican sources in order to guarantee their priesthood. Such a situation presents interesting ecumenical possibilities; however, the Catholic Church has not precisely defined the role of the co-consecrator nor examined officially the orders of the Polish National Catholic church.

An institute for the study of Anglicanism has been established at the Benedictine Abbey of St. Matthias in Trier, West Germany. The abbot, Dom Laurentius Klein, O.S.B., explained that the studies at the institute will be undertaken with a view toward entering into constructive dialogue with Anglicans.

An international commission of Anglican and Roman Catholic scholars has been meeting for several years to see what steps can be taken to reconcile Canterbury and Rome. The goal of the commission is "Full organic union between our two communions."

When Pope Paul VI concluded his sermon at the canonization of the 40 English martyrs he surprised some by hinting at a possible uniate status for Anglicans within the Roman Catholic Church. Said the pope: "There will be no seeking to lessen the legitimate prestige and the worthy patrimony of piety and usage proper to the Anglican Church when the Roman Catholic Church . . . is able to embrace her ever-beloved sister in the one authentic communion of the family of Christ."

Further Reading

Albright, Raymond W., *A History of the Protestant Episcopal Church* (New York, Macmillan, 1964).

Chorley, E. C., *Men and Movements in the American Episcopal Church* (New York, Scribners, 1946).

DeMille, George E., *The Episcopal Church Since 1900* (New York, Morehouse-Barlow, 1955).

Williamson, William B., *A Handbook for Episcopalians* (New York, Morehouse-Barlow, 1961).

Chapter VI

THE METHODISTS
'All the World Is My Parish' — *John Wesley*

WHAT began as a revival of tired eighteenth-century Anglicanism has become the second largest single Protestant church in the United States. Since the 1939 reunion of the three main Methodist bodies, the *United Methodist Church* has embraced 99 per cent of the estimated 10,800,000 white Methodists.

A few years ago *Life* magazine described the Methodist Church in these words: "In many ways it is our most characteristic church. It is short on theology, long on good works, brilliantly organized, primarily middle-class, frequently bigoted, incurably optimistic, zealously missionary and touchingly confident of the essential goodness of the man next door."

John Wesley, Methodism's chief founder, emerges as one of the noblest and most appealing figures in Protestantism. Catholics as well as Protestants admire his genuine piety, zeal, and organizational abilities. As the Catholic scholar Moehler has said: "Under other circumstances he would have been the founder of a religious order or a reforming pope."

Not noted as a theologian himself, Wesley founded a church which assigns to dogma a relatively minor role. If any attribute fits Methodism from Wesley's day to this it is activism. The founder once remarked, "The distinguishing marks of a Methodist are not his opinions of any sort. His assenting to this or that scheme of religion, his embracing any particular set of notions . . . are all quite wide of the mark. Whosoever imagines that a

Methodist is a man of such or such an opinion is grossly ignorant of the whole affair." Since 1924 American Methodists have been excused from subscribing to any statement of belief or creed. Instead they promise "loyalty to Christ."

Ranked with Luther and Calvin as one of the Big Three of the Protestant reform, Wesley differed from the other two in that the milieu in which he labored was not a Catholic but a Protestant land. Many of his admonitions have been forgotten and certain developments in twentieth-century Methodism would certainly distress him, but we must turn to Wesley to gain an insight into this huge American denomination and the reasons for its phenomenal success on this continent.

John and his youngest brother Charles were born in a Church of England parsonage at Epworth. His mother, Susanna, had been one of 25 children and John was her fifteenth and Charles her eighteenth.

Life in the rector's large family was orderly and scholarly and John in particular valued the guidance of his strong-willed mother. Eventually both sons entered Oxford where they organized a Holy Club in the amoral university atmosphere. Rules for the Club included fasting on Wednesdays and Fridays, Bible reading, diligent study, two hours of daily prayer, frequent communion, almsgiving, and visiting the poor and imprisoned. Adolescent scoffers labeled the members Bible Moths and Methodists because of their regular habits of prayer and strict self-discipline. John's favorite devotional book was *The Imitation of Christ* by Thomas a Kempis.

When the Holy Club, forerunner of Methodism, was disbanded the brothers volunteered for a mission to recently settled Georgia. Both had been ordained Anglican priests and adhered to the High Church party which later nurtured the Oxford Movement. Their hope was to convert the heathen Indians in Oglethorpe's new American colony.

During the sea voyage to America Wesley saw the lack of faith in his own heart as he witnessed a band of Moravians calmly singing psalms and hymns during a raging storm. These spiritual descendants of John Huss, the Czech heretic burned three centuries earlier, had also been sent from their German headquarters to spread the Christian message in the New World.

Wesley spent two unhappy years in Georgia. He found the Indians indifferent to the gospel. He himself was involved in the first of a series of unfortunate love affairs. Finally a judicial body accused him of various church offenses such as insisting on confession before Holy Communion as dictated by his unbending High Church conscience. He returned home to England disappointed and frustrated.

Still fascinated by the simple faith of the Moravians, he made contact with their missionaries in London. From them, especially from Peter Bohler, he accepted the doctrines of justification by faith alone and of instantaneous conversion.

One evening in 1738 Wesley attended a religious society meeting on Aldersgate Street. A lay preacher was reading Luther's preface to the Epistle to the Romans. "I felt my heart strangely warmed. I felt I did trust in Christ, Christ alone for salvation; and an assurance was given me that He had taken away my sins, even mine, and saved me from the law of sin and death," Wesley later related. This experience at 8:45 p.m. on May 24, 1738, marks the beginning of the Wesleyan revival in Protestantism. The young Anglican priest now felt he had received the same faith which he had admired in the Moravian missionaries.

Few Anglican churches would admit the Wesleyan enthusiasts to their pulpits. Undeterred, the brothers took to the open air and began to preach in the fields, barns, and private homes. They sought out the neo-pagan miners, factory workers, slum dwellers rather than the wealthy and offered them a warm, emotional message which had never come from the cold established church. They were joined by the eloquent George Whitefield, a Holy Clubber and the converted son of a saloon keeper, who also labored as an evangelist in Georgia but with greater success.

All three of the first Methodist preachers instructed their converts to remain within the Church of England. They had no desire to found another sect. Methodists were urged to receive the sacraments in the established church although they might gather to study scripture, testify, sing hymns, and hear sermons in Methodist classes. They were encouraged to become a leaven in the Anglican church, a sort of Protestant Third Order. Since few clergymen joined the revival, Wesley reluctantly consented to the use of licensed lay preachers.

Theology received scant attention. Practical religion was the goal. If any theological principle received emphasis, it was the insistence on man's free will in opposition to Calvinist predestination. This represented a return to Catholic doctrine which flatly denied that God elected some to salvation and damned others to hell.

Their doctrinal views approximated those of Jacob Arminius (1560-1609), a Dutch theologian, who contradicted the absolute predestination taught at Geneva. Arminianism insisted that Christ died for all men, that He offers His grace to all men rather than to a body of the elect. As predestination has been relegated to the shelf in modern Presbyterian and Reformed theology, the sharp differences between Methodists and Calvinists have been blurred.

Assurance of salvation became another original Methodist tenet. Wesley taught that a man who has experienced a second blessing or entire sanctification can be absolutely sure he will reach heaven. Such a man can lose all inclination to evil and gain perfection in this life. Wesley never claimed this state of perfection for himself but he insisted that the attainment of perfection was possible for all Christians. Here the English reformer parted company with both Luther and Calvin who denied that man would ever reach a state in this life in which he could not fall into sin. Today the Wesleyan doctrine of perfection has been soft-pedaled by The Methodist Church but finds champions in the smaller Methodist bodies and the Holiness sects spawned by Methodism.

Since Wesley claimed a conversion which he could pin point to the day, hour, and minute, he assumed that all genuine conversion is the instantaneous operation of the Holy Spirit. At one time Methodists expected all converts to testify to a miraculous and instantaneous conversion. This requirement has been abandoned. Adults joining The Methodist Church today need not relate their spiritual experience nor admit to having such an experience.

From the night of the Aldersgate meeting until his death at 88 Wesley followed a back breaking schedule of preaching, writing, traveling, and organizing his Methodist classes. Initially he was assisted by his Moravian friends and he even made a trip to their headquarters at Herrnhut to observe their way of life at firsthand. Within a few years he had broken with the Moravians over the practice of "stillness." In stillness the brethren suspended all work, study, and prayer and waited for a special blessing from God. The Wesley brothers also disagreed with Whitefield when he turned to Calvinism and began to mix Methodism and predestination.

Once asked by what authority he dared to preach in the open fields as a Church of England priest, Wesley replied, "To save souls is my vocation; all the world is my parish." He preached 42,000 sermons and covered an estimated 250,000 miles on foot and horseback throughout the British Isles. The democratic structure of Methodism was admittedly a facade during his lifetime since he ruled his society as an ecclesiastical dictator.

Never a successful suitor, he finally married a shrewish widow with four children. Quarrels and humiliations marked the match and they separated. He learned of his wife's death only after the funeral and it has been said that his only child was Methodism.

John's relations with his more conservative brother became strained as he drifted further from the High Church orbit which Charles never left. While Charles devoutly believed in the Real Presence and the apostolic succession, his older brother came to accept a symbolic interpretation of the Eucharist and undertook to ordain priests himself. Among Charles' 6500 hymns are the popular "Hark, the Herald Angels Sing" and "Jesus, Lover of My Soul." He has been called the poet of the revival, John, the organizer, and Whitefield, the orator.

Critics commonly charged the Wesleys with being Jesuits in disguise bent on subverting the established church to the interests of the papacy. Certainly the Wesleys restored the positive principles of the Reformation to English and continental Protestantism and stripped Protestantism of its negative features. They opposed extrinsic justification, predestination in the Calvinist sense, and the depreciation of good works. To this extent the revival may be considered a return to the traditional Catholic positions.

Furthermore, they urged fasting and abstinence, daily prayer and devotions, frequent communion. They accorded an importance to good works which was foreign to Lutheranism. They not only taught that man is changed by justification and sanctification but that he could attain perfection — a far cry from Luther's "sinful and sinning" Christian. Most of these Catholic inclinations were diluted and lost as Methodism accommodated itself to the conditions of the American frontier.

The first authorized Methodist missionaries were dispatched to the colonies in 1769, only ten years before the American Revolution and fully 150 years after the other denominations had staked out their claims. Francis Asbury stands as the greatest figure in American Methodism and to his foresight and energy must be credited much of the amazing growth of this tardy denomination. Like Wesley he spent a great part of his life in the saddle. He perfected the system of circuit riders, devoted lay preachers who brought religion to the people in isolated cabins and frontier towns. Equipped only with Bible, hymn book, and a set of sermons they preached six days a week, urging all who would listen to "flee from the wrath to come." Their main audience were the poor and underprivileged. They conserved the effects of their conversions by setting up classes under class leaders.

Methodism suffered a near fatal setback during the Revolution even though it gained some numerical strength. Many colonists looked on Methodism as an English importation and their suspicions were buttressed by two pamphlets in which Wesley disowned the agitation for independence. "We Methodists are no republicans and never intend to be," wrote Wesley. All but one of the Methodist preachers sent to America by Wesley were Tories who fled to Canada or England during the war.

Discredited by their pro-British attitude during the conflict, the Methodists retained strength below the Mason and Dixon lines and recouped losses by concentrating on the expanding frontier. Here their zealous lay preachers could outnumber the college-trained Congregationalist, Episcopalian, and Presbyterian ministers. Here their proclamation of man's free will made more sense to the independent frontierman than the fatalism of Calvin. When Bishop Asbury began his preaching Methodism counted scarcely a few hundred members in the American colonies; at his death he could survey a thriving church of 200,000 souls.

As in England, the Methodists were directed to receive baptism and Holy Communion from Episcopalian priests. Naturally they soon petitioned to receive the sacraments from the same Methodist preachers who visited their homes and conducted their worship services. The Bishop of London refused to ordain preachers in the colonies so in 1784 Wesley assumed the power to ordain ministers himself. When he ordained two men and sent them to America Methodism moved from the status of a revival movement in Anglicanism to that of a separate church.

He justified his action by claiming that bishops and presbyters were identical in the primitive church, at least at Alexandria, and that therefore priests like himself could lawfully ordain other priests. He then consecrated Thomas Coke as superintendent for the Methodists in the United States and he in turn consecrated Asbury. Both men assumed the additional title of bishop over Wesley's ineffective protest. Brother Charles disassociated himself from these actions and declared, "I can scarcely believe it that in his eighty-second year my brother, my old, intimate friend and companion, should have assumed the episcopal character, ordained elders, consecrated a bishop, and sent him to ordain our elder preachers in America." "My brother has put an indelible stigma upon his name," he added.

The *Methodist Episcopal Church* was organized officially at the Christmas Conference of 60 preachers in Baltimore in 1784. Wesley died proclaiming his loyalty to the church of which he was a priest: "I live and die a member of the Church of England, and none who regard my judgment will ever separate from it."

Wesley had prepared an abridgment of the Anglican Thirty-nine Articles which was accepted as a doctrinal statement by the Americans. They added another article to Wesley's 24 which recognized the independence of the colonies. Among other doctrines the articles affirmed justification by faith, the sufficiency of the scriptures, and the baptism of infants. "The Romish doctrine concerning purgatory, pardon, worshipping and adoration, as well of images as of relics, and also invocation of saints, is a fond thing, vainly invented, and grounded upon no warrant of scripture, but repugnant to the Word of God," according to the Wesleyan articles. The sacrifice of the Mass was termed a "blasphemous fable and dangerous deceit." Other sources of Methodist belief are Wesley's *Notes on the New Testament* and 53 collected sermons.

A demand for greater lay participation in church government led to the formation of the *Methodist Protestant Church* in 1830. Slavery drove a deeper wedge into Methodism in 1844 when the Southerners seceded and formed the *Methodist Episcopal Church, South*. Reunion of the three branches was not effected until 1939 although no doctrinal issues were involved. At this time the Southern faction was pacified by constructing a segregated Central Jurisdiction for 340,000 Negro members regardless of place of residence. The five white jurisdictions were mapped out on a geographical basis. This racial compromise struck many Methodists as a betrayal of Christian brotherhood and the 1956 General Conference adopted a constitutional amendment to dissolve the Negro jurisdiction gradually.

The *United Methodist Church* came into existence in 1968 when *The Methodist Church* and the *Evangelical United Brethren Church* formed one church.

The reluctance of American Methodist bishops to sanction preaching in the German language had led to the formation of two independent German Methodist denominations: the *United Brethren in Christ* and the *Evangelical Church*. These two bodies, similar in doctrine, polity, and national origin, merged in 1946 at Johnstown, Pennsylvania, to form the *Evangelical United Brethren Church*.

Philip Otterbein studied for the Reformed ministry in Germany and came to America in 1752. He began to preach Arminian doctrines and to conduct revivals and prayer meetings with Martin Boehm, a Swiss Mennonite preacher. Had there been no language problem their converts would have been absorbed into Methodism. As it was they formed their own United Brethren Church in 1800 with themselves as bishops. A minority seceded in 1889. The 24,000 members of the *United Brethren in Christ (Old Constitution)* oppose secret societies and participation in war.

A development parallel to that of the United Brethren led to the founding of the Evangelical Church, once called the Evangelical Association. In this case Jacob Albright, an ex-Lutheran, began to preach in eastern Pennsylvania but his plan for a German Methodist branch was vetoed by the Methodist hierarchy. In 1803 he organized a separate church whose adherents were variously known as Albright people or Brethren or German Methodists. The greatest period of expansion of this body was during the administration of Bishop John Seybert, elected in 1839. A serious schism disrupted the denomination from 1894 to 1922 when the two factions reunited in the Evangelical Church.

Both the United Brethren and the Evangelicals generally confined their evangelism to the German population in this country. Of course, most of their converts came from Lutheran, Reformed, or Mennonite backgrounds. At the time of the merger in 1946 the United Brethren reported 450,000 members and the Evangelicals about half that number. By the time of the 1968 merger with The Methodist Church the EUB Church was reporting 758,000 members with particular strength in Pennsylvania.

The great majority of Negro Methodists are found in separate denominations outside The Methodist Church, such as the *African Methodist Episcopal Church,* the *Christian* (formerly Colored) *Methodist Episcopal Church,* and the *African Methodist Episcopal Zion Church.* Together they enroll about 2,500,000 members. Both the A.M.E. and A.M.E. Zion churches were organized before 1800 by Negroes who resented discrimination by their white coreligionists. The C.M.E. church gathered the Negro remnant of the Methodist Episcopal Church, South, after the Civil War and remains the smallest of the three major Negro bodies with 466,000 members. These Negro bodies follow the same theology and polity as the United Methodist Church but little intercourse exists between white and Negro churches. Bishops of the three Negro Methodist churches have met to discuss a possible merger.

By the middle of the nineteenth century most Methodists had become fairly prosperous and conservative. Methodism has followed the typical pattern from sect to church even though from the beginning it lacked two sectarian characteristics: congregational government and adult baptism. The upper middle class now dominates the United Methodist Church, once the church of the English workingman. In a recent year the Methodists claimed 24 U.S. senators, 69 representatives, and ten state governors.

A dozen tiny Methodist sects totaling only 160,000 members include the fundamentalist *Free Methodist Church* which still emphasizes entire sanctification and elects superintendents instead of bishops, and the equally strict *Wesleyan Church.*

No religious body of Christians outside the Catholic Church is so highly and efficiently organized as the United Methodist Church. Organizational problems and the social gospel receive the attention which other churches direct toward theology and liturgy. Laymen play a large part in Methodist projects and a layman with any special talent can find a suitable niche in Methodism.

National committees in the church are set up for missions, the local church, education, evangelism, lay activities, Christian social relations, temperance, world peace, social and economic relations, hospitals and homes, chaplains, and pensions. Methodism is big business with over $4 billion invested in 40,000 churches and institutions.

Despite its efficiency the Methodist Church has recorded an unimpressive growth record in recent years of less than 1 percent a year. It ranks 43rd out of 46 denominations in per capita giving according to a survey of the National Council of Churches.

Full authority in church matters rests with the General Conference. This body, consisting of equal numbers of locally elected laymen and ministers, meets every four years. Laymen were first admitted in 1872; before this the complaint of the Methodist

Protestant faction was probably justified. General Conference decisions are incorporated in the 890-page *Discipline* which roughly corresponds to the Code of Canon Law.

Personal moral standards rule out alcohol and tobacco although lay members who indulge are no longer excommunicated. At one time Methodism in this country also banned dancing, card playing, all forms of gambling, and the theater but these are now tolerated. Methodists led in the formation of the Women's Christian Temperance Union and the Anti-Saloon League and take a large share of the credit for the 18th Amendment and the Great Experiment. The United Methodist Church still officially lobbies for national prohibition, condemns beer and cigarette advertising on radio and TV, tries to ban beer from army and navy establishments.

Among Protestant denominations Methodists take first place in missions, hospitals, and colleges. Some of their 78 colleges and universities have all but severed their ties with the denomination but others remain definitely Methodist: Syracuse, Boston, Emory, Duke, Drew, Denver, and Southern Methodist. The Church operates 360 schools and institutions of higher learning overseas. Methodists established the Goodwill Industries in 1907 to help handicapped persons help themselves by repairing and selling old furniture and clothes. Seventy-two hospitals in the U.S. are run by the United Methodist Church.

Nowadays most Methodist ministers who became full members of the annual conference hold the B.D. degree. Methodism still depends also on lay preachers whose training is received via correspondence and short courses. A ministerial candidate may attend any of the 12 seminaries maintained by the church, among which are Garrett, Drew, Duke, Candler, Perkins, and Boston.

About 400 women are serving as Methodist ministers but few have become pastors. The 1956 General Conference accorded full clergy rights to women. The 800 deaconesses in this country receive a fixed salary, regular leaves of absence, and provision for retirement. The Methodist deaconess movement has experienced little growth in recent years but deaconesses operate a number of hospitals and homes.

Bishops are elected and their main duties are administrative. The 68 active U.S. bishops ordain ministers, appoint them to parishes and supervise church activities in their areas. The bishops are elected at the Jurisdictional Conferences, consecrated by three bishops, and expected to retire before 72. The Council of Bishops serves as the executive branch of Methodism just as the General Conference is the chief legislative branch. Methodists hold that the difference between a bishop and an ordinary minister is purely one of administrative responsibility.

Wesley prepared a revised liturgy from the Book of Common Prayer but it was never widely adopted. Methodists are liturgical individualists who resist all attempts to impose a uniform pattern of worship on the local congregation. As in most Protestant denominations a trend toward beauty in the worship service has reintroduced gowns, candles, crosses, a central altar.

A typical form of worship would be: call to worship, hymn, prayer of confession, silent meditation, words of assurance, Lord's Prayer, anthem, responsive reading, *gloria patri*, affirmation of faith, scripture lesson, pastoral prayer, offertory, hymn, sermon, prayer, invitation to Christian discipleship, doxology, benediction, silent prayer, and postlude. An alternate form is used when the Lord's Supper is observed. One form of Sunday worship and two forms for the Lord's Supper are presented in the *Discipline* but the local church need not use these liturgies.

Weekly communion was one of Wesley's frequent spiritual prescriptions but few Methodist churches today observe the Lord's Supper oftener than quarterly or monthly. The communicants kneel at the altar rail, receive bread and grape juice in a communion service which is considered symbolic as in the Reformed tradition.

Methodists deny that baptism produces sanctifying grace or takes away sin. The sacrament may be administered by sprinkling, pouring, or immersion although sprinkling is most widespread. Infants as well as adults are baptized. Confirmation, which is not believed to be sacramental, is conferred by ministers as well as bishops.

The great bulk of Methodists reside in the United States. Within a few years after the founder's death British Methodism split into half a dozen sects. These groups developed a nonepiscopal form of church government and never emphasized the Puritan concern for personal morals which has preoccupied their American cousins. The world's 20,000,000 Methodists co-operate in the World Methodist Conference.

Successful itself in reuniting the three main Wesleyan bodies, the United Methodist Church takes an active and prominent part in the ecumenical movement. A Methodist layman, Dr. John R. Mott, was instrumental in calling the World Missionary Conference in Edinburgh in 1910 which turned out to be the beginning of the Protestant ecumenical movement. Dr. Albert Outler of Southern Methodist University attended all sessions of Vatican II and has been a leading figure in Protestant-Catholic dialogue.

Methodism is distantly related to a score of other denominations, Arminian in doctrine and sometimes claiming the authentic mantle of Wesley for themselves: the Salvation Army, countless Holiness sects, and the General Baptists.

In many respects the Wesleyan revival represented a distinct reversal of Protestant direction in the eighteenth century. Wesley's emphasis on free will, his insistence on the need for good works, his doctrine of conversion, his encouragement of fasting and abstinence, frequent communion, the value of a personal devotional life set early Methodism on a path verging toward Catholicism.

Wesley himself, however, knew little of Catholic doctrine and his picture of the sacraments and the theology of the Church was often a caricature. His estrangement from the High Church position of his youth and the transplanting of Methodism to the American frontier carried the movement more directly into the Protestant camp.

Further Reading

Davies, Rupert E., *Methodism* (Baltimore, Penguin Books, 1963).

Harmon, Nolan B., *Understanding the Methodist Church*, rev. ed. (Nashville, Methodist Publishing House, 1961).

Outler, Albert C., *John Wesley* (New York, Oxford University Press, 1964).

Chapter VII

THE BAPTISTS

'No Human Founder, No Human Authority, No Human Creed'

BAPTISTS carry the Protestant principle of justification by faith alone to its logical conclusion. Since infants are incapable of such an act of faith, they cannot receive the grace of baptism. Hence, only persons able to make a profession of faith in Christ may be admitted to baptism.

Likewise, since the Baptists deny the sacramental character of baptism in favor of a symbolic interpretation, they see immersion as the most dramatic symbol of burial and rebirth in Christ. Immersion is certainly the ancient form of baptism and was practiced by the Latin rite of the Catholic Church until the twelfth century. The modern Baptists deny that baptism removes the stain of original sin. Baptism by a non-Baptist Christian may be considered valid in some Baptist churches but not in all of them.

To define a Baptist, we may say that he is a follower of Jesus Christ who has been baptized by immersion and belongs to a local congregation which is identified by the name Baptist. Some Baptists would add that he must be committed to the Baptist principles of religious liberty.

Religious liberty and freedom of conscience have perhaps characterized the Baptists more than their concern about the first sacrament. Whereas the Episcopalian and Presbyterian acknowledges the authority of the larger church and the Congregationalist recognizes the authority of the local community of Christians, the Baptist denies any spiritual authority over the individual. The local congregation is autonomous and receives no directives or liturgies or regulations from denominational headquarters.

Baptists view the Protestant Reformation as a job only half done. Luther and Calvin, they believe, allowed too many unbiblical practices and beliefs to remain — such as infant baptism —to merit the allegiance of Bible-believing Christians. Baptists see the genuine Reformation as taking place in America in the rise of the Baptist movement. And this was a movement which did away with all creeds, infant baptism, sacraments, the episcopal and presbyterial systems of church government, ritual in worship, and what Baptists regard as unscriptural modes of baptism.

At one time an effort was made to expel President Harry Truman from the Southern Baptist Convention because he was reported to have enjoyed a shot of whiskey from time to time. Truman snorted that no one in the Convention had any power to expel him or anyone else. In this case the president was a better Baptist theologian than his critics. Baptist churches have no machinery to excommunicate members or to enforce doctrinal or ethical standards.

Each Baptist congregation hires and fires its minister, sets its own worship patterns, examines and baptizes members. In some congregations, the members choose and ordain their own ministers although in others the ordination is performed by a group of Baptist churches.

The Baptist family, numbering 22,875,000 adult members, constitutes by far the largest American Protestant denomination. Every third Protestant in the United States is a Baptist. About a third of the Baptists are Negroes and the bulk of Negro and white members live in the South. In Alabama, Georgia, and Mississippi almost 60 percent of all church members are Southern Baptists. Baptists constitute a majority of church members in ten of 11 states of the old Confederacy. Millions of children in Baptist families are not included on the church rolls because they are not old enough to be baptized. The emergence of this radical, independent sect into a position of numerical superiority in this country has influenced American Protestantism in the direction of individualism, anti-ritualism, and sectarianism.

Most Baptists belong to one of the four largest groups: the *American Baptist Convention* (called Northern Baptist until 1950) with 1,454,000 members; the fast growing *Southern Baptist Convention* with more than 11,330,000; the *National Baptist Convention of the U.S.A., Inc.*, original Negro body, with 5,500,-000; and a 1916 offshoot of the latter organization, the *National Baptist Convention of America*, which reports 2,669,000. Twenty-three other Baptist groups are represented in this country, many of them claiming only a handful of adherents.

Some Baptists like to claim Christ or John the Baptist as their founder; the first Christian congregation, they believe, was the First Baptist Church of Jerusalem. But history does not tell us of any organized Baptist groups until the early seventeenth century. Their spiritual ancestors, once removed, were the Anabaptists of Reformation times who despaired of the theological positions of Luther, Zwingli, and Calvin. They yearned for a church of saints not a church of saints and sinners. These Anabaptists called for a voluntary association of adult Christians rather than a state church into which all citizens were born and baptized. These early radical reformers also agitated for separation of Church and State, complete sovereignty of the local congregation, communal living, pacifism, and Biblical literalism. They were persecuted by both Protestants and Catholics. By 1535 the Anabaptist movement had been largely suppressed by force except for a remnant gathered by the ex-priest Menno Simons.

A refugee congregation of English separatists in Amsterdam accepted the doctrine of believer's baptism from the Mennonites around 1607. John Smythe and Thomas Helwys shepherded this first English Baptist congregation in Holland but Smythe himself left to join the Mennonites. A handful returned to England with Helwys and carried their Baptist principles with them. As these pioneer Baptists pondered the symbolic meaning of baptism, they began to prefer immersion rather than the pouring mode used by the Mennonites. The first church to baptize by immersion was a London congregation in 1638. Theologically most of the original English Baptists were Arminian, but Baptists of this persuasion now form a small minority since most Baptists have adopted a more or less Calvinist theology.

Some names which stand out in the history of the English Baptist movement are John Bunyan, author of *Pilgrim's Progress,* John Milton of *Paradise Lost,* Daniel Defoe, the creator of *Robinson Crusoe,* and William Carey, the pioneer Protestant missionary to India.

Roger Williams, the founder of the first Baptist church in America, remained a Baptist for only four months. A Nonconformist clergyman, he left England in 1630 and sought religious freedom in the Puritan Massachusetts Bay Colony. Instead of freedom he found himself accused of heresy and was exiled. Indians gave him shelter and he founded a settlement of his own at Providence. In 1639 he had become convinced of the Baptist position and was rebaptized, but within a few months he resigned his pastorate of this first Baptist church in the New World. Williams continued to search for religious truth until his death.

Little expansion was undertaken during the first century of the Baptist movement in America. The sect would register its tremendous gains in the late eighteenth and the nineteenth centuries by an appeal to the lower classes, the Negro, the frontiersmen, and the Southerner. Thousands of unschooled Baptist preachers carried the gospel to the settler in his frontier cabin. These preacher-farmers found a rich soil on America's frontier for their principles of separation of Church and State, church democracy, simple worship services, and freedom of conscience. They offered no creeds but the Bible itself. Defections by the Disciples and the Adventists amounted to nothing more than temporary setbacks to Baptist growth.

The Baptists brought the Christian gospel to white man and Negro. Today most American Negroes are either Baptists or Methodists. Negro Baptists number 7,500,000 and the Concord Baptist church in Brooklyn with over 12,000 members is the largest Protestant congregation in the world.

Often called the problem child of American Protestantism,

the Southern Baptist Convention is conservative and cautious in its co-operation with other churches. Statistics indicate it is the fastest growing major denomination and an average of 1000 new members are baptized every day. This denomination has grown from 325,000 in 1845, the year of its secession from the northern group over the issue of slavery.

The big Southern slaveholders were usually Episcopalians or Presbyterians but the Baptists lined up with them in opposition to abolition. When the Baptist Foreign Missions Society refused to appoint any slaveholder as a missionary, the Southern churches seceded and formed their own Convention. The Rev. Richard Furman, who wielded great influence in the South, declared that "the right of holding slaves is clearly established in the Holy Scriptures, both by precept and example."

In 1950 the Southern Baptists decided to expand their evangelistic efforts to all states of the Union. This strained relations with the Northern Baptists but transformed the Southern Baptist church from a regional to a national one. For example, there are now 36 Southern Baptist churches in the New York City area and more than 1,000 in California. These churches attract not only transplated Southerners but Baptists unhappy about the liberalism or tepidity of former church homes. The American (Northern) Baptists have recently started congregations in such cities as Richmond, Dallas, and Tulsa.

In 1963 the Southern Baptists overtook the Methodist Church to claim the title the largest single Protestant church in the nation. Its aggressive evangelistic campaigns, its well-organized Sunday School program, and its frank espousal of the "old-time religion" help to explain its success. Billy Graham, a Southern Baptist minister, succeeded Billy Sunday as America's best known revivalist.

The largest congregation in the Southern Baptist Convention, the First Baptist Church of Dallas, operates with an annual budget of more than $2 million. Its pastor, the Rev. W. A. Criswell, has also served as president of the Convention.

Aggressively missionary-minded, the Southern Baptists support 2,165 missionaries in home missions; special efforts are made to convert migrant workers, Puerto Ricans, Indians, Mexican

Americans, and Jews. Their 2,300 foreign missionaries labor in 53 countries on four continents with the largest mission fields in Japan, Nigeria, and Brazil. They seek Negro converts in Africa but generally do not encourage Negro membership in the U.S. Only 510 out of some 35,000 Southern Baptist churches report even one black member and most of these churches are outside the South.

Southern Baptists traditionally support complete separation of church and state but find no paradox in vigorous efforts to impose community Blue laws, enforce prohibition, fight the legalization of gambling, or stop the teaching of evolution in the public schools.

The Convention meets once each year but its decisions cannot commit the denomination, any congregations, or any individual Baptist to a particular position. As many as 15,000 "messengers" represent local churches at these annual meetings.

Neither the National Council of Churches or the World Council has Southern Baptist representation. A book currently used in Southern Baptist Sunday Schools states: "The National Council of Churches of Christ has led the denominations affiliated with it, in the main, away from the fundamental truths of the gospel." (p. 61, *Baptist Distinctives* by W. R. White). He adds: "We believe that the more popular ecumenical movements are too artificial, arbitrary, and mechanical. They are not the result of spiritual growth. They are too much the manipulations and compromises of zealous men. They have been and are far removed from the biblical concept of Christian union" (pp. 62-3). And finally Dr. White declares: "All this talk of tolerance and good will among the religions is perfectly sincere on the part of Protestants and Jews, but it is the smoke screen of an attack by the Romanists." (p. 67).

The American Baptist Convention participates in ecumenical activities, and is one of the founders of the National Council of Churches of Christ in America and of the World Council of Churches. It has a long history of missionary work in Asia, Africa, and Central America, Mexico, and the Carribean Islands. The emphasis of these missions has been to educate the converts and develop them as leaders of the churches in their own countries, including administration of the work. American Baptists have only 350 missionaries overseas but they have many thousands of trained national evangelists, pastors, teachers, medical workers, administrators, and other leaders in the mission churches. While merger of the American and Southern Baptist Conventions seems remote, there are generally brotherly relationships between them.

Protesting what was called "modernism" in the former Northern Baptist Convention a group of Baptists organized the *General Association of Regular Baptist Churches* in 1932. The number of churches affiliated with this conservative association has increased from the original 22 to more than 1000. Their original indictment of the parent body charged that the Northern Baptists honored members who denied the inspiration of the Bible, the divinity of Christ, the redemption, and the resurrection. They claim 154,000 members.

The 184,000 *Free-Will Baptists* continue to oppose Calvinist predestination with their slogan of "free grace, free salvation, free will and free communion." Of Welsh origin, many Free-Will Baptists in the north were absorbed into the American Baptist Convention in a merger in 1910. The Negro counterpart, the *United Free-Will Baptist Church,* claims 100,000 members.

The *Landmarkers,* members of the American Baptist Association, add a strong premillennial conviction to a thoroughgoing fundamentalism. This group of 782,000 Baptists experienced a doctrinal schism in 1950 which led to the formation of the *North American Baptist Association* which now reports 174,000 members in southern and midwestern states.

Primitive Baptists, also known as Hardshell, Old School, and Antimission Baptists, oppose Arminian compromises with Calvinism, instrumental music in worship services, and church societies. As usual, white and Negro groups support separate denominations.

Nine tenths of the world's Baptists reside in the United States. This means that the largest Protestant denomination in this country occupies a relatively small niche in world Protestantism which is overwhelmingly Lutheran, Anglican, and Reformed. Fear of compromising local church autonomy has also kept most Baptists, including those in the huge Southern Baptist Convention, from exerting a proportionate influence in the National and World Councils of Churches. An undetermined number of Baptists, perhaps half a million, live in Soviet Russia and 200,000 are reported in England. Baptists in mission fields include 350,000 in India, 110,000 in Brazil, 142,000 in Burma, and 95,000 in the Congo. There are about 145,000 Canadian Baptists. The 25,000,000 member Baptist World Alliance meets every five years. It was established in London in 1905 but now maintains headquarters in Washington, D.C.

Several decades ago a Baptist minister might have found that a college degree was actually a handicap in his clerical career since the Baptists did not look upon higher education with complete favor. Yet the Baptists can point to such institutions as the University of Chicago, Carleton, Colby, Kalamazoo, Baylor, Wake Forest, Denison, Stetson, and others as Baptist-founded.

Educational standards for Baptist clergymen are rising rapidly, especially in the larger conventions. A local congregation may choose to ordain a grade school graduate as minister but the national bodies advocate college and seminary training. In the more stable branches of the Baptist family the local church submits the name of a candidate for the ministry to a committee composed of members of several churches. If approved, the ordination is performed by a council. In some Negro groups the number of ordained ministers is nearly double the number of active ministers.

The increasing use of symbolism and ritual which is obvious in most Protestant denominations has found fewer proponents among the Baptists. Symbols in Baptist architecture and church decoration are limited to the cross, Bible, anchor, banner, globe, and gate. Few Baptist preachers wear any type of vestment or gown, and no set liturgy is prescribed. Most churches baptize in pools in the church proper although some use rivers and streams. Communion may be administered on a monthly, quarterly, or annual basis. What other denominations consider sacraments, the Baptists consider ordinances with no supernatural significance.

Most Christian churches, including the Catholic Church,

admit the validity of other modes of baptism. Eastern rite Catholics continue the ancient form of immersion and a Catholic may be validly baptized by immersion or pouring. The sacrament need not be administered by a Catholic, much less a Catholic priest, in order to be valid.

As early as the first century, however, the Church began to baptize infants. Origen writes: "The Church received from the Apostles the tradition of giving baptism to infants." The New Testament admittedly does not command the baptism of infants but the Catholic sacramental view of baptism assumes the desirability of baptizing infants. Luther was driven to ingenious explanations for his acceptance of justification by faith and infant baptism. According to Protestant principles it would seem that the adult baptism of the Baptists, Disciples of Christ, Mennonites, Seventh-day Adventists, Brethren, and Jehovah's Witnesses is more consistent.

Despite its meteoric rise to the position of largest American Protestant denomination, the Southern Baptist Convention faces some urgent problems. The world and especially the Southern states have experienced rapid change. The Supreme Court and the federal government have made civil rights decisions which have destroyed the old racial patterns in the South. A Roman Catholic has been elected president of the country. The ecumenical movement has won the allegiance of most of the leaders of the major Protestant churches. The South itself is experiencing a move toward urbanization and industrialization which must affect the lives of the people in these states in a thousand ways. Questions of Biblical interpretation have divided Southern Baptist seminaries and colleges as have questions of racial policy and social action.

Except for some modernists in the northern branch, the Baptists preach a Christianity based firmly on the divinity of Christ and the central facts of His incarnation and redemption of mankind. They accept the doctrines of the Trinity, the virgin birth, original sin, heaven, and hell. In some areas they have carried Protestant principles to conclusions which the original Reformers hesitated to draw. Unlike some denominations which have catered to the upper classes, the Baptists have worked with the humble people and have developed an amazing spirit of personal evangelism. Estimates have placed two thirds of the Baptists in the lower economic class. Yet the Rockefellers, multi-millionaire H. L. Hunt, and a number of Texas oil barons also claim the Baptist label.

Hans Herzl, only son of the founder of Zionism, turned from Judaism to the Baptist faith and finally became a Catholic in 1924. After his final conversion he wrote, "I came to know them (the Baptists) as a sect of good, zealous Christians whose life was lived in the spirit of the Holy Scriptures."

Further Reading

Armstrong, O. K. and Marjorie Moore, *The Indomitable Baptists* (Garden City, N.Y., Doubleday, 1967).

Hays, Brooks and Steely, John E., *The Baptist Way of Life* (Englewood Cliffs, N.J., Prentice-Hall, 1963).

Newton, Louie D., *Why I am a Baptist* (New York, Nelson, 1957).

Torbet, Robert G., *A History of the Baptists,* rev. ed. (Valley Forge, Pa., Judson Press, 1963).

Chapter VIII

THE DISCIPLES OF CHRIST AND CHURCHES OF CHRIST

'No Creed But Christ'

PLEDGED to the twin objectives of Christian unity and the restoration of the church in its New Testament form, the *Disciples of Christ* represent the most successful indigenous Christian denomination in the United States. During its relatively short 150 years this church has grown to become the sixth largest Protestant denomination in the country.

Paradoxically the unity-minded Disciples movement simply added another denomination to the roster of Protestant churches and sects. In fact, later disagreement over the precise nature of New Testament Christianity led to the schism of the conservative *Churches of Christ*. Another schism within the Disciples looms over the horizon. Thus the Campbellite restoration movement has already contributed two more denominations to the crowded American religious scene.

Closely akin to the much larger Baptist denomination, the Disciples also insist on baptism of adults by immersion. This insistence on adult baptism by a particular mode separates them from the vast majority of Protestants and doomed their efforts at a reunion of Christendom to an early failure. Disciples observe the Lord's Supper every Sunday while Baptists usually hold a communion service only four times a year. This difference between 52 and four communion services a year seems to be the main one which distinguishes the Disciples from the American (northern) Baptists.

Disciples pride themselves on being members of a creed-less church. "No creed but Christ" is a familiar maxim, and they will admit to their fellowship and to their communion table all baptized persons who wish to participate. Neither the Apostles' nor the Nicene creed finds any place in the liturgy and no Disciple, minister or layman, need affirm belief in any specific Christian dogma. As a result you will find Disciples who approach unitarian positions and others who would be logically classified as fundamentalists, although most of those in the latter category would likely gravitate toward the Churches of Christ. "Study your Bible and believe what you wish" would be typical Disciples' advice to a potential convert who expressed some reservations about a point of traditional Christianity such as the virgin birth, Christ's miracles, a literal heaven and hell.

The sectarian de-emphasis of any clergy-laity distinction continues to characterize the Disciples to a greater extent than most Protestant bodies. Lay elders and deacons may baptize, serve the communion elements, and preach; for legal reasons only an ordained minister may perform marriages. The Disciples of Christ minister is simply an elder among elders, hired and fired by the local congregation. He may be called "Reverend" by outsiders but Disciples themselves observe no ecclesiastical amenities when referring to their professional, full-time clergy. More and more pastors of the larger churches in the denomination now possess college and seminary degrees. Women are accorded full clergy rights but few are serving as pastors.

The Disciples movement grew out of a coalition of a number of nineteenth-century "back-to-primitive-Christianity" revivals, but the denomination owes its greatest debt to the Campbells, Thomas and Alexander. Thomas came to the United States from Ireland early in the century and became minister of a small Seceder Presbyterian church in western Pennsylvania. His liberal views and invitations to non-Presbyterians to partake of the Lord's Supper scandalized his colleagues and in 1809 he and his followers withdrew from Presbyterianism and formed the nondenominational Christian Association of Washington county, Pennsylvania.

That same year his son Alexander arrived in this country and joined his father as a free lance preacher. Both declared their guiding principle to be: "Where the scriptures speak, we speak; where the scriptures are silent, we are silent." Both Campbells thought it was possible and desirable to strip Christianity of all post-New Testament accretions. Every doctrine must be preceded by a Biblical "Thus saith the Lord." Father and son offered this common denominator Christianity as an antidote to rampant sectarianism.

Whereas the Christian Association was more of a fellowship than a church, the Campbells took the next step and organized a separate church at Brush Run, Pa., several years later. They had also been persuaded that adult baptism by immersion was the only valid baptism. They themselves were immersed in 1812. Their newly proclaimed stand on baptism drew them closer to the Baptists and they affiliated with that denomination in a union that lasted for 17 years.

Son Alexander, who had assumed leadership from his father, edited the *Christian Baptist* magazine in whose pages he denounced creeds, clergymen, church organs, mission societies, seminaries, Sunday Schools, Catholicism, and other "nonscriptural" innovations. Over the years the Campbells, champions of the doctrine of free will, grew restive in the Calvinist Baptist fold. They also objected to the labeling of the Baptist church as a "denomination" since they called their own movement a "restoration" and "brotherhood." In 1830 the Campbells severed their Baptist ties and from then on the Campbellites were known by the term "Disciples of Christ."

Meanwhile in Kentucky and Ohio an ex-Presbyterian minister with unitarian tendencies, Barton W. Stone, was urging Christians to discard all divisive doctrines and unite in one "Christian" body. Other anti-Calvinists in New England were forming similar fellowships of "Christians."

Shortly after withdrawing from the Baptists the Disciples entered into a union with the bulk of Stone's "Christians." Those "Christians" in the East who refused to enter the merger continued their corporate existence until 1931 when they fused with the Congregational church in the Congregational Christian church. By this time the doctrinal views of the 100,000 "Christians" were indistinguishable from unitarianism.

The "common sense" approach of the Disciples, the ability of their evangelists, and the wide scope afforded laymen contributed to the denomination's success on the American frontier. Two preachers, Walter Scott in Ohio and Pennsylvania and "Racoon" John Smith in Kentucky, won thousands of converts.

By 1860 the Disciples movement counted 200,000 members although statistics of the early Disciples and Christian groups are unreliable. Since Campbell approved of neither slavery nor abolition his church managed to avoid schism during the Civil War. By keeping intact during the conflict the Disciples won an advantage over the sundered Baptists, Methodists, and Presbyterians.

Alexander Campbell, contentious and vain, delighted in challenging clergymen of rival denominations to debate current theological issues. He was bitterly critical of all ministers and priests, whom he accused of being the "cause of all division, superstition, enthusiasm, and ignorance of the people." In 1837 he engaged in a lengthy debate with Roman Catholic Bishop John Purcell of Cincinnati.

Henry Clay moderated a debate between Campbell and a Presbyterian divine in 1843 which lasted for 16 days. Each speaker examined the question of infant baptism in a series of 64 speeches.

Campbell's 60 theological volumes interest no one today except perhaps Disciples ministerial candidates. He railed against mission societies but became head of the first national missionary board. He denounced seminaries and higher education and ended his career as president of Bethany College. He accused the clergy of greed and avarice and died the wealthiest man in West Virginia, a successful businessman, sheep raiser, and author. He scorned instrumental music, Sunday Schools, choirs, and Bible societies as unscriptural and eventually incorporated all these devices into his own sect.

He renamed his *Christian Baptist* magazine the *Millennial*

Harbinger and his extreme millennial views sometimes embarrass his twentieth-century spiritual children. The Protestant churches must drop all sectarian barriers because the end of the world was nigh, warned the editor. Later he mellowed on this issue as on many others and he finally predicted that the Second Coming could be expected about A.D. 2000.

Many of his followers failed to notice his many reversals of position; they remembered only his earlier injunctions. By 1906 the conservative and progressive wings had split into the *Churches of Christ* and the *Disciples of Christ.* Today the two branches are separate denominations with no formal and little informal fellowship or co-operation.

The outsider is understandably confused by the use of similar names. Disciples churches rarely include the term "Disciples" in their church name. They are commonly known as First Christian church, Main Street Christian church, etc. Some Disciples churches also use the term "Church of Christ" but no Churches of Christ church is ever identified as a "Disciples" church. The Disciples *Yearbook* lists some unusual church titles: Plumber's Landing, Weeping Mary, Rock of Ages, Gum Neck, The Last Chance, Sinners Union, Dripping Springs, and Little Bethlehem.

Each congregation is completely autonomous. Each church interviews prospective ministers, hires, and fires without supervision by any conference or administrative body. The individual church may be high or low in its liturgy, fundamentalist or rationalist in theology.

Most Disciples churches are equipped with a built-in pool for immersion baptisms. A Disciples minister's manual suggests a supply of leaded robes for men and women, heated water, and banks of flowers around the pool and warns that "humiliating experiences can be related of shallow baptistries."

The Disciples, unlike most Protestants, schedule a weekly communion service. At this service the minister takes a seat while laymen preside. One elder briefly discusses the significance of the Lord's Supper and the other elder offers the prayer over the bread and wine. The Disciples invite all those present to participate in the communion service but the Churches of Christ limit communion to those duly baptized by immersion. The elders serve the bread and wine to the deacons who bring the elements to the worshippers in the pews.

Some Disciples churches are known as "open membership" churches; these congregations will receive as full members transfers from other Christian denominations who have not been baptized by immersion. They will not themselves baptize infants or use any form by total immersion. Other Disciples congregations still insist on baptism by immersion of all who ask for full membership. Disciples theologians differ on the question of the validity of infant baptism.

Local churches may choose to join district and state conferences and most Disciples churches belong to the voluntary Christian Churches (Disciples of Christ), International Convention with headquarters in Indianapolis. All who attend the annual convention may vote and nothing the convention recommends binds an individual church or Disciple. This convention is a mass convention rather than a representative assembly. Local churches may or may not contribute funds for the support of the convention.

Concerted efforts on the national level by The Christian Church (Disciples of Christ) are handicapped by the weak central authority. Even financial support of the headquarters in Indianapolis is completely voluntary; only about half of the 5,800 local congregations contributed anything to this headquarters.

Almost all of the Disciples of Christ live in half a dozen of the South and Middle West states. The Disciples report only seven churches in the New England area; there are only 123 individual Disciples in Wisconsin and 3,783 in Minnesota. Yet in such states as Indiana, Ohio, Kentucky, Illinois, Texas, Oklahoma, and Missouri the Disciples play a major role in church life.

Outside of the U.S. the Disciples report some 210,000 members in 15 countries and of these more than half live in the Congo. There are also 35,000 members in Australia, 8,000 in Puerto Rico, and 7,200 in England.

A traditional suspicion of higher education stunted the denomination's expansion in this area although Butler, Drake,

Phillips, Texas Christian, and College of the Bible are Disciples institutions. For a denomination of 1,592,000 members in the United States their one hospital, six homes for the aged, and six orphanages reveal only a slight interest in social welfare institutions.

Two Disciples were instrumental in founding and editing the *Christian Century,* now the leading interdenominational Protestant journal of opinion. They were W. E. Garrison and Charles Clayton Morrison. President James A. Garfield was a former Disciples preacher and poet Vachel Lindsay was also a member of the sect. Former President Lyndon B. Johnson joined the Disciples of Christ as a teen-ager and maintains membership in the Johnson City, Texas, congregation.

The fundamentalist Churches of Christ keep no records and are even more loosely organized than the Disciples since they have no annual convention, and no local, state or national associations. Most of their 16,000 affiliated congregations are found in Texas, Tennessee, Kentucky, Alabama, Arkansas, and Oklahoma. Although not officially identified as Churches of Christ institutions such schools as Harding, David Lipscomb, George Pepperdine, and Abilene Christian belong to this tradition.

Students of the Churches of Christ movement list at least five distinct groups. They differ on such matters as the proper form of worship, the support of church colleges, the use of the common vs. the individual communion cups, the operation of Sunday Schools, and the use of various translations of the Bible. Total membership of the Churches of Christ has been estimated at 2,500,000.

All music is *a capella* since they find no mention of organs in the Bible (or, for that matter, hymn books, pews, electric fans, and the English language). Their periodicals are carefully identified as "unofficial" and their colleges as "nonsectarian."

Criticism of the alleged modernism of the Christian Church (Disciples of Christ) has been voiced for several decades. In 1927 the Restorationists or Independents began to set up rival Bible colleges and to support separate agencies and publications. At least a third of the Disciples now favor the more fundamentalist Restorationists. They support the North American Christian Convention and sometimes are known as members of the Church of Christ Number Two or the Church of Christ (Instrumental).

For all practical purposes the Campbellite revival has added three (four counting the 5,800-member Christian Union church) to the American religious scene. And all this in the name of Christian unity.

What should not be denied, however, is the devotion of so many Disciples ministers and laymen to the ecumenical movement. Despite the failure of Campbell's vision of unity these Christians remain in the forefront of efforts to find such unity. If the Disciples of Christ movement can survive further division and can somehow combine the principle of congregational autonomy with a minimum of needed centralization, it should continue as an influential, though regional, American church.

Further Reading

Adams, Hampton, *Why I am a Disciple of Christ* (New York, Thomas Nelson, 1957).

Garrison, W. E. and A. T. DeGroot, *The Disciples of Christ* (St. Louis, Christian Board of Publication, 1954).

Chapter IX

THE UNITED CHURCHMEN

Congregational Christians,
Evangelical and Reformed Merged in 1957

ALTHOUGH a number of denominational mergers have been completed in recent years, most of these could be termed family reunions rather than marriages. Churches which had divided over some issue such as slavery or language came together to form a united church once more. Other churches which represented almost identical constituencies found common grounds for forming a single denomination.

In this respect the formation of the *United Church of Christ* in 1957 was unique in American Protestantism. *Congregationalism,* a product of English Separatism, came to these shores with the Pilgrim Fathers and became a virtual state religion for the New England Yankees. On the other hand the *Evangelical and Reformed Church,* a fusion of two German denominations in 1934, found its adherents among the descendants of German immigrants in Pennsylvania and the Middle West. Congregationalism rested upon the complete autonomy of the local congregation and refused to recognize the power of any bishop, synod, or council over the congregation. The Evangelical and Reformed Church operated under a modified presbyterian system of church government. Congregationalists refused to bind members or churches with creeds while the Evangelical and Reformed were committed to uphold the Heidelberg Catechism, Luther's Short-er Catechism, and the Augsburg Confession.

In some parts of the country the local United Church of Christ congregations may still be identified by the older names. In New England, for example, some UCC churches will be known as Congregational while other UCC churches in the Middle West might still be popularly known as Evangelical and Reformed or E and R churches. What adds to the confusion is that nearly 1,000 Congregational Christian churches refused to join the 1957 merger; they retain the Congregational name and have formed associations of like-minded churches.

Opposition by a minority of Congregationalists blocked the merger through court action for five years. Opponents of the union contended that they would be untrue to their most distinctive Congregational belief by uniting with a presbyterian church such as the Evangelical and Reformed. They lost their case and the proponents of union obtained large majority approvals in their respective church councils.

To understand this new religious synthesis called the United Church of Christ, we must examine the backgrounds of its two diverse components. This youngest Protestant denomination numbers about 2,000,000 communicants in the United States and represents the same type of ecumenical approach whose counterpart we find in the older United Church of Canada and the Church of South India.

For the origins of Congregationalism we must look to the Separatist movement in England and for the Evangelical and Reformed Church to continental Calvinism and to attempts in Prussia to blend Lutheranism with Calvinism.

"No bishops" had been the battle cry of English Presbyterians who preferred a representative form of church polity which nevertheless exercised a measure of control and supervision over member congregations. This did not satisfy everyone. More radical wings of the Separatist movement denied any authority over the local congregation. "No head, priest, prophet, or king save Christ" was their motto. Each church, composed of the predestined elect, should be free to frame its own creed or no creed and to choose its own minister and church officers. Furthermore, they agreed with the more moderate Puritans that all vestiges of popery be driven from the church. These radicals came to be known as Independents or Congregationalists.

Persecution drove many Congregationalists to tolerant Holland, among them the future Pilgrims. Perhaps the most flourishing community was that at Leyden under the pastorate of the gentle John Robinson. This congregation had been organized by poor people of the hamlet of Scrooby who finally sought refuge in Europe's religious sanctuary.

As time passed these English Separatists found economic conditions harsh in their new home and they saw their children adopting the customs of a foreign land and intermarrying with the Dutch. They wished to preserve their English heritage. A group decided to sail to the New World where they could re-establish their religious community but the majority remained in Holland with their pastor. They arranged transportation through some merchant adventurers; by the time they set sail from England on the Mayflower the majority of the 101 passengers were non-Separatists. When they sighted Cape Cod in 1620 the adult males among the Separatists signed the Mayflower Compact but once ashore the distinctions between the Congregationalists and the "Strangers" disappeared.

Starvation, cold, and disease faced the Pilgrim Fathers but they buried their dead and labored to build their colony at Plymouth. Half the settlers died within six months. Later wealthy Puritans, originally non-Separatists, landed at nearby Salem. Between 1628 and 1635 more than 20,000 Puritans arrived at the Massachusetts Bay Colony and they eventually exchanged their own presbyterian preferences for the congregationalism of their Pilgrim neighbors. The two settlements merged in 1691 and Congregationalism became the established religion of the New England colonies.

Only church members could vote (1708 voters out of 15,000 settlers in the Massachusetts Bay Colony). Everyone was required to pay taxes for the support of the established church. This special status was not abrogated in Connecticut until 1818, in New Hampshire until 1819, and in Massachusetts until 1834.

While it may not be entirely fair to say that the Pilgrims

came to this country to worship God in their own way and make everyone else do likewise, they certainly were not champions of religious freedom. They came to the New World to find freedom for themselves rather than to provide it for others. Persecuted in England they became self-righteous persecutors in America. Dissenters were firmly invited to leave. Four Quakers were hanged on Boston Commons. Heresy and witchcraft were vigorously extirpated and Puritan treatment of Roger Williams and the Baptists, Anne Hutchinson, the Quakers, and any episcopal sympathizers is well known. The Salem witchcraft trials of 1692 found a theocracy in religious frenzy. Nineteen men and women were hanged in Salem for trafficking with the devil.

The Puritan theocracy forbade dancing, card playing, smoking, mince meat pies, the observance of Christmas, and all musical instruments save the drum, trumpet, and jew's-harp. "No one shall travel, cook victuals, make beds, sweep house, cut hair or shave and no woman shall kiss her children on the Sabbath Day," declared the Puritan divines. But just as the Congregational heirs of Puritanism jettisoned strict Calvinism for theological liberalism, so they also abandoned Puritan morality to the Methodists, Baptists, and Holiness sects.

Despite the excesses and witch trials and bigotry, the Puritan theocracy made an enormous contribution to American life. The Puritans developed the town meeting system. They established standards of sobriety and the industry which helped American men and women tame a continent. They furnished the Minute Men and gave us the Thanksgiving holiday.

An observer in the early nineteenth century would probably have assumed that Congregationalism or the "New England Way" would continue to be the largest and one of the most influential churches in the nation. That it lost this pre-eminence to become one of the smaller major denominations was the result of several factors.

Early in the 1800's Congregationalism split into two parties: Trinitarian and Unitarian. The Unitarians lopped off all but one of Boston's 14 congregations, captured Harvard and the original Pilgrim church at Plymouth, and dominated the religious scene in eastern Massachusetts.

Another reason for Congregationalism's decline was the Plan of Union which was devised in 1801 to minimize denominational competition in the West but which usually worked to the advantage of the Presbyterians. Before its repudiation in 1852 the Plan is said to have resulted in a loss of 2000 Congregational churches outside of New England to the better organized Presbyterians. Up to the 1957 merger Congregationalism remained primarily a New England institution with smaller memberships in New York, Ohio, Illinois, Iowa, and California.

Reliance on state recognition and support led to complacency in Congregational ranks and the upstart Methodists and Baptists forged ahead to become the leading Protestant denominations in the country. Like the Presbyterians and Episcopalians, the Congregationalists insisted on an educated clergy and lacked the trained manpower to compete with the Methodist circuit riders and the Baptist preachers.

Congregationalists organized the American Board of Commissioners for Foreign Missions in 1810 and dispatched the first missionary team to India in 1812. Others went from New England to South Africa, Ceylon, and Turkey. Descendants of Congregationalist missionaries to Hawaii not only converted many of the natives but obtained control of much of the economy of the islands.

Few Congregationalists held slaves but many supported Abolitionism. Harriet Beecher Stowe, daughter of a Congregationalist minister, wrote *Uncle Tom's Cabin*. After the Civil War the Congregationalists set up 500 schools for Negroes in the former Confederate states and also founded such institutions as Howard, Fisk, Hampton Institute, Dillard, and Tougaloo.

Congregationalism has always demonstrated a concern for higher education; church members founded Harvard, Yale, Dartmouth, Bowdoin, Amherst, Smith, Williams, Oberlin, and 40 other colleges most of which have since passed from church control. When Harvard capitulated to Unitarianism the Congregationalists founded Andover seminary to inculcate orthodox Calvinism. The educational level of Congregationalists, clergy and laity, has traditionally been among the highest of all Protestant groups.

In 1931 the Congregationalists merged with the 100,000-

member *Christian Church,* sometimes known as the Baptist Unitarians. This group denied the divinity of Christ and rejected all creeds since it arose from the same religious ferment which produced the creedless Disciples of Christ and Churches of Christ. The first overtures for a merger were made in 1895. The new church was known as the *Congregational Christian Churches.*

Calvinism originally formed the theological basis of Congregationalism although the Congregationalists minimized formal creeds and confessions. Then as now the local congregation could compose a creed of its own, adopt the Apostles' Creed, or remain creedless.

Theoretically the power of the local Congregational Church was unlimited. It could fix doctrine and ritual, hire and fire ministers, choose its own officers. Theory and practice differed and there are those who maintain that a Congregationalist had no more freedom than a Methodist and Lutheran. Strict educational and moral standards for the ministry were enforced and a church had to be accepted by the churches in its district before it could use the title "Congregational." Group pressure can sometimes bring about more uniformity and conformity than elaborate governmental structures. Beyond the local churches were the Associations, the Conferences, and the General Council. The decisions of these regional, state, and national bodies had no binding power on the congregations. The problem of preserving the essentials of Christianity in a Congregational polity was never solved and in many cases the essentials were not preserved. A few Congregational churches could be characterized as fundamentalist but most taught a mixture of liberalism, modernism, sentimentalism, social gospel, and unitarianism.

As in the Evangelical and Reformed Church, women were ordained to the ministry but generally served smaller rural churches. A Congregationalist leader estimated in 1956 that half the Congregational ministers had been recruited, educated, and ordained by other Protestant churches. In fact, 170 Congregational churches were served by ministers who retained their standing in other denominations. Ministers who embraced Congregationalism were not required to undergo reordination.

Early Congregational worship and architecture were severely

plain: lengthy sermons, Bible reading and psalms, unadorned meeting houses. Christmas was called a popish holiday and its observance cost the celebrant five shillings. Today Christmas finds a place in the Congregationalist year as well as the Puritan's own contribution to the calendar, Thanksgiving Day. Organs and hymns were gradually introduced and the service was shortened from three hours to one. An altar, cross and candles, cassock, surplice and stole which would have scandalized their Puritan ancestors are accepted by modern Congregationalists.

At the time of the merger with the Evangelical and Reformed Church the Congregational Christian Churches counted 1,342,000 adult members, mostly in New England. Each Congregational Christian church is free to accept or reject the union with the E and R Church.

Whereas almost all E and R congregations joined the United Church of Christ, hundreds of Congregational Christian churches refused. The *National Association of Congregational Christian Churches* claims 110,000 members in 300 churches. These churches believe that basic congregational principles were compromised by the merger with the E and R body. Another group, the *Conservative Congregational Christian Conference,* claims 15,000 members in 92 churches.

The Evangelical and Reformed Church itself was the youngest of the major denominations since it traced its beginning as a single church to a union in 1934 of two German-Swiss churches. As separate churches the Reformed Church antedated the century-old Evangelical Synod by almost 300 years.

Not all areas in Germany which had abandoned the ancient faith accepted Lutheranism. Certain sections such as the Palatinate adopted a Reformed theology in the Heidelberg Confession of 1563. This confession attempted to strike a middle course between Lutheranism and Calvinism which differed mainly on the doctrine of the Real Presence.

A number of Palatinates left their homeland for America after the devastation of the Thirty Years' War. A Reformed minister, Michael Schlatter, organized these scattered German settlements in Pennsylvania but the American church remained under Dutch control until 1793. In the early 1800's two groups led by

Philip Otterbein and John Winebrenner seceded and started churches of their own: the United Brethren in Christ and the Church of God.

A merger of two German Reformed synods in 1863 and the wider use of the English language strengthened the Reformed Church in the United States (not to be confused with the Reformed Church of America, a Dutch body). Units of the Hungarian Reformed Church were absorbed in 1924.

The other party in the 1934 union, the Evangelical Synod of North America, represented the 1817 union of Reformed and Lutherans in Prussia. King Frederick William III desired religious unity in his realm and decreed the union as a solution of religious differences between the Reformed and the Lutheran majority. He chose the 300th anniversary of Luther's revolt for the royal decree.

Members of this United Evangelical Church of Prussia began to enter the United States almost a century after their Reformed cousins. They formed their church in 1840. Although most of the charter members were Lutherans this church has drifted far from orthodox Lutheranism and its absorption into the United Church of Christ is evidence of the extent to which it had accepted more liberal theological assumptions.

Both participants in the 1934 merger were organized by German immigrants; both employed the German language in their pioneer days; both preached a Lutheran-Reformed theology; both were governed by a presbyterian polity. At the time of the merger in Cleveland the Reformed Church counted 348,000 members and the Evangelical Synod, 281,000. An unusual feature of this action was that the two denominations united first and worked out the details later. Church boards were not consolidated until 1941.

Three of the most distinguished Protestant theologians in the United States were ordained Evangelical and Reformed ministers: Reinhold and H. Richard Niebuhr and Paul Tillich. The Niebuhrs grew up in an E and R parsonage and Tillich transferred his membership from the German church.

Pennsylvania, Missouri, and Ohio were the Evangelical and Reformed strongholds; a large proportion of the members resided in these three states and two others: Indiana and Illinois. In this respect E and R membership complemented the New England strength of Congregationalism.

Calvin Coolidge was the only U.S. president who was a Congregationalist although members of this tradition have furnished more than their share of public servants. Some Congregationalists have won fame by founding new religions: Mary Baker Eddy, foundress of Christian Science, and Charles Taze Russell, organizer of the Bible groups which became known as Jehovah's Witnesses.

The United Church has become more of a national church than either of the former denominations although it has scarcely any adherents in the South. As a matter of fact the growth of the separate parties to the merger has hardly kept pace with the natural increases in population in this country.

The two churches in the 1957 merger reported a combined membership of 2,192,674. By 1971 this had fallen to 1,997,000 attributable in part to the defection of congregations which opposed the merger.

Unlike many denominations which have abandoned their city parishes in the face of invasions by Puerto Ricans, Negroes, and Southern whites, the United Church refuses to retreat entirely to suburbia. In Brooklyn, Chicago, Harlem, and even in San Francisco's hippie colony the church of the Pilgrim fathers attempts to meet the challenges of metropolitan living in the 1970s.

Further Reading

Horton, Douglas *The United Church of Christ* (New York, Thomas Nelson, 1962).

Starkey, Marion L., *The Congregational Way* (Garden City, N.Y., Doubleday, 1966).

Chapter X

THE QUAKERS
Follow the Inner Light

QUAKERS, members of the *Religious Society of Friends*, often consider themselves representatives of a third form of Christianity, neither Catholic nor Protestant. At other times they concur with many non-Quakers who see Quakerism as Protestantism carried to its logical conclusion.

Luther rejected the pope, the visible church, five of the seven sacraments, the value of tradition as a rule of faith, the sacrificial element in worship. Calvin dispensed with the rule of bishops, minimized the role of music and art in worship. Congregationalists did away with centralized church government of any kind and Baptists damned infant baptism as unscriptural.

The Quakers dispensed with all sacraments, all ritual, any professional ministry. On the other hand, the familiar Protestant formulae—total depravity, justification by faith alone, and the sole sufficiency of the scriptures—are foreign to Quaker thought. Further, the Quakers declare that the ultimate religious authority rests in no church, individual, tradition, or Bible but within each individual.

An understanding of the Quaker's Inner Light is essential to an understanding of this radical but influential phase of the English Reformation. By the Inner Light which each man must follow the Quakers do not mean conscience. Conscience itself is illumined by the Inner Light. This Inner Light is rather the immediate influence of the Holy Spirit, that which is of God in each soul. Like most mystics the early Quakers found themselves helpless to express their experiences in words.

In some basic theological positions Quakerism comes closer to Roman Catholicism than to Protestantism. The Quaker rejects the classical Lutheran view of human nature as totally depraved as a consequence of original sin. Most Quakers would uphold the inherent goodness of man. They believe that perfection and freedom from sin are possible in this life. The founder of the Society of Friends early preached against the Calvinist doctrine of predestination; Quakerism denies that God has divided mankind into the elect and the damned. Finally the Quaker does not ascribe to the Bible the same final authority as do Protestants.

Quaker writer Rufus Jones probably spoke for most of his co-religionists when he said: "Friends are not much interested in abstract theories and statements about God. They prefer to begin with personal experience of Him."

The Friends have never been numerous and there are probably about as many in the world today as there were in 1700. In the United States, now the chief Quaker center, they count 115,000 members which is approximately the same number reported in the 1906 religious census when the nation's population was less than half what it is today.

Most of the customs and mannerisms which once set them apart from the world as a "peculiar" people have disappeared. The group mysticism of the English lower classes has become a respected denomination for the middle class American. Their witness against war and their active interest in social questions continue and they have won the universal admiration of their countrymen.

Like Luther and Wesley, the founder of the Quakers had no intention of founding another church or sect. George Fox, born in 1624, had little opportunity to attend school or study. He was apprenticed to a shoemaker at the age of 12 but developed a dissatisfaction with his religious life and that of his Puritan neighbors. One day as a youth of 19 he was shocked at the sight of two clergymen engaged in a drinking bout at a fair. In a vision he said he heard the voice of God tell him: "Thou seest how men give themselves over to vanity. Forget about them. Keep aloof from them and in the future be as a stranger to them."

He decided to break with home, friends, church, and trade and he began four years of wandering about England. Fox came to the conclusion that man arrives at truth not by study or Bible reading or listening to sermons but by following the Inner Light whereby God speaks directly to each soul. Of what use, then, is learning and ritual and church organization? Quakers take the year 1649 as their founding date.

The young enthusiast found many converts for his views among the dozens of sects which dotted the English countryside: Seekers, Ranters, Baptists, and mystics of all types. He found many who disliked the Anglican establishment and kindred spirits who had reacted against the harshness of Calvinism.

The Quaker founder believed that God granted the Inner Light to all; Fox had no place in his system for elect and reprobate. He denied that man was depraved and he set up perfection and freedom from all sin as a spiritual goal. Even the atonement was rejected since the Quakers believed that no one, not even God, could atone for another's sins. They reverenced the Bible but considered it a Word of God and not *the* Word of God.

Imprisoned for a total of six years, Fox endured dogged persecution throughout his life. Once condemned to death for his religious views he missed execution only through the intervention of powerful friends. Nevertheless he maintained a full schedule of preaching and won many followers, especially in northern England.

On one occasion he was brought before a judge and accused of blasphemy. Fox startled the magistrate by shouting, "The time has come for even judges to quake and tremble before the Lord." "Oh," mocked the judge, "so you are quakers, are you?" The name stuck although it has never been officially adopted and the term "Friends" is sometimes preferred. Fox's converts had previously called themselves "Children of Light" and "Friends of Truth."

Quaker ideas of social equality contributed to their persecution in seventeenth-century England. They refused to acknowledge any special privilege among men which meant that they would doff their hats to no human and address no one with the then complimentary "you." Instead they used the plain "thee" and "thou." They opposed taking oaths on Biblical grounds and as implying a double standard of truth, one for the marketplace and one for the courtroom. Objecting to the pagan origin of the days of the week they renamed Sunday "First Day," Monday "Second Day," and so on. Simple dress, simple speech, sober habits were prescribed. Participation in war was strictly forbidden. Music, art, fiction, and the theater fell under Quaker ban. As a result of their attitudes more than 13,000 Quakers were imprisoned and hundreds died in prison during the Stuart Restoration and the reign of Charles II.

At their meetings for worship neither preaching nor ritual had a place. The only ritual was silence. Quakers waited quietly for inspiration from God and occasionally one or another of the assembled Friends would stand to testify or present a religious thought. Since they abhorred ritual of any kind they neither baptized nor observed the Lord's Supper.

The Quaker withdraws to the silence of the weekly meeting only to find spiritual nourishment and inspiration to go back into the world. There is no such thing as a Quaker hermit or a Quaker monastery where contemplatives cut themselves off from men and affairs.

In all Quaker meetings the members seek decisions not by majority rule but by the "sense of the meeting" which means unanimity. Women hold equal power and status with men.

Elders and overseers are appointed to serve each monthly meeting. The elders arrange for worship, marriages, and funerals, while the overseers assume responsibilities for the pastoral care of members. The Clerk is the chief administrative officer of the meeting.

A Quaker bride and groom repeat their marriage vows during a meeting for worship after obtaining the consent of the meeting to the union. Each declares: "In the presence of the Lord and of these our friends, I take thee, . . . to be my wife (or husband) promising with divine assistance to be unto thee a loving and faithful husband (or wife) so long as we both shall live." Then all those present sign the marriage certificate as witnesses.

Pioneer work in the social field was undertaken by the Quakers and millions of people have benefited from their efforts. They were among the first to urge proper care for the poor, aged, and insane; they fought slavery and battled for just treatment of the American Indians; they promoted temperance, prison reform, and equality of the sexes.

Two other names besides Fox are associated with Quaker history in a special way: Robert Barclay, the theologian of Quakerism, and William Penn, the founder of Pennsylvania.

Barclay was Fox's Melanchthon. He drew up the systematic presentation of Quaker doctrine. A Presbyterian in his youth, Barclay was sent to Paris to study under his Catholic uncle who taught at a Jesuit college. The Jesuit Fathers taught Barclay scholastic philosophy, Catholic theology, the Church Fathers, Latin, and French. Fearing his conversion to popery his parents withdrew him from the college. Back in England he finally joined the new Quaker movement in 1666 and employed his Catholic-sponsored education in the interests of this mystical sect. His chief work was *Apology for the True Christian Divinity*.

Penn, son of an English admiral, had embraced the principles of Quakerism and planned to establish a haven for his persecuted brethren. The king owed Penn's father a large sum of money and was happy to settle the debt by chartering a tract of land in the New World to Penn in 1681.

The first Quaker missionaries to America, two women, had been condemned as witches and sent back to England within five weeks of their arrival. The Massachusetts Puritans resisted and harassed the revolutionary Quakers in every way possible. Four intrepid Quakers who followed the women were hanged on Boston Commons and their coreligionists were imprisoned, whipped, and tortured.

Penn arrived in his colony in 1682 and found Swedes, Englishmen, and Dutch already settled. He assured them that they would be governed by their own laws as before. Following his religious convictions he soon concluded a model treaty with the Indians. He granted freedom of worship to all Christians, including Catholics, and laid out the streets of his City of Brotherly Love, Philadelphia.

Meanwhile, in England the Act of Toleration of 1689 released the Quakers from some of the harsher penalties and by the time of Fox's death two years later there were at least 50,000 Friends in the British Isles (twice as many as today).

Quakers prospered in the American colonies and by 1700 Quakers owned not only Pennsylvania but New Jersey and Delaware, controlled Rhode Island and the Carolinas, and had strength in New York and Maryland. They constituted the greatest single religious community in the New World at this time.

Eventually the Quakers lost not only preponderance in the colonies but shrank to comparative numerical insignificance in American religious life. They lost political control of Pennsylvania in 1756 when they voluntarily relinquished their seats in the state assembly rather than vote for war against the Shawnee and Delaware Indians. Schisms, doctrinal disputes, lack of trained leaders, quietism, defection, membership purges, and a reluctance to proselytize furthered Quaker decline.

Quietism infected the movement for many decades. This enervating philosophy, which has appeared in many religious systems, teaches that God operates in man only when man silences all his usual activities: prayer, study, and work. Its infection of Quakerism might have been anticipated. As a result of this philosophy, planning, organization, and foresight are neglected. Such Catholic Quietists as Molinos, Fenelon, and Madame Guyon were popular among the Quakers. Membership dipped from 60,000 in 1700 to 17,000 half a century later.

The movement depended almost entirely on birthright members who might grow indifferent to the original Quaker message. At other times purges crossed hundreds of names from the membership rolls. No replenishing evangelistic campaigns were conducted.

But the most serious organizational disruption of Quakerism sprang from the schism of Elias Hicks. A modernist theologian bordering on unitarianism, Hicks apparently rejected the divinity of Christ and the existence of original sin. He led a large group of rural Quakers from the main body in 1827. The Hicks-ites never adopted Hicks' theology in toto but this split handi-capped Quaker activities for nearly a century until the original differences melted away. A smaller group called the Evangelical Friends or Wilburites broke away in 1837 in the expected con-servative reaction.

It was not easy to be a Quaker. They were expected to wear a distinctive garb (see the Quaker Oats package), oppose all wars, refuse to swear oaths, adopt peculiar habits of speech, ignore the traditional Christian holidays, and marry within the group. The periodic purges expelled backsliders. Even today no orthodox Quaker gambles, plays the stock market, or drinks.

Quakers early opposed slavery in all its forms. Led by the gentle John Woolman they dismissed all slaveholders from their ranks and threw their weight behind the abolitionist crusade. Today they continue to fight segregation and racial intolerance.

Eventually compromises diluted Quakerism. The silent meeting often gave way to a programmed meeting differing only slightly from a simple Protestant service. Next came pro-fessional pastors. Those groups with programmed services came to be known as Friends Churches in contrast to the original Friends Meeting.

Officially the Quakers continue to oppose war but as more young Quakers volunteered for military service the attitude to-ward soldier-members softened. Estimates put 8000 Quakers in the armed forces during World War II, 1000 as noncom-batants, 1000 as conscientious objectors, and 100 in prison. Those who did serve in the military services were no longer ostracized as they would have been in the earlier days of the sect.

The peculiarities which once set Quakers apart from the rest of the community have become private family customs.

The monthly meeting for worship and business is the basic unit of Quaker polity. This meeting convenes for silent or pro-grammed worship, keeps records of births, deaths, and mar-riages, appoints committees, and conducts the necessary busi-ness. These meetings come together in quarterly meetings and they in turn comprise the yearly or Five Years meetings of which there are 28 in the United States and Canada.

Largest of these Quaker bodies is the *Society of Friends (Friends United Meeting)* which reports about 70,000 members in 514 churches. This is a union of 25 autonomous yearly meetings in the U.S., Canada, East Africa, Cuba, and Jamaica. It maintains headquarters in Richmond, Ind., and was once known as the Five Years Meeting. Claiming to represent some 20,000 of the total membership is the Association of Evangelical Friends which leans toward a more fundamentalist orientation.

The Hicksites form the *Religious Society of Friends (General Conference)*. Although this group never officially adopted the theological platform of Elias Hicks they tend to be more rationalist and modernist in their outlook. The General Conference is made up of 31,000 Friends in seven yearly meetings in Baltimore, Canada, New England, Illinois, Indiana, New York, and Philadephia.

In 1965 four independent yearly meetings — Ohio, Kansas, Oregon, and Rocky Mountain — formed the *Evangelical Friends* Alliance. They favor an evangelical Protestant theology, sponsor revivals, seek associations with holiness churches. They give their membership at 30,000.

Smaller Quaker bodies include the *Pacific Yearly Meeting of Friends* (1,600) and the *Religious Society of Friends (Conservative)* whose 1,700 members continue the Wilburite tradition.

Most American Quakers will be found in Pennsylvania, North Carolina, Indiana, Kansas, Ohio, and California. Outside of the U.S. and England the largest number of Friends live in Kenya (31,555), Madagascar (7,726), Bolivia (3,000), Ireland (1,875), Guatemala (1,500) and Australasia (1,500). About 4,000 men and women belong to the Wider Quaker Fellowship. They sympathize with Quaker positions but do not wish to cut the ties with their own churches.

Representatives of the various Quaker branches formed the American Friends Service Committee in 1917. Since then the committee has spent millions of dollars on war and disaster relief work, rehabilitation, and care of conscientious objectors. Many non-Quakers contribute to the committee's financial support. Together with the Friends Service Council (London) it received the Nobel Peace Prize in 1947.

The Quakers operate ten small but distinguished colleges including Swarthmore, Earlham, Friends University, and Whittier. Quaker pastors receive training at a number of interdenominational seminaries. A Quaker seminary has been opened at Earlham.

This relatively small denomination has seen two of its members occupy the White House in this century: Herbert Hoover and Richard Nixon. The latter maintains membership in the Whittier Friends Meeting near Los Angeles. Other well-known American Quakers have included John Greenleaf Whittier, Johns Hopkins, Ezra Cornell, and Susan B. Anthony.

Quakerism flourished during the lifetimes of its original triumvirate: Fox, Barclay, and Penn. Since then it has accomplished much in the way of social action and philanthropy but it has hardly held its own membership-wise. Millions of Americans applaud Quaker activities but never seriously consider joining the sect and no one ever asks them to do so.

With few members and few converts the Quaker movement in this day demonstrates what even such a small band of people can do to serve mankind. The Quakers are mystics but they do not ignore the world while they cultivate their own spiritual lives. As Penn wrote: "True godliness does not turn men out of the world but enables them to live better in it, and excites their endeavors to mend it."

Further Reading

Bacon, Margaret H., *The Quiet Rebels: The Story of the Quakers in America* (New York, Basic Books, 1969).

Brinton, Howard, *Friends for 300 Years* (New York, Harper & Brothers, 1952).

Sykes, John, *The Quakers* (Philadelphia and New York, Lippincott, 1958).

Chapter XI

THE PERFECTIONISTS

Christians Seek 'Baptism of the Holy Spirit' in Numerous Holiness Churches

SEVERAL dozen sects comprise the Holiness movement (popularly known as Holy Roller) which grew out of post-Civil War revivals. These revivals stressed Wesley's doctrine of entire sanctification or Christian perfection which had been quietly eased out of the regular Methodist churches.

Today these numerous Holiness groups are characterized by emotionalism, swingy gospel hymns, faith healing, strict morality, premillenialism, revivals, and camp meetings. We can distinguish two branches of the Holiness movement, a right and a left wing, perfectionist and pentecostal.

Included in the perfectionist wing are such bodies as the *Church of the Nazarene,* the *Church of God* (Anderson, Indiana), and *Christian and Missionary Alliance.* The pentecostal wing embraces those groups which maintain that speaking in tongues, glossolalia, is a necessary and natural accompaniment of the baptism of the Holy Spirit.

All these groups from the sedate Church of the Nazarene to the most primitive hillbilly cult believe they have restored the Biblical and Wesleyan doctrine of entire sanctification to its proper and central position in the Christian life.

According to the theology of holiness or, as it has been termed, the theology of the Holy Ghost, a Christian can receive a subsequent blessing after justification which frees him from all sinful desires. His nature is then freed from all depravity wrought by original sin. Whereas repentance is considered the prime requisite for baptism, consecration is the main requisite for holiness. All Christians are called to this holiness experience, an instantaneous transformation wrought by faith.

No one denies that Wesley, departing from the pessimism of Luther and Calvin regarding human nature, taught the doctrine of holiness and that his teaching on this subject has all but been disowned by modern Methodists. Many would deny that Wesley's teaching was carried to the extremes of some Holiness enthusiasts in the United States. By the end of the Civil War the doctrine was seldom mentioned in Methodist circles. When the postwar revivals renewed interest in holiness the devotees of the Latter Rain movement first formed prayer groups within the existing churches and eventually broke away to form their own congregations.

More radical or ecstatic elements claimed that the gifts showered on the Apostles at Pentecost were necessary signs of holiness. They especially encouraged speaking in tongues which the Nazarenes, for example, have never countenanced.

A revival meeting in a medium-sized Indiana community illustrates the appeal of these groups. In this case an evangelistic team from Texas was imported to stage a six-night revival and healing campaign under the auspices of a local Holiness church.

About 200 people had assembled in the armory when the master of ceremonies began the hymn fest with piano accompaniment. A young lady in an orange blouse sang a solo entitled "Wicked Life." After half an hour of lively singing the M.C. asked that all those willing to contribute five dollars for the expenses of the meeting step forward to receive special prayers. No one did but he repeated the invitations for those with one dollar, fifty cents, and finally small change.

After several more gospel songs which the audience seemed to know by heart, the M.C. introduced the white-suited evangelist. His 40-minute sermon berated the larger churches for neglecting divine healing and for wasting money on medical missionaries and drugs. His talk was interrupted ritually time and again with "Amen," "Hallelujah" and "Praise God."

Finally he invited all those seeking healing to raise their hands and then to stand while everyone else was to bow his head and resist the temptation to peek. They were then asked to come to the platform; seven or eight people complied. Among the complaints were deafness, sore legs, fallen arches, and internal disorders. A white-haired lady of 80 and a lad of nine were among the petitioners.

"I command you, Satan, in the name of Jesus Christ to leave this woman," screamed the perspiring evangelist as he slapped his palm on a woman's forehead. Most of those participating mumbled that they felt better and had been miraculously cured. The 80-year-old grandmother showed no signs of regaining her hearing and the young healer calmly told her daughter that her mother evidently was not a true Christian and lacked genuine faith. A gentleman with fallen arches hobbled up to the front of the auditorium, submitted to the exorcism, praised God that he had been cured, and hobbled back to his seat. During the healing service a number of those in the audience rocked on the seats with closed eyes and upraised hands and uttered frequent ejaculations.

After the healing, the evangelist himself led several familiar hymns and then asked all who wished to be prayed for to hold up their hands. As with those who wished healing they were then urged to stand up and step forward. About 30 responded. They retired to the anteroom and the air was soon filled with groans, shrieks, and moans. The meeting closed with a hymn. The preacher pointed out that some of his books could be purchased under the "Saved By His Blood" banner in the rear of the hall. He announced that the next night's sermon topic would be "What Dr. Kinsey Dare Not Put in His Book." The service had lasted about two hours.

Obviously people who demand this type of religious experience will not find it in the established churches. They find it in thousands of storefront churches, revival tents, and camp meetings.

One of the largest Perfectionist bodies of the Holiness movement, the *Church of the Nazarene*, represents a merger of a number of smaller sects whose members were drawn from Methodism. These congregations sprang up around the country between 1890 and 1900 and the formal organization was completed at Pilot Point, Texas, in 1908. The original merger brought together 10,400 members and this church now claims 372,000 members in more than 4,500 congregations. Sociologists see in the Nazarene church an excellent example of a body in transition from sect to church. Within another generation or two it will no doubt take its place along with the Baptist, Methodist, Congregational, and Presbyterian churches as a "respectable" established church.

The word "Pentecostal" was deleted from the church name in 1919 and all Nazarene colleges have dropped the "Holiness" designation from their names.

The Church of the Nazarene closely resembles Methodism in theology, polity, and worship. Once it attains full "church" status the church might well consider a merger with the United Methodist Church of which it is an offspring.

All Nazarene ministers and local church officials must testify that they have experienced instantaneous entire sanctification. They believe in divine healing but do not disparage or ignore medical science. Their moral code exemplifies the Puritan attitudes of most Holiness sects. For example, their general rules for church membership condemn "profaning the Lord's Day, either by unnecessary labor, or business, or patronizing or reading of secular papers, or by holiday diversions." Another section bars "Songs, literature and entertainments not to the glory of God; the theater, the ballroom, the circus, and like places; also, lotteries and games of chance; looseness and impropriety of conduct; membership in or fellowship with oathbound secret orders or fraternities."

Nazarenes invariably rank high in the per capita donation to the church among Protestant denominations. A recent year revealed a per capita (not per family) donation of $147. General superintendents take the place of Methodism's bishops and are elected to four-year terms. The sect operates six small liberal arts colleges in addition to Bible schools and a graduate theological seminary; headquarters are maintained at Kansas City, Mo. Ministers are ordained after completing a four-year college Bible course but many now enroll for graduate work at the seminary.

Both the Free Methodist and Wesleyan churches have continued to uphold entire sanctification and should be included as part of the Holiness movement. Recently the Wesleyan Methodist Church merged with the Pilgrim Holiness Church to form the Wesleyan Church. The next logical step would be a union of the Free Methodists and Wesleyans.

Sunday School attendance of the *Church of God* (Anderson, Indiana) exceeds church membership: 250,000 in Sunday School compared to 144,000 communicants. Now highly organized, this sect was begun as a protest against church organization and shares a distaste for the term "denomination" with the Disciples of Christ. It prefers to be called the Church of God Reformation Movement but adds the geographical location of its headquarters to distinguish it from the innumerable Church of God sects. Daniel S. Warner, a thrice married Winebrennarian preacher, began this sect in 1880. His second wife attempted to wrest control of the sect from the founder but he managed to retain control and obtained an uncontested divorce. Headquarters were moved to Anderson in 1906 where the church also maintains a college and publishing house. Like the Nazarenes, the members of this church are moving in the direction of church status. A full-time professional ministry, growing emphasis on education, and development of church organization accelerate this evolution.

Although most Holiness leaders came from Methodist and Baptist backgrounds, the founder of the *Christian and Missionary Alliance* was a former Presbyterian preacher, A. B. Simpson. Members of other Protestant denominations support the evangelistic work of this organization much as they lend support to the Salvation Army. Like the Army, the Christian and Missionary Alliance has developed into a denomination itself with a particular emphasis on skid row and foreign missions. It reports 120,-000 members in more than 1100 congregations.

Membership in the various Holiness churches continues to outstrip the more traditional Protestant denominations and these members put most other churchgoers to shame in the category of financial sacrifice, but the amazing growth in the

Holiness tradition has been among the Pentecostals rather than the Perfectionists.

Further Reading

Redford, M. E., *The Rise of the Church of the Nazarene* (Kansas City, Mo., Nazarene Publishing House, 1951).

Chapter XII

THE PENTECOSTALS

Gift of Speaking in Tongues
Claimed by Pentecostals

"GOLAM kebah shakar elemont."

"The Lord is praised on the highest mountains," interprets an earnest young lady sitting near the front of the small Pentecostal chapel.

"Folant remdad marino," continues the dignified gentleman who might well be an insurance salesman or real estate broker.

". . . and in the depths of the oceans," explains the interpreter.

This is a meaningful religious experience for the members of the congregation even though an observer hears nothing but incoherent mumbling. The gentleman is thought to have received the baptism of the Holy Spirit and is now giving evidence of this gift by speaking in tongues.

The tongue-speaker, the interpreter, and the other Pentecostals are convinced that the gifts bestowed on the infant Church on the day of Pentecost have been restored to the church in these latter days. And paramount among these gifts is glossolalia, or the gift of speaking in a language which the speaker has never known or studied. "They were all filled with the Holy Ghost, and began to speak with other tongues, as the Spirit gave them utterance." (Acts 2:4.)

The millions of Pentecostals around the world do not agree

on every detail of theology but all Pentecostals believe that every Christian can expect a second baptism, subsequent to conversion. Furthermore each spirit baptism is demonstrated by some form of motoric manifestation of ecstasy, almost always speaking in tongues. A few are privileged to receive the gift of tongues which may be exercised throughout their lives; most speak in tongues only at their second baptism. The Pentecostals claim to represent a modern day revival of primitive Christianity.

A common statement of Pentecostal belief would be that proclaimed by the Assemblies of God: "All believers are entitled to, and should ardently expect, and earnestly seek, the promise of the Father, the Baptism in the Holy Ghost and fire, according to the command of our Lord Jesus Christ. . . . This experience is distinct from and subsequent to the experience of the new birth." (*Statement of Fundamental Truths*, 7.)

Furthermore, "The Baptism of believers in the Holy Ghost is witnessed by the initial physical sign of speaking with other tongues as the Spirit of God gives them utterance. (Acts 2:4.) The speaking in tongues in this instance is the same in essence as the gift of tongues (1 Cor. 12:4-10, 28) but different in purpose and use." (*Statement of Fundamental Truths*, 8.)

Linguists have difficulty identifying these tongues when they have been tape-recorded and studied. To this objection the Pentecostals point out that there are more than 2,800 languages being spoken around the world and that no one linguist or even a corps of linguists could possibly recognize more than a handful. It could also be that the language is one no longer spoken by modern man or a language used by the angels rather than by humans.

Since the start of the Pentecostal movement around 1900 this branch of Christianity has grown at a remarkable rate. Dismissed for years as "holy rollers," the Pentecostals have forged ahead by energetic missionary activity. Some scholars estimate the world Pentecostal membership at 8,500,000, including more than two million in the United States. This does not include children or "fellow travelers."

The various Pentecostal bodies furnish about four times as many foreign missionaries as you would expect from this number of adherents. In Chile 14 percent of the population now belongs to Pentecostal churches. In Brazil the Assembleias de Deus claims almost 1 million members. Elsewhere in Latin America the Pentecostals win more converts than all of the mainline Protestant churches put together.

One Pentecostal preacher, Oral Roberts, rivals Billy Graham in popularity and in radio and TV audiences. The largest single Pentecostal church, the Assemblies of God, reports more than 625,000 members in this country and enrolls twice this number in its Sunday Schools. You could visit at least 350 Pentecostal churches and missions in New York City alone.

Sweden reports the largest percentage of Pentecostals of any nation; the Pentecostals in that country form the largest religious body outside of the state Lutheran church. Large Pentecostal constituencies are also found in Norway and Finland.

What has catapulted Pentecostalism into the religious headlines in the past few years has been the appearance of tongue-speaking in such staid churches as the Episcopalian, Lutheran, and Presbyterian. These so-called neo-Pentecostals prefer to remain in their own churches and exercise their gift of tongues in prayer circles or private devotions. They may join the blessed Trinity society and subscribe to the sophisticated *Trinity* magazine, the neo-Pentecostal journal.

Glossolalia was first reported outside the Pentecostal churches in 1960 when the rector of a fashionable Episcopalian church in Van Nuys, California, began to speak in tongues. The resulting controversy led to the rector's resignation but soon glossolalia made its appearance in other churches: Methodist, Lutheran, Reformed, Baptist, Presbyterian, Episcopalian. Even Roman Catholics — priests, Sisters, laymen — have reported the reception of the gifts of Pentecost including speaking in tongues. Groups of Catholic Pentecostals at the University of Notre Dame and other Catholic universities have sparked the movement in the Catholic Church.

The amazing growth of Pentecostalism and its aggressive missionary programs have prompted some writers to call Pentecostalism the cutting edge of Protestantism.

The Norwegian scholar Nils Bloch-Hoell has called Pentecostalism "the primitive Christianity of the less educated." These churches appeal mainly to those of limited income, social standing, and education but millionaires and professors can also be found in the ranks of Pentecostal and neo-Pentecostal groups.

A three-year study at the University of Minnesota concluded that the Pentecostal movement is not limited to "the discontented, the deprived, or the deviant." Prof. Luther P. Gerlach who directed the study stated: "Our own judgment is that most of them are outstandingly stable individuals." He attributed the rapid growth to several factors: An effective recruitment system usually through friends or relatives, a simple master plan from the Bible which gives members a high degree of confidence, a flexible organization, and an experience (speaking in tongues) that produces a fervent commitment to the cause.

Most Pentecostal churches are store-fronts or small rented halls and buildings, but you can also discover Pentecostals who worship in contemporary church buildings in middle-class suburbs. One of the most influential Pentecostal groups, the Full Gospel Business Men's Fellowship, appeals to professional and businessmen of Pentecostal and neo-Pentecostal persuasion.

The roots of Pentecostalism can be found in the Wesleyan revival of the 18th century. John Wesley taught that committed Christians could expect to receive a baptism of the Holy Spirit subsequent to conversion which would enable them to achieve perfection or complete holiness. Over the years this doctrine of entire sanctification received less and less attention in mainstream Methodism; only the tiny Free and Wesleyan Methodist churches put any great emphasis on perfectionism or "holiness."

After the Civil War some American Methodists took a renewed interest in Holiness. Bloch-Hoell observes, "The Holiness Movement in which the Pentecostal Movement had its main roots, was a Puritan reaction against a supposedly stiffening institutionalism and secularism in the greater American churches." (*The Pentecostal Movement,* p. 12). The Methodist bishops tried to constrain Holiness enthusiasm but thousands of Holiness people seceded. They formed separate churches of which the largest is the Church of the Nazarene.

Speaking in tongues was rarely reported in Christendom

from 100 A.D. to 1800. Some heretical groups such as the Montanists claimed this gift and glossolalia appeared among the Quakers, Shakers, and members of the Catholic Apostolic Church (Irvingites). Article 7 of the Mormon Articles of Faith claims the gift of tongues for the Latter-day Saints but its exercise has been circumscribed since some early unfortunate experiences.

A Methodist minister in the Holiness tradition, Charles F. Parham, opened a small Bible school in Topeka, Kansas in 1900. The school's only textbook was the Bible and the students were drawn from Methodist, Holiness, and Baptist backgrounds. Parham believed in the baptism of the Holy Spirit and asked his 40 students to search the Scriptures to see whether they could discover any physical evidence of this second baptism. The students completed their assignment and came to the conclusion that the one consistent evidence that this baptism had been received was that the baptized began to speak in tongues.

Parham and the students prayed earnestly that they would receive this baptism of the Holy Spirit and give evidence by speaking in tongues. On Jan. 1, 1901, Miss Agnes Ozman spoke in tongues at a school prayer meeting and became the first person to demonstrate glossolalia in the Pentecostal revival.

Others followed Miss Ozman and soon many of the students as well as the minister were speaking in tongues. Parham taught that the modern church should possess all the gifts of Pentecost, that every Christian could expect to receive a second baptism, and that every Christian so baptized should give initial evidence by speaking in tongues. This remains the common belief of all Pentecostals and of most neo-Pentecostals. For the next few years Parham and his students carried the Pentecostal message to various communities in the South and Southwest.

Now the scene shifts to Los Angeles. In 1906 the city had a population of about 230,000, mostly recent arrivals. A Negro lady who belonged to the Church of the Nazarene invited a Holiness preacher of her race to deliver a series of sermons in Los Angeles. Preacher W. J. Seymour, lame and blind in one eye, had attended a Pentecostal Bible school in Houston. He accepted the invitation to come to California.

After one sermon the more conservative Nazarenes closed the door on Seymour. The Negro preacher then began to instruct potential converts in a private home; later his followers took over a ramshackle building at 312 Azusa Street which had been used as a livery stable.

The Azusa mission in the Negro ghetto of Los Angeles became the worldwide center of early Pentecostalism. By the end of 1906 the movement claimed 13,000 adherents in the United States and Canada and had outposts in India, Norway, and Sweden. At first the Pentecostals tried to spread their doctrine in the established denominations but they were soon forced to organize separate churches.

Holiness preachers from around the country came to Los Angeles to receive their second baptism. They planted the new ecstatic religion in New York, Chicago, and other cities. The Norwegian Pentecostal, T. B. Barratt, who introduced the revival to Europe, received his baptism at the mission.

Today dozens of distinct churches fit into the Pentecostal category, besides numberless store-front Pentecostal chapels. Largest by far of the U.S. Pentecostal bodies is the Assemblies of God with a membership of 626,000 in 8,570 churches in the United States and nearly 1,675,000 in other countries. This denomination has increased its membership tenfold since 1925.

The *Assemblies of God* was organized in Hot Springs, Arkansas, in 1914 and now reports members in every state of the union and 75 foreign countries. It operates nine Bible institutes and colleges in this country and 80 such schools overseas. The sect supports 884 foreign missionaries.

The Assemblies of God does 80 percent of all evangelical work on American Indian reservations, has commissioned 13 missionaries to convert the Jews, provides 50 ministers to the deaf. It offers correspondence Bible courses for prisoners and works with teen-age gangs. Some 400 local congregations conduct religious services in jails.

Springfield, Missouri is now headquarters of the Assemblies of God. Here the church employs 600 men and women on a $3 million annual payroll. Its printing plant produces 11 tons of literature every day. This city is also the home of the main college of the denomination: Central Bible College. It confers B.A. and M.A. degrees. An estimated 12 million listeners hear "Revivaltime," a weekly radio program broadcast by 523 stations.

Negroes participated in the birth and early spread of Pentecostalism and several of the larger churches are composed entirely of Negroes. *The Church of God in Christ* was founded in the 1890s as a Holiness church, but founder C. H. Jones brought his followers into the Pentecostal fold. This body has grown from 31,000 members in 1936 to 413,000 in 1971.

Another Negro church, the *Apostolic Overcoming Holy Church of God* (75,000 members) was founded in 1916 by a former Methodist minister. Members not only speak in tongues but engage in ecstatic dancing during revival services. They follow a Puritan ethic which discourages the usual vices as well as slang, the use of snuff, and idle talk. The 29,000-member *United Holy Church of America, Inc.* began as a Holiness church in North Carolina in 1886 and adopted Pentecostal positions.

Many churches bear the name Church of God and most of these hold Pentecostal views. The first *Church of God* started after a revival in Tennessee in 1886 and now maintains headquarters in Cleveland, Tennessee. It has 200,000 adherents in this country and Canada and about as many in the missions. Its overseer, A. J. Tomlinson, was impeached in 1923 and this led to numerous schisms.

A unitarian Pentecostal church, the *United Pentecostal Church*, is said to enroll about 225,000 members. It denies the doctrine of the Trinity and insists that Father, Son, and Holy Spirit are one Person and that Person is Jesus Christ. This position is also known as the "Jesus Only" doctrine. Converts who had previously been baptized in the name of the Trinity must be rebaptized in the name of Jesus only.

The flamboyant Los Angeles evangelist Aimee Semple McPherson founded the *International Church of the Foursquare Gospel* which is classified as a Pentecostal body. She employed every kind of publicity device to attract people to her huge Angelus Temple. Less Puritanical than most Pentecostals, she was married three times. Bloch-Hoell discusses this aspect of Aimee Semple McPherson "who, in the course of a few years, developed from a strictly puritanical matron to a luxury-loving and extravagant grande dame." (op. cit., p. 117.)

Her son, Rolf, now heads the Foursquare church which enrolls almost 160,000 members in the United States and sponsors an ambitious foreign mission program. Ministers are trained at the L.I.F.E. Bible college which counts 700 students.

The best known Pentecostal preacher in the nation—Oral Roberts—was ordained by one of the smaller churches: the *Pentecostal Holiness Church*. This church claims 90,000 members, of whom 66,000 are Americans.

Roberts himself joined the United Methodist Church in 1968 and has been ordained a United Methodist minister. The Oral Roberts Evangelistic Association in Tulsa employs 415 people. Rev. Roberts serves as president of the new Oral Roberts University in Tulsa which may well become the largest and leading Pentecostal college. It includes a graduate school of theology.

Other Pentecostal bodies include the *Pentecostal Church of God in America* (115,000), the *Pentecostal Assemblies of the World* (45,000), *Elim Missionary Assemblies* (4,000), *International Pentecostal Assemblies* (7,500), and *Pentecostal Church of God of America, Inc.* (115,000). Smaller bodies could be numbered by the dozens.

Although American in origin, Pentecostalism finds that most of its adherents now live outside of the United States. We find more than one million Pentecostals in Brazil, 500,000 in Chile, and at least 500,000 in other Latin American countries. Pentecostal missionaries have reaped a large harvest in Africa, especially in Nigeria and South Africa. The 45,000 Norwegian Pentecostals have furnished a large army of missionaries. In Italy the Pentecostals support 300 churches and have 55,000 members. The 50,000 English Pentecostals belong to the Assemblies of God, Elim Four Square Gospel Alliance, and the Apostolic Church.

Baptism of the Holy Spirit is usually sought in a prayer meeting which may well last three hours. The individuals prepare themselves by prayer, fasting, Bible reading, and hymn singing. The baptism may come when a minister or others in the congregation lay hands on the individual.

Pentecostal churches are usually bare auditoriums devoid of altar, art, vestments, candles, and liturgical appurtenances. The piano lends itself better to gospel hymns than the organ although a trumpet, piano accordion, or even drum may accompany the pianist.

Doctrinally the Pentecostals are Protestant fundamentalists who rely on a literal interpretation of the Bible. They abhor higher criticism of the Scriptures and condemn the teaching of evolution as unbiblical.

Pentecostals accept the Trinity, original sin, the divinity of Jesus, the virgin birth, the resurrection. In some areas of theology as in their view of human nature they come closer to Roman Catholicism than to classical Protestantism, but Pentecostals usually view Catholicism as a corrupt and superstitious form of Christianity.

A prominent Pentecostal theologian comments:

"As regards salvation by justification, we are Lutherans. In baptismal formula, we are Baptists. As regards sanctification, we are Methodists. In aggressive evangelism, we are as the Salvation Army. But as regards Baptism in the Holy Spirit, we are Pentecostal, inasmuch as we believe and preach, that it is possible to be baptized in or filled by the Holy Ghost just as on the day of Pentecost."

An attempt to provide some unity in world Pentecostalism was made in 1947 by organizing a world conference. The American Pentecostals seem to prefer more structural unity than the Scandinavians. Since 1958 the conference has been called the Pentecostal World Conference; it meets every three yars.

Pentecostals sometimes participate in local ministerial associations but boycott the National Council of Churches and the World Council of Churches. Some Pentecostal churches support the National Association of Evangelicals. Yet two small Pentecostal bodies from Chile joined the World Council at its New Delhi meeting.

Many Pentecostals fear that the World Council may be leading unwary Protestants back to Rome, is infected with a modernist theological bent, and has been infiltrated by Communists. One prominent Pentecostal scholar, Dr. David Du Plessis, attended the Second Vatican Council as an observer but did not represent any particular Pentecostal church.

Puritanism influences the moral code of Pentecostal churches. A Jesuit priest observes that the Pentecostal convert in Latin America gives up drinking and smoking, saves his money, puts in a full day's work, avoids luxuries and is sought after by employers as a sober and conscientious employee. Many Pentecostal bodies forbid liquor, tobacco, mixed bathing, dancing, bobbed hair, cosmetics and jewelry, secret societies, labor unions, the theater, card playing, and motion pictures. Although most Pentecostals belong to the lower economic class, they live frugally and can therefore afford to support the extensive missionary and evangelistic programs of their churches.

In a short history of less than 70 years Pentecostalism has grown to become a major force in world Protestantism. Its growth rate and its devotion to missionary work indicate it has hardly reached its peak. Adherents find a fellowship in Pentecostal churches that they never found in the older churches.

Students of the movement, and especially of the phenomenon of tongue-speaking, adopt one of three attitudes. One school which includes many other fundamentalists condemns Pentecostalism and tongue-speaking as the work of demons. Another school accepts the possibility of genuine glossolalia. A third school, which would include most Catholic observers, considers glossolalia a purely psychological phenomenon. They believe that under certain emotional stresses individuals can lose control of their vocal powers and utter strange sounds which others call tongues.

The authenticated cases in which a person actually speaks a foreign language interpreted by someone who knows the language are extremely rare. Usually the sounds bear no relation to a known language. The mysterious powers of the subconscious cannot be ruled out in the few apparently genuine cases; an individual might be speaking a language used by a neighbor or heard on a radio and stored in the subconscious until released in an emotional and religious ecstasy. Similar natural explanations can also account for most of the healings produced by Pentecostal preachers.

Bloch-Hoell states: "The Pentecostal Movement still lacks university-trained ministers, scholarly theology, liturgical tradition, and Church art, and because of its strong emotionalism, presents the picture of a primitive form of Christianity. (op. cit. p. 172.)

Few religious movements as young as Pentecostalism can report as amazing a numerical growth. The next decades will be decisive for the movement. The influence of the neo-Pentecostals, the worldwide ecumenical movement, the higher educational standards for Pentecostal ministers, and the advances in medicine and psychology will affect the Pentecostal revival.

Further Reading

Bloch-Hoell, Nils, *The Pentecostal Movement* (New York, Humanities Press, 1965).

Damboriena, Prudencio, *Tongues As of Fire: Pentecostalism in Contemporary Christianity* (Washington and Cleveland, Corpus, 1969).

Hoekema, Anthony, *What About Tongue Speaking?* (Grand Rapids, Mich., Eerdmans, 1966).

Nichol, John T., *Pentecostalism* (New York, Harper & Row, 1966).

Ranaghan, Kevin and Dorothy, *Catholic Pentecostals* (Paramus, N.J., Paulist Press Deus Books, 1969).

Sherrill, John L., *They Speak With Other Tongues* (New York, McGraw-Hill, 1964).

Wilkerson, David, *The Cross and the Switchblade* (Westwood, N.J., Spire, 1964).

Chapter XIII

THE SEVENTH-DAY ADVENTISTS
A Prophetess Combines
Fundamentalism and Recrudescent Judaism

AT FIRST glance Seventh-day Adventists seem to be simply conservative Protestants who emphasize the Second Coming of Christ and go to church on Saturday instead of Sunday. Closer examination reveals several basic departures from traditional Protestant theology and practice.

While Catholics and most Protestants agree that man's soul is immortal, Adventists insist that man is mortal. Man does not *have* a soul; he *is* a soul. At death the soul enters a state of deep sleep or unconsciousness until the Second Coming when those who have accepted Christ as their Savior will receive immortality. The wicked are resurrected one thousand years later at the close of the millennial reign of Christ and are annihilated by fire together with Satan.

Therefore, while the righteous may receive the gift of immortality and the wicked may be brought back to life briefly before their cremation, man's nature is basically mortal. Justin Martyr championed the view that the souls of the just enter heaven only after the resurrection and echoes of this belief may be found in present-day Eastern Orthodoxy.

Adventists believe that the followers of Christ will be raised from the dead and reign with Him in heaven for a millennium. During this time the earth will be depopulated, a wilderness and prison for the devil.

138

Adventists attribute the belief that people go to heaven or hell immediately after death to the infiltration of pagan mythology into Christianity. They attempt to prove from the Bible that the dead are asleep until the Second Coming.

At the close of the millennium the Holy City, New Jerusalem, will descend to earth. In it will be Christ and His faithful. From its walls they will witness the resurrection and final destruction of the wicked. Then they will dwell for eternity in an earth made pure once more.

Catholics and Protestants, on the contrary, teach that man has both a body and a soul. His soul is immortal. At death each man is judged and assigned to heaven, hell, or purgatory (Protestants generally reject the idea of a place of temporary punishment and purification).

The Catholic Church teaches that the Second Coming of Christ will precede the Last Judgment. The millennium is not a literal 1000 years but indicates the entire period between the Incarnation and the Last Judgment. At the resurrection man's soul is reunited with his body with special characteristics of glory for the saved. The earth will be destroyed.

Adventists propagate their eschatological doctrines with an aggressiveness and sense of urgency which has brought them a good measure of success. To many they appear as prophets of gloom and doom. Embarrassed by several awkward date-setting episodes in their pioneer days, they carefully avoid such pitfalls today. Their revivalists and preachers, however, produce all types of natural catastrophies, wars, A- and H-bombs, modern inventions, and moral lapses as evidence that mankind is living in the latter days.

Total abstinence from liquor and tobacco is not only recommended but considered a sure test of Christian faith. Any who have not eschewed cigarettes and beer are refused baptism and adherents who lapse into such habits are promptly excommunicated.

The movement likewise commands an observance of the Jewish dietary laws, forbidding the eating of pork and other unclean flesh itemized in the Old Testament. In fact, for health reasons, most Adventists are vegetarians.

The Seventh-day Adventist and Mormon churches are the two best known denominations which base their financial structure on the tithe. Adventists expect each member to tithe his gross income since this is the divine plan for church support as revealed in the Bible. Adventism adopted tithing in 1858. The basic tithe or 10 per cent goes to the support of the ministry. Over and above this other offerings provide for church buildings, maintenance, parochial schools, publishing plants, missions, relief work, etc. Many Adventists contribute 20 percent or more of their income to the church; virtually all members in good standing tithe. Although Adventism counts few wealthy devotees, an Oregon businessman turned over his $10,000,000 lumber company to the church.

With funds received from tithes the SDA Church employes some 57,000 men and women as missionaries, teachers, printers, medical personnel, etc. This means that one Adventist out of every 31 is a full-time salaried employe of the Church. Salaries of these Church workers, even college presidents and physicians, fall far below what they could receive in secular employment.

Statistics consistently show the Adventist church at the head of the list of Protestant denominations in per capita contributions. A recent year indicated a per capita contribution of $350, probably many times that of American Catholics. This should be multiplied by a factor of three or so to obtain the average family contribution: about $1,000.

Their observance of the seventh-day Sabbath has become almost an obsession. Their literature insists time and again that man's most important responsibility in this life is the correct choice of God's seal (the Saturday Sabbath) or the beast's sign (Sunday). Those who changed the Christian observance from the Judaic Saturday to Sunday are branded as tools of Satan. Christians who persist in keeping Sunday as the Lord's day become accomplices in this nefarious plot to disobey God's own commandment.

Since history plainly records that the Catholic Church changed the Christian observance in memory of Christ's resurrection on Easter Sunday, Adventists hold the popes and "Romanism" responsible for deception. However, Protestants find themselves far more vulnerable to Adventist attacks on this score since they hold the Bible to be the sole rule of faith. "Search your Bible from Genesis to Revelation and show me any authorization for a Sunday Sabbath observance," challenges the Adventist.

Here Adventism dramatizes Protestant dependence on Catholic tradition. At least two Protestant leaders saw the inconsistency of this position and observed the original Sabbath: Melanchthon and the Moravian's Count Zinzendorf.

Catholics point out that the word Sabbath means "rest" and the third commandment commands man to rest every seventh day and to offer special worship to God. The Jews chose Saturday for their Sabbath while the early Christians chose Sunday. Writing in the fourth century St. Augustine comments, "The Apostles and their contemporaries sanctioned the dedication of Sunday to the worship of God."

Adventists, preoccupied with what they consider the letter of the law, reason that since all other Christian churches have tampered with God's commandment without Biblical leave, these churches must be apostate. Thus the Seventh-day Adventist church alone constitutes the remnant church in these last days. This charge in the face of today's "live and let live" ecumenism arouses bitter feeling among other Protestants. Some of the harshest anti-Adventist tracts circulate among fundamentalists who would otherwise find common cause with the Adventists.

Next to the Catholic Church and the Lutheran Church-Missouri Synod, the Seventh-day Adventist sect operates the largest parochial school system in the United States. Worldwide the sect conducts 6,200 church schools and academies with more than 342,000 students. It manages to educate about half of its young people in church institutions. On the higher education level in this country it operates 12 coeducational colleges and two universities—Andrews University, in Berrien Springs, Mich., and Loma Linda University at Loma Linda, Calif. The latter concentrates largely on medical education, annually turning out some 300 physicians, dentists, and graduates in related fields. Andrews University's major emphasis is the training of theologians, though degrees in other liberal arts areas are also granted by both institutions. Adventists make enormous sacrifices to provide religious training for their young people from kindergarten to college and even to medical and dental school.

Adventism is booming. Worldwide membership recently passed the 1,700,000 mark with about 400,000 Seventh-day Adventists in this country. The extraordinarily generous support from the tithe enables the sect to finance a missionary, publishing, and educational effort out of all proportion to its numbers. The extensive school system graduates thousands of loyal and Bible-indoctrinated followers.

Among Protestant groups only the Southern Baptists send more missionaries overseas than the Adventists; in 1970 the Seventh-day Adventists supported 1,467 such missionaries.

It all began during the early decades of the past century when some Protestant clergymen and laymen began to study Bible prophecy. Many calculated that the Second Coming was at hand and would certainly occur during their lifetimes. Someone has estimated that 300 Anglican ministers and twice that number of Nonconformists in England were heralding the imminent personal return of Christ in the 1820's and 1830's. This enthusiasm found converts in England, the continent, and the New World.

William Miller, a War of 1812 veteran, a converted deist and Baptist farmer-preacher, spearheaded the American version. Miller concentrated on the Books of Daniel and Revelation. His chief discovery was that the 2300 days in Daniel 8:13, 14 meant years. Figuring from the year 457 B.C., the date of the commandment to restore Jerusalem, he announced that the Second Coming could be expected in 1843. He began preaching this news in 1831.

People flocked to the movement from the old line Protestant churches and hundreds of ministers enrolled under Adventism's banners. But 1843 came and passed. The date was revised to Oct. 22, 1844. By this time at least 50,000 people were known as Adventists, and Miller issued a call that his followers come out of "Babylon." By Babylon he meant the other Protestant communions. Many sold their possessions, settled their affairs, and awaited the Great Day. The press helped to publicize the event. But Oct. 22, 1844, also came and passed.

Disillusioned, thousands abandoned religion entirely as a monster hoax; others drifted sheepishly back to their former church homes in "Babylon." Miller died lonely and forgotten, expelled by the Baptists in 1845. But a tiny band of diehards in Washington, New Hampshire, remained true to Adventism and reopened their Bibles to see what had gone wrong. They were First-day Adventists.

This group of New England Millerites formed the nucleus of the present Seventh-day Adventist church. They insisted, despite rather convincing evidence to the contrary, that the 1844 date was correct. Finally one of their number hit upon the explanation that the error was not in the date but in interpreting the date in terms of an earthly event. What really happened on Oct. 22, 1844, was that Christ had entered the most holy place in the heavenly sanctuary. Here He offered His blood as the purchase price for man's redemption.

A master stroke, this explanation rescued the wobbly movement from complete collapse. Satisfied that they had not been deceived by Miller, they rekindled their Adventist hopes and also resolved never again to set a date for the Second Coming.

All the leaders in the reorganized Adventist church such as Joseph Bates, James White, and his wife Ellen White (nee Harmon) had been closely associated with the pre-1844 Millerites. Of this trio Mrs. White became the undoubted leader. Never a church officer or minister, she was and is considered a prophetess by Seventh-day Adventists. She dictated many of her 20 books and 3000 articles while in a trance and her writings are held to be inspired.

Mrs. White, a Methodist in her early youth, guided the SDA church for nearly 70 years, dying in 1915. She has been elevated to a role comparable to that of Mrs. Eddy in Christian Science. Here again Adventists cross swords with fellow fundamentalists who reject Mrs. White's visions and inspiration altogether.

By 1855 the church had gained enough adherents in Michigan to establish a national headquarters in Battle Creek. The present name of the church was adopted in 1860 and in 1903 headquarters were shifted to Takoma Park, a suburb of Washington, D.C.

From a visiting Seventh-day Baptist the Adventists picked up their second distinctive doctrine. Prophetess White confirmed this doctrinal standard by announcing that an angel had shown her the tablets of the Ten Commandments with a great halo of light surrounding the defiled Fourth (Catholic Third) commandment.

The 1906 religious census reported a SDA membership of 62,111. Fifty years later this enrollment had quadrupled in this country with even greater gains outside continental United States. Few denominations have done as well. The church registers its largest membership in California, Oregon, Michigan, Washington, and Florida.

Standards of personal conduct among Adventists are strict. Of course, no Adventist may drink or smoke. Other prohibitions include card playing, dancing, attendance at the movies or theater, costly or immodest apparel, jewelry, and lodge membership. Use of coffee, tea, and pepper is discouraged.

They observe the Sabbath from sundown Friday to sundown Saturday. Adventists attend Sabbath school and church services on Saturday and abstain from all buying, selling, and unnecessary labor. Most food is prepared Friday before the Sabbath begins as in Orthodox Jewish households. Bible reading and study of church publications are recommended for the rest of the Sabbath.

Converts are instructed in the essentials of Adventism, and must promise to tithe, observe the Sabbath, and practice total abstinence before they are admitted to baptism. Baptism of adults by immersion is the rule.

Their worship service resembles that of other nonliturgical Protestant denominations. A foot washing ceremony in separate rooms precedes the quarterly observance of the Lord's Supper. To Adventists as to others in the Reformed tradition this constitutes merely a memorial service; all those attending are invited to the communion table. Only grape juice is used.

Incidentally, the Seventh-day Adventists refuse to observe

Easter which they claim is a pagan and unscriptural holiday.

Seventh-day Adventists once attempted proselytizing campaigns incognito, not revealing sponsorship of revivals and community meetings. Now, however, their evangelists are instructed to identify their services, and the hidden sponsor is the exception rather than the rule. Their widespread "Voice of Prophecy" radio program and "Faith for Today" TV series are also now presented with Adventist credit lines.

No church sponsors a more ambitious foreign mission program. Adventist medical, educational, and religious work is now carried on in 189 countries by some 57,000 salaried workers. The only nations not penetrated by indefatigable SDA evangelists are Afghanistan, Crete, and Vatican City. An ex-priest by the name of M. B. Czechowski inaugurated Adventist evangelism in Europe in the nineteenth century. Today three out of every four Seventh-day Adventists reside outside the United States which indicates the success of this missionary endeavor. For example, the entire population of Pitcairn Island of *Mutiny on the Bounty* fame has embraced the faith.

Health reform became a plank of the Adventist platform following a revelation to the prophetess in 1863. Members show a concern for health seldom found among other fundamentalists. In their chain of 119 hospitals and sanitariums and 163 clinics Adventist doctors, nurses, dietitians, X-ray technicians, and dentists care for more than 3,555,000 patients each year. SDA institutions graduate 100 physicians and 420 nurses annually. Although they emphasize drugless healing and hydrotherapy they do not neglect surgery or modern medication. *Life and Health* magazine features popular health articles with a SDA twist regarding alcohol and tobacco.

An Adventist layman, Dr. J. H. Kellogg, invented corn flakes and changed the menus at millions of American breakfast tables. Adventists started the pioneer Battle Creek (Michigan) sanitarium for treatment of nervous disorders and introduced the techniques of hydrotherapy and physical therapy.

A flood of literature pours from 42 Adventist printing presses of which 34 are overseas. About 75 new book titles are issued yearly besides 348 periodicals in 228 languages. A bimonthly magazine entitled *Liberty* advocates separation of Church and State and serves as an organ of the National Religious Liberty Association. Adventists oppose tax-supported welfare measures for parochial school pupils, including their own. Their publications regularly blast Blue Laws urged by fellow Protestants.

Adventist scholars are thoroughly antievolutionist and have supplied this school with some of its most respected controversialists such as Prof. George McCready Price. They believe the earth was created in six literal days.

Seventh-day Adventists are not pacifists and do not seek exemption from military service. They call themselves "conscientious co-operators" rather than "conscientious objectors" since they do not dodge army service but only object to bearing arms. To prepare their young men for medical duty the sect operates 35 training programs each year. About 12,000 Adventists served as medical corpsmen during World War II and an Adventist corporal is one of the few noncombatants to receive the Congressional Medal of Honor.

Local church government is technically congregational. Actually the district conference appoints pastors and co-ordinates area activities and the General Conference wields great power. Pastors are called "Elder" or "Pastor." Seminary training is required for ordination but many receive a bachelor's degree in theology from a church college which serves the purpose. Women as well as men serve as grade school and Bible class teachers.

Adventists do not consider themselves bound by a creed. Nevertheless the annual *Yearbook* includes a statement of "Fundamental Beliefs of Seventh-day Adventists." They reject predestination and seem to stress man's co-operation in the work of justification more than most evangelicals.

Not all Adventists whose faith survived the Millerite debacle were attracted to Seventh-day Adventism. Four other Adventist sects, of which three are moribund and minuscule, are listed in religious directories. The *Advent Christian Church* which upholds the conscious state of the dead and the eternal punishment of the wicked and the observance of Sunday counts 30,000 members in the United States. The other tiny sects are the *Church of God (Abrahamic Faith)*, *Life and Advent Union*, and *Primitive Advent Christian Church*.

The SDA doctrines of soul-sleep after death and the annihilation of the wicked have been appropriated by Jehovah's Witnesses whose founder, Russell, received his introduction to millennialism in Adventism. However, Seventh-day Adventists differ from their Watchtower cousins in a number of respects, among which are the Saturday Sabbath, the character of the millennium, military service, voting and civic responsibilities, and the tithe.

The Seventh-day Adventists play no part in the contemporary ecumenical movement since they believe that their church alone qualifies as the remnant church and obeys all God's commandments in a literal way. They do not, however, claim to be the only true Christians. In their *Questions on Doctrine* we read: "We fully recognize the heartening fact that a host of true followers of Christ are scattered all through the various churches of Christendom, including the Roman Catholic communion." (p. 197). The same Adventist text declares: "We respect and love those of our fellow Christians who do not interpret God's Word just as we do."

Further Reading

Froom, L. R. E., *The Prophetic Faith of Our Fathers* (Washington, D.C., Review and Herald, 1946-54, 4 vols.)

Herndon, Booton, *The Seventh Day* (New York, McGraw-Hill, 1960).

Seventh-day Adventists Answer Questions on Doctrine (Washington, D.C., Review and Herald, 1957).

Chapter XIV

OTHER PROTESTANTS

**American Protestantism Comprises
More Than 220 Churches and Sects**

EVERY second American Protestant is a Baptist or Methodist and 80 per cent of the Protestant Christians in this country belong to the 13 largest denominations. Nevertheless we find hundreds of smaller groups which are classified as Protestant for census and tabulation purposes. Acually, some of these are Protestant only in the sense in which they are not Catholic: Mormonism, Christian Science, Unitarianism, Spiritualism, and others. Many are subdivisions of denominational families such as the Two-Seed-in-the-Spirit Predestinarian Baptists and the Lumber River Annual Conference of the Holiness Methodist Church. Scores of sects belong to the Holiness and Pentecostal family and some are religious curiosities such as the "House of God, Which is the Church of the Living God, the Pillar and Ground of Truth, Inc." and the "House of David."

This chapter will examine a number of significant but smaller churches in the Protestant tradition. These include the Moravians, the Mennonites, the Reformed and Christian Reformed, the Brethren or "Dunkers," the members of the Salvation Army, and the Mission Covenanters. All of these churches represent more or less distinct traditions and could not convenently be grouped with other denominations.

The Moravians

One of the two Protestant bodies which predate the Reformation, the Moravian Church received its inspiration from John Huss, a Bohemian priest and rector of the University of Prague who was burned at the stake for heresy in 1415. (The other pre-Reformation Protestants are the Waldensians in northern Italy.)

Huss appealed to the authority of the Bible alone, rejected the doctrine of purgatory and the invocation of the saints, and demanded the cup for the laity. His followers disagreed among themselves after his execution but a small group organized themselves in 1457 as the Unity of the Brethren or Unitas Fratrum. They wielded influence in Bohemia, Poland, and Moravia for more than two centuries. By the time Luther was nailing his Ninety-five theses to the Wittenberg church door this Bohemian Protestant church numbered about 175,000 members in 400 congregations.

The Counter-Reformation and the Thirty Years' War all but obliterated the Hussites, most of whom were absorbed into the Catholic, Lutheran, and Reformed churches. A few diehards kept alive Hussite beliefs and traditions and this underground church found a distinguished leader in the educator John Amos Comenius.

Count Nicholas Ludwig von Zinzendorf, a Lutheran layman, sponsored the Moravian revival in the eighteenth century. He turned over a corner of his Saxony estate to a nucleus of the Unitas Fratrum, nominally Catholic, with the thought that they would act as a leaven in the Lutheran establishment.

Eventually the Moravians at Herrnhut became a separate church and chose Zinzendorf as their bishop. The first large-scale Protestant missionaries, they worked among Negro slaves on St. Thomas Island in the West Indies beginning in 1732 and among the Indians in Georgia (1735). As we have seen, a band of Moravian missionaries traveling to the New World impressed John Wesley, the founder of Methodism, with their piety and faith. Moravianism multiplied its influence on Protestantism through Wesley and the Wesleyan revival.

Bethlehem and Nazareth in Pennsylvania and Salem in North Carolina became centers for American Moravianism. Zinzendorf himself visited this country in 1741 and for many years Moravian settlements in America were closely supervised from the German headquarters. Changes in the middle of the nineteenth century brought autonomy in church government to the American members.

Today the *Moravian Church in America* includes two provinces. The 49 congregations in the Southern province are all within 120 miles of Winston-Salem and enroll about 22,000 members. The Northern province takes in the rest of the country and reports 38,000 communicants in 113 congregations.

Total Moravian membership worldwide exceeds 300,000. American Moravians maintain missions in Alaska, Nicaragua, and Honduras while other Moravians staff missions in ten other areas. Herrnhut itself is now a village of 2,000 in East Germany while Bethlehem, Pa., has become a steel city of 75,000.

This church follows a church year and a liturgical form of worship but the Moravian churches themselves have no altars. A distinctive Moravian custom is the love feast which consists of coffee and buns; the Lord's Supper is observed half a dozen times a year. The Moravian liturgies for Christmas Eve, Holy Week, and Easter Dawn attract many people because of their beauty and solemnity.

Besides the major Moravian body in the U.S. there is the 6,000 member *Unity of the Brethren*. Until 1962 this group was known as the Evangelical Unity of the Czech-Moravian Brethren in North America. It enrolls descendents of immigrants who began arriving in Texas in 1850 and is similar to the Unitas Fratrum.

A tiny component of world Protestantism the Moravian Church has made an important contribution through its missionary programs, its influence on other Protestants such as Wesley, and its liturgy and hymns.

The Mennonites

Once the Reformation sundered the unity of Western Christendom, more radical groups than the Lutherans and Reformed urged a complete return to what they considered primitive Christianity. Chief among these sects were the various Anabaptist bodies which insisted that infant baptism was unscriptural. Adults who had been baptized as infants had to submit to rebaptism, hence the name Anabaptist.

These early Anabaptists became the object of intense persecution by state and church officials. The first martyr in 1527 was bound hands to knees, rowed to the middle of a lake, and dumped overboard to drown. Later thousands of others throughout Europe would be broken on the rack, left to rot in prison, beheaded, and burned.

The Anabaptists taught nonresistance to evil which meant that they refused to serve in the army. They preferred an untrained and unsalaried ministry chosen by lot and believed the church should be a brotherhood of believers without hierarchy or titles. They would not swear any oaths or hold any public office.

Menno Simons, a Catholic priest for 12 years, left the Church to join the conservative Anabaptist wing. He systematized its organization and theology and provided such outstanding leadership to these despised Anabaptists that their movement became known by his name, the Mennonites.

Around the world some 480,000 adults belong to the Mennonite family of churches and of these the largest number are North Americans. But this is a spiritual family which has been plagued by schisms since its earliest days. Over the centuries Mennonites have quarreled over whether a second band of suspenders constitutes worldly luxury and whether one or two people should wash and wipe the feet in the foot washing ceremony. In the U.S. alone the estimated 170,000 baptized Mennonites belong to at least 19 different church bodies.

Many of the most serious divisions have sprung from the use of the ban or "shunning." The Anabaptists have always sought to establish a voluntary church of saints in contrast to a state church which embraced saints and sinners, children and adults, believers and mere conformists. In order to preserve the exclusive character of their congregations the Mennonites have resorted to excommunication more than most churches.

The Amish, for example, enforce the ban to the extent that an excommunicated husband cannot eat at the same table or have sex relations with his wife. He is completely ostracized from the community and his own family. Moderate and progressive Mennonites still enforce excommunication and strongly discourage marriage outside of the religious family but do not apply the ban as the Amish do.

Jacob Amman, a Swiss bishop, thought the church was not strict enough in enforcing the ban. He traveled around the Mennonite communities urging a return to traditional ways; his followers began to withdraw from the main body in 1693. No Amish remain in Europe but they can be found in Pennsylvania and several Middle Western states.

In Holland the number of Mennonites has declined from an estimated 160,000 in 1700 to fewer than 38,000 today. They may have diluted their Anabaptist principles in the eyes of many American Mennonites but they have prospered and sit on the boards of some of the largest Dutch corporations, hold distinguished professorships, serve in the cabinet, and contribute members out of all proportion to medicine and the sciences in that country.

Outside of North America and the Netherlands the largest bodies of Mennonites are reported in Soviet Russia (40,000), India (30,000), the Congo (40,000), Germany (11,000), and Indonesia, (21,000).

Lancaster, Pennsylvania, became the center for Swiss Mennonites in the United States although later immigrations brought the church to the Midwest. Mennonites are universally respected as scrupulously honest and God fearing. Despite a reluctance by some to adopt mechanized farming methods they are known to be excellent farmers.

Almost half of the Mennonites in the U.S. belong to the *Mennonite Church* whose members were once known as the Old

Mennonites. These 86,000 Mennonites occupy what might be considered a middle ground between the ultraconservative Amish and the progressive General Conference Mennonite Church. But all Mennonites in North America share a relatively conservative theology in the context of contemporary Protestantism.

The Mennonite Church finds its strength in Pennsylvania, Virginia, Indiana, Ohio, Iowa, and Ontario. This group supports 11 high schools, three colleges, a hospital, two nursing schools, three children's homes, and four homes for the aged. Most of its members are farmers but a growing number are going into other occupations such as teaching, medicine, and business.

Membership in this church has quadrupled since 1900, mostly through a high birth rate. Its ranks have been augmented by former Amish who have become dissatisfied with the sect's strict rules. It sponsors the Mennonite Hour which is carried by several hundred radio stations and maintains 220 overseas missionaries.

A statement of doctrine declares: "That mixed marriages between believers and unbelievers are unscriptural, and marriage with divorced persons with former companions living constitutes adultery." These Christians also hold that it is unscriptural to "follow wordly fashions, engage in warfare, swear oaths, or join secret societies."

A somewhat more progressive stance characterizes the *General Conference Mennonite Church* which was organized in Iowa in 1860. This church has always sought the union of all Mennonites and has fostered seminary training for ministers, foreign missions, and church publications. It has 36,000 members in the U.S. and almost 17,000 in Canada; an estimated two-thirds are of Dutch ancestry and the rest Swiss.

Russian-German immigrants who started to enter America in 1874 organized the *Mennonite Brethren of North America*. Most members now live in Kansas and Oklahoma but there are others in several Western states. There are slightly more Mennonite Brethren in Canada (15,454) than in the U.S. (13,425). This small church supports the work of 224 missionaries in 16 countries. Their efforts have won 20,000 adherents in India and

8,700 in the Congo; home missions serve the American Indians and Mexican Americans in the Southwest.

Most picturesque and traditional of the many Mennonite factions are the *Old Order Amish.* These 20,000 Amish impose the strict ban on backsliders, prescribe dress regulations, oppose all education beyond grammar school, worship in homes and barns instead of churches, and speak a dialect known as Pennsylvania Dutch. They do not believe in missions, Sunday Schools, or church conferences.

Their communities stretch from Lancaster County through Ohio, Indiana, and Illinois to Iowa and they own some of the richest farm lands in the nation. The Amish make no compromises with the world or the idea of progress. Their motto is "The old is the best and the new is of the devil."

Amish parents consider their lives a success if all their children have married Amish, live on farms, and remain within the Amish faith. Young people join the church through baptism in their late teens and subscribe to the Ordnung or rules of their particular branch. In general these rules forbid the use of electricity, telephones, central heating, automobiles, tractors with pneumatic tires, buttons, and higher education. Certain Amish groups add prohibitions against mirrors, high heels, silk clothing, bright colors, photographs, pressed trousers, and the like.

A church which excommunicates anyone who buys an automobile, goes to high school, or marries outside the faith is bound to lose some young people. But since the average Amish family has 7 to 9 children the total Amish community grows each year. When one Amishman died in Indiana in 1933 he was said to have 565 living descendents.

These four major bodies—the Mennonite Church, General Conference Mennonite Church, Mennonite Brethren Church, and Old Order Amish—claim 85 percent of U.S. Mennonites but there are at least 15 other branches.

The Amish and other Mennonites invariably win the respect of their neighbors for their honesty, simple living, and industriousness. Their witness for peace is perhaps needed more now than during the past centuries. Yet their penchant for doctrinal hair-splitting and their addiction to outmoded ways of life have undercut any message they might have for other Americans.

The Reformed

Calvinism took early root in Holland and Dutch colonists brought their Reformed Church to New Amsterdam. Their Collegiate church in New York City, organized in 1628, is the oldest Protestant church in the nation with an uninterrupted ministry. Members of this Dutch Calvinist church also founded a college at New Brunswick which later became Rutgers.

Church affairs were closely regulated by the Classis of Amsterdam until 1771 when the American branch won the right to train and ordain its own ministers. By 1830 the exclusive use of the Dutch language had ceased. A later Dutch immigration which began in 1847 gave this denomination a sizable Middle West constituency. The present name, which eliminates a national label, was adopted in 1867. This *Reformed Church in America* reports 383,000 communicants. Its best known minister is Norman Vincent Peale, pastor of Marble Collegiate Church in New York City and author of the best-selling *The Power of Positive Thinking;* he began his ministerial career as a Methodist.

Efforts to merge the Southern Presbyterians and the Reformed Church in America were scuttled in 1969. The defeat of the proposal, which was approved by the top officials, was attributed to objections by conservative Reformed members in the Middle West.

This church is broadly characterized by theological conservatism, a semi-liturgical posture in worship, and a confessional basis which is summarized in the Heidelberg Catechism, the Belgic Confession, and the Canons of the Synod of Dort.

The Christian Reformed

A protest against laxism in the Dutch Reformed Church led to the formation of the strict *Christian Reformed Church* in 1857. Ministers of five congregations accused the mother church of diluting Calvinism, slighting the doctrine of predestination, and tolerating Masonry and other secret societies. Within a decade the protesters had won few followers but immigrants from Holland and anti-Masonic dissenters from the parent body added new strength.

This church supports a seminary in Grand Rapids, Michigan, two colleges, and operates 246 parochial grade schools for parents of 50,000 pupils who wish to educate their children in uncompromising Calvinism. Since its founding the Christian Reformed Church has held fast to the rigid Calvinism of the Heidelberg, Dordrecht, and Belgic Confessions. This church belongs to neither the National nor World Councils of Churches. It has experienced a rapid growth in recent years and now reports 281,000 members. The Christian Reformed Church reflects 16th-century Geneva Calvinism in 20th-century America.

The Brethren

To some of the people of Schwarzenau, Germany, in the early years of the 18th century the spiritual level of established Lutheran and Reformed churches was too low for dedicated Christians. Influenced by Anabaptist and Pietist teaching they formed a new church in 1708 under the leadership of Alexander Mack, Sr. One member of the first congregation of eight baptized Mack by immersing him three times in the name of the trinity and Mack in turn baptized the others. The *Church of the Brethren* was born.

In a few years persecution would drive almost all of the Brethren from their homeland to the New World. Welcomed by William Penn, one group settled at Germantown near Philadelphia in 1719. A second group, led by Mack himself, lived for a few years in Holland and arrived in America in 1729. When a third party left Germany in 1733 the organized life of the Brethren movement came to a close in Europe.

The Brethren were also known by other names; sometimes they were identified as German Baptists and sometimes as Dunkers from the German word *tunken* which means to dip or immerse.

Today more than 185,000 members belong to the 1,100 congregations of the Church of the Brethren in the United States. This is the largest of half a dozen churches comprising the Brethren movement. Most Church of the Brethren congregations are found in Pennsylvania, Maryland, Virginia, Ohio, Indiana, and Illinois. Another 19,500 Brethren belong to overseas congregations. Of these there are 10,000 Brethren in Nigeria, 9,000 in India, and small groups in Ecuador and Canada.

In doctrine the Brethren share the basic beliefs of other evangelical Protestants. They belong to the National Council of Churches and World Councils of Churches. Yet the Church of the Brethren observes certain distinctive rites and holds positions not held by mainline Protestants. For example, the Brethren like the Quakers and Mennonites belong to one of the historic peace churches. Young men can claim conscientious objector status by simply giving evidence of membership in the Church of the Brethren or other Brethren bodies.

The Brethren observe four ordinances: baptism, the love feast, anointing for healing of the sick, and laying on of hands. The candidate for baptism kneels in the water and is immersed three times in the name of the Father, Son, and Holy Spirit. Infant baptism is rejected as a violation of free choice in religion. Those who may have been baptized by pouring or sprinkling in other denominations and wish to join the Brethren church need not be rebaptized.

The love feast, observed once or twice a year, takes up the entire evening and includes three parts. In the first part the congregation divides itself into men and women and performs the foot washing ceremony. The entire congregation then enjoys a full meal which is regarded as the counterpart of the original Lord's supper. Finally the Brethren partake of the bread and wine of the communion service. The Brethren understand the eucharist in the memorial sense rather than in terms of a Real Presence. Communion may also be scheduled at other times throughout the year apart from the complete love feast.

Those who are sick or in danger of death may be anointed with oil. This rite is common in Roman Catholicism and Eastern Orthodoxy but rare in Protestantism. Finally the Brethren employ the laying on of hands in baptism, the installation of deacons, ordination of ministers, commissioning of missionaries, and anointing of the sick.

The Church of the Brethren refuses to accept any creed since it regards the New Testament as its "rule of faith and practice." It rejects the Old Testament as a proper guide for Christians since as one Brethren writer comments "the Old Testament has war, and slavery, and divorce, and revenge and cultus which no longer fit into the Christian ideal." All other Protestants value both the Old and New Testaments as the Word of God.

The Brethren present the simple life as the ideal. They are asked to avoid all ostentation and extravagance such as jewelry and costly clothes. Brethren are expected to observe total abstinence, avoid secret societies, refrain from oaths.

Local Churches follow a congregational polity but the Annual Conference of representatives has final authority; this is not necessarily binding on local congregations. Church general offices are in Elgin, Illinois.

The Church of the Brethren supports six liberal arts colleges which enroll about 5,000 students. It has a graduate school of theology in Chicago. Originally churches were served by an unsalaried ministry but full-time ministers now care for most churches.

This church is noted for its relief work overseas and in this country. It organized the Brethren Service Committee after World War II. The Brethren Volunteer Service enrolls young men for one and two year tours of service and antedated the Peace Corps. Young men choosing alternative service in lieu of military service may also join the BVS. A Brethren project to send heifers to needy farm families overseas has been supported by many other denominations.

Divisions within the parent church during the past century have given rise to a number of other Brethren bodies. In 1881 a group of about 3,000 Brethren objected to what they considered liberalism in the church. Debate raged over the role of revivals, Sunday Schools, methods of feet washing, and "worldly" dress.

The dissidents formed the *Old German Baptist Church*, also known as the Old Order Brethren. Most of the 4,200 Old Order Brethren live in Pennsylvania, Ohio, Indiana, Kansas, and California.

In 1882 another group of Brethren withdrew because they thought the church was too conservative; they organized the Brethren Church (Progressive). This church eventually split into two branches. The Grace Brethren, also known as the *National Fellowship of Brethren Churches*, favor a Calvinist theology and maintain headquarters at Winona Lake, Indiana. They report 31,000 adherents. The other branch, the *Brethren Church*, has headquarters in Ashland, O., and has about 17,000 members. Two other tiny Brethren bodies are the *Dunkard Brethren Church* and the *Fundamental Brethren Church*.

Other denominations such as the *Plymouth Brethren, Moravian Brethren, United Brethren*, and *River Brethren* are identified as "Brethren" but have no connection with the Church of the Brethren.

The Brethren try to live lives of simplicity, peace, temperance, and brotherhood in a world which often prefers sham, war, and dissension.

The Salvationists

In its war against "slumdom, rumdom and bumdom" the *Salvation Army* adopted a military form of organization which suggests a comparison with a Catholic religious order. Popular opinion often views the Salvation Army as a relief agency with religious undertones. On the contrary, the Army is an evangelical Protestant sect which carries out its religious mission through social service.

Founded by a saintly Methodist minister in England, the "Christian Mission" carried the gospel to the vicious slums of London. But William Booth found his poor converts felt unwelcome in the "respectable" churches, Methodist or Anglican, and he found it necessary to provide separate worship services and church facilities. The name, Salvation Army, and the military organization were adopted in 1878 and Booth became General Booth.

General Booth's devoted wife and mother of his eight children died in 1890 but the General continued his tireless efforts for the down and out. He visited America every four years. He was honored by kings and presidents, received honorary doctorates from Oxford and Brussels Universities. He died blind and penniless at the age of 84.

Clergymen were officers of this army with titles from lieutenant to general. Converts became recruits and soldiers and wore a military uniform after they had signed the "Articles of War" against liquor, tobacco, and vice. Orders come from the top and are obeyed by junior officers. The Salvation Army officer wears a uniform at all times, receives "marching orders" to a new post, progresses through a system of ranks, receives a salute, takes his vacation as a "furlough," participates in "knee drills" or prayer meetings, and is lowered into his grave to the sound of taps.

Officers are recruited from the ranks of soldiers and are selected to attend an intensive two-year course at one of the four schools for Officers Training in the United States. On graduation he or she is commissioned a lieutenant. Salvation Army officers may perform marriages, preach, christen children, and serve as armed forces chaplains. They agree to marry within the Army family and to serve at their post for life. A wife holds equal rank with her husband.

No longer does the Army confine its activities to skid row. Extensive programs for children and families have been developed. A decade ago 80 per cent of those who sought help from the Salvation Army had alcohol problems but now 70 per cent have drug problems. Accordingly the Army has had to change its priorities. The street meeting with brass band and preaching, however, continues to be a basic Army evangelistic technique.

Converts are expected to don the military uniform as soldiers and commit themselves to saving sinners although they may keep their secular occupations. Many are reluctant to devote their lives to this work and are free to join other churches. About 5500 officers in the U. S. supervise the volunteer local officers and soldiers in the Army's widespread activities: citadels (local churches), relief associations, summer camps, hospitals, homes for unmarried mothers, publications, nurseries and day schools, orphanages. No Protestant church approaches the scope of the Army's welfare work.

Theologically the Salvation Army follows the original Wesleyan emphasis including belief in the Baptism of the Holy Spirit or entire sanctification as preached by the Holiness sects. They uphold man's free will and deny that man's spiritual powers were utterly destroyed by the Fall, contrary to Luther and Calvin. With the Quakers they reject baptism and the Lord's Supper as unnecessary rituals. Booth debated whether to continue the Lord's Supper and his decision was based on three factors: the use of wine in the service might tempt his alcoholic converts, the public might object to women officers administering the communion, and the interpretation of the Eucharist had divided Christians in the past. The Salvation Army offers classical Methodism without sacraments.

In place of baptism the Army conducts the Dedication of Children using the following formula: "In the name of the Lord and of the —— Corps of the Salvation Army, I have taken this child, who has been fully given up by his parents for the salvation of the world. God save, bless, and keep this child. Amen." Other ceremonies in the Army are the swearing in of soldiers, the presentation of colors, covenant services, and marriage. The Army reports 329,000 officers and soldiers in the U.S.

Two defections from the Salvation Army led to the organization of groups with similar objectives but more democratic principles. The first, the *American Rescue Workers*, was begun just two years after the Army invaded this country in 1880. In 1896 General Booth's son and his wife seceded and started the *Volunteers of America*. This sect now numbers 32,000 members and has done outstanding work among prisoners, parolees, and their families. Unlike the Salvationists, the Rescue Workers and Volunteers observe baptism and the Lord's Supper.

The Covenanters

A protest against the formalism of the state Lutheranism of Sweden began in mission societies within the Lutheran Church and developed into the *Evangelical Covenant Church of America.*

Transplanted to the United States by Swedish immigrants, the church was formally organized in Chicago in 1885. The majority of Swedes who remained Christian, however, allied themselves with the Swedish Lutheran Church, or Swedish Methodist and Baptist groups. Since the local Covenant church is independent and autonomous its members are sometimes known as Swedish Congregationalists.

This church values the historic Christian confessions, especially the Apostles' Creed, but emphasizes the sovereignty of the Word of God over all creedal interpretations.

A few non-Swedes have affiliated with this church which seems to be moving further from Lutheran orthodoxy. It supports North Park College and Seminary and reports 66,000 members. For many years it was known as the Mission Covenant Church.

Further Reading

Moravians

Gollin, Gillian Lindt, *Moravians in Two Worlds* (New York and London, Columbia University Press, 1967)

Schattschneider, Allen W., *Through Five Hundred Years; A Popular History of the Moravian Church* (Bethlehem, Pa., Comenius Press, 1956).

Mennonites

Dyck, Cornelius J., ed., *An Introduction to Mennonite History* (Scottsdale, Pa., Herald Press, 1967).

Hostetler, John A., *Amish Society* (Baltimore, Johns Hopkins Press, 1963).

Smith, C. Henry, *The Story of the Mennonites,* 3rd ed. (Newton, Kansas, Mennonite Publication Office, 1950).

Mennonite Encyclopedia, 4 vols. ed. by Harold S. Bender and C. Henry Smith (Scottsdale, Pa., 1955-59).

Brethren

Kent, Homer A., *250 Years Conquering Frontiers: A History of the Brethren Church* (Winona Lake, Ind., Brethren Missionary Herald, 1958).

Mallott, F., *Studies in Brethren History* (Elgin, Ill., Brethren Publishing House, 1945).

Salvationists

Bishop, Edward, *Blood and Fire* (Chicago, Moody Press, 1964).

Chesham, Sallie, *Born to Battle: The Salvation Army in America* (Chicago, Rand McNally, 1965).

Neal, Harry Edward, *The Hallelujah Army* (Philadelphia, Clinton, 1961).

Nygaard, Norman E., *Trumpet of Salvation: The Story of William and Catherine Booth* (Grand Rapids, Mich., Zondervan, 1961).

Chapter XV

THE CULTISTS
Many Travel Side Streets
on America's Religious Map

ALTHOUGH the term "cult" can have an unfortunate pejorative connotation, it simply describes a minority religious body whose teachings are considered unorthodox or spurious by members of the majority faiths. This chapter examines four such cults which retain some Christian content while the following chapters consider the larger groups which are usually identified as cults: Mormonism, Christian Science, and Jehovah's Witnesses.

Space limitations preclude description of all the many cults active in this country especially those which lack any Christian orientation such as Theosophy, Scientology, I AM, the Hare Krishna movement, Rosicrucianism, Satanism, witchcraft, the Self Realization Fellowship, and the assorted Southern California cults.

In general, the cults appeal to a special revelation such as that claimed by Emanuel Swedenborg or Joseph Smith, Jr. or they revere certain scriptures such as *Science and Health With Key to the Scriptures* whose divine inspiration is denied by mainline denominations. If Christians see cultists as standing outside the central Christian tradition, some cultists are just as confident that they alone constitute the true church and all others give allegiance to apostate churches. The Mormons and Jehovah's Witnesses hold this view.

Some groups are classified as cults by certain scholars and

as nothing more than smaller denominations by other scholars. For example, the prophetic role of Mrs. Ellen G. White in Seventh-day Adventism leads such Protestant writers as Prof. Anthony Hoekema and J. K. Van Baalen to group the Adventists with other cultists.

The cults we will describe do not belong to the National or World Councils of Churches and seldom participate in even local church associations. Cultists may be popularly known as Protestants and may be included in Protestant membership statistics but fundamentally they are no more Protestant than Catholic. The fact that these cults have arisen in Western societies since the Reformation is no reason to classify them as Protestant. Typically they deny basic Protestant positions on the sole sufficiency of the Bible, the priesthood of all believers, etc.

The Swedenborgians

After a distinguished scientific career a latter day Leonardo da Vinci by the name of Emanuel Swedenborg turned to religion. A PH.D. at the age of 21, he had mastered the mathematics, anatomy, and science of his day, traveled throughout Europe, and written 60 books and pamphlets when, at the age of 55, he announced that he had received the power to live in two worlds, the material and the spiritual.

This respected Swedish scientist abandoned science to produce 29 volumes in Latin which described the spirit world in detail and presented his own peculiar version of the Gospel. He recounted his spirit conversations with St. Paul, Luther, infidels, angels, popes, and Moslems. He had earlier rejected the doctrine of justification by faith alone as had his father, a Lutheran bishop. Now he discounted the Trinity and other traditional Christian beliefs. He claimed to have witnessed the Last Judgment which took place in 1757.

Swedenborg devised an allegorical interpretation of the Bible in which stones always represented truth, houses meant intelligence, snakes were carnality, cities were religious systems, and so on.

At death, Swedenborg explained, man awakens in the spirit world and continues a life quite similar to his earthly existence. Eventually each man goes to the realm in which he will feel most at home: heaven, the spirit world (similar to purgatory), or hell. Bachelor Swedenborg revealed that marriage continues in the next world as an eternal relationship although there may be some reshuffling of partners. He carefully described the flora and fauna of heaven as well as the appearance of the inhabitants of other planets such as Mercury, Jupiter, Mars, and the Moon.

Despite these bizarre revelations Swedenborg continued to enjoy the respect of his fellow Swedes. He seldom attended the state Lutheran church because he complained that spirits kept interrupting the sermons and contradicting the minister. He also won a reputation as a seer by disclosing a number of secrets and reporting events at a distance such as the details of a Stockholm fire some 300 miles from his home.

He did not found a church. An English printer and some Anglican clergymen initiated the Swedenborg movement in 1783, eleven years after the seer's death in London. Lancashire became the main center for the *Church of the New Jerusalem.* The original American branch was founded in Baltimore in 1792 and a secession produced a second, smaller body in 1890. Together the Americans make up about half of the world's 12,000 Swedenborgians.

The larger body, the General Convention, maintains a theological seminary at Cambridge, Massachusetts, and most of its members may be found on the Atlantic seaboard. Swedenborg's works are offered in inexpensive editions and a modest advertising program has been launched but no one seems particularly interested in the Swedish seer. Barron, the financial expert, and Helen Keller are probably the best known Swedenborgians. The father of William and Henry James was a Swedenborgian.

Nevertheless Swedenborg exerted an influence on modern Spiritualism by claiming immediate contact with the spirit world. His view on eternal marriage was elaborated by the Mormons. The Swedenborgian cult, however, is now intellectually stagnant and declining in membership.

To devout New Churchmen Emanuel Swedenborg was a "divinely illuminated seer and revelator." To the founder of

Methodism, John Wesley, he was "one of the most ingenious, lively, entertaining madmen that ever set pen to paper." To most Christians he remains unknown.

The Spiritualists

Attempts to pierce the veil of death and communicate with the spirits of the departed are recorded in man's earliest history. But modern spiritualism began with the Fox sisters in Hydesville, N.Y., and March 31, 1848, is usually given as the founding date.

The Fox family which included two little girls, Kate and Margaret, occupied a cottage known by their neighbors to be haunted. Strange nocturnal rappings and noises had been heard in the house for some time and on March 31 little Kate addressed the noisemaker: "Here, Mr. Splitfoot, do as I do." The spirit responded and a rapping code was devised.

The two sisters, exploited by an older sister Leah, went on tour and staged public demonstrations of the mysterious rappings in many American cities. The new religion attracted hundreds of thousands of enthusiasts and gave rise to a flood of spiritualist publications. Horace Greeley of the *New York Tribune* contributed many newspaper columns of publicity to the Fox exhibitions.

Margaret eventually entered a common law marriage, gave birth to a son, turned to drink, and finally startled the Spiritualist world by announcing her conversion to Catholicism. She admitted the whole thing was a hoax and demonstrated how she and her sister Kate had produced the loud rappings by snapping their toes. "I know that every so-called manifestation produced through me in London or anywhere else was a fraud," she confessed. Her expose failed to shake the faith of the hardcore believers and Margaret herself eventually recanted and returned to Spiritualism to eke out a living.

Meanwhile Andrew Jackson Davis, the Poughkeepsie seer, provided a systematic Spiritualist theology and terminology in 33 volumes supposedly written with spirit aid. He, rather than the discredited Fox sisters, is considered by many devotees to be the real founder of the religion but the Fox sisters are esteemed by most Spiritualists and the Hydesville cottage has become a shrine.

Spiritualism reached its membership peak within five years after its dramatic arrival on the American scene. By the first part of the present century it had all but disappeared, only to be revived after World War I. American Spiritualism never achieved the respectability of English Spiritualism which counted A. Conan Doyle (and presumably Sherlock Holmes) and Sir Oliver Lodge among its propagandists. Exposures and fraud have harried the Spiritualist cause in the United States. The enthusiasm of Episcopal Bishop James A. Pike and the resurgence of interest in the occult in the 1970s have given American Spiritualism a boost.

Spiritualist mediums use various physical devices to prove their powers of spirit communication. These include the time-tested rappings, the ouija board, slate writing, spirit photography, levitation, telekinesis (moving heavy objects without visible means), clairvoyance, knowledge of foreign tongues, and automatic writing. In a typical seance the medium sits with a circle of devotees and attempts to establish contact by rappings or voice with the deceased. At times a go-between or "control" relays messages from the deceased to the medium. Healing services are also conducted by some Spiritualists.

Harry Houdini, the magician, claimed he could duplicate any Spiritualistic phenomena by legerdemain. He exposed dozens of mediums and published his findings after 25 years' study in *A Magician Among the Spirits*. A number of Societies for Psychical Research have studied alleged Spiritualistic phenomenon in the United States and Europe.

Spiritualists ignore most Christian doctrines although they sometimes seek incorporation as a Christian church. They usually refer to Christ as an exceptionally able medium and adduce the annunciation, transfiguration, and resurrection as spirit phenomenon. The theology of Spiritualism pays little attention to God and ends up as a base ancestor worship. The highest ideal apparently is to be assured that one's loved ones are happy

and contented in the spirit world. Spiritualism is singularly free
of ethical or social content.

Spiritualists describe seven levels of life after death and
claim that most of mankind begin their upward evolution in the
third or Summerland sphere. The religion is universalist and no
one ends up in hell. The first of the seven levels is thought to
start about 300 miles above the earth's surface and the seventh
heaven begins at 18,000 miles. Life in Summerland seems to resemble life on earth except that sorrow and evil are missing.
The dead marry their soul mates, live in houses, wear clothes,
keep pets. The trite and contradictory messages received from
the "other side" disappoint many who investigate Spiritualism
from a religious motive.

Women dominate the movement but men usually hold the
top national offices. About 500 local congregations are grouped
in a dozen denominations. The oldest (1893) and largest is the
National Spiritualist Association of Churches which prescribes
rituals for worship, baptisms and funerals and ordains clergymen,
licentiates, and mediums. Congregations are likely to meet in
private homes or hotel rooms rather than church buildings. Other national organizations are the *National Christian Spiritual
Alliance* and the *International General Assembly of Spiritualists,*
a co-operative federation which claims 164,000 members. Most
Spiritualist churches meet in rented halls, hotel rooms, or private
homes. Perhaps 180,000 Americans are affiliated with recognized Spiritualist churches but many times this number can be
considered fellow travelers to the spirit world.

All Spiritualist spokesmen admit that fraudulent mediums
abound in the movement but they insist there remains a hard
core of sincere devoted mediums. Some associations seek to
raise the educational requirements for Spiritualist clergymen,
and a seminary in Wisconsin, the Morris Pratt Institute, offers
a course for would-be mediums. Summer sessions are featured
at Lily Dale, N.Y., and Chesterfield, Ind.

Spiritualism may attract some bereaved Christians by
offering an assurance from the other world that the departed
loved one is safe and happy. For others it supposedly offers
tangible evidence of a hereafter which some Protestant churches

seldom mention. Many people dabble in Spiritualism and drift in and out of the movement. Spiritualism's religious impulse is slight. Not worship of God but chats with the dead is its motivation.

The Unity School of Christianity

Unity School of Christianity, which grew out of New England Transcendentalism and New Thought, propagates its religion of optimism and healthy mindedness from a 1300-acre farm and headquarters near Kansas City. Unity is often confused with Christian Science. Unlike it, however, Unity acknowledges the reality of sin, sickness, and death, but teaches that God works through man's right thinking to overcome these difficulties.

Each year millions of copies of a half dozen attractive periodicals and pamphlets are mailed from the 100-man printing plant at Lee's Summit. These include *Unity, Weekly Unity, Daily Word,* and *Wee Wisdom.* Many Protestants and Catholics read Unity literature without ever bothering to investigate Unity's philosophy and religious basis.

Myrtle and Charles Fillmore were debt ridden and sickly before discovering the transforming principles of Unity. Both had studied many of the New Thought ideas, including Christian Science, and the new religion which they taught after 1889 was based on Mrs. Fillmore's healing. She experienced a change in her bodily condition as she believed, "I am a child of God and therefore I do not inherit sickness."

Devotees were encouraged to think good thoughts, dismissing the delusion that sickness and death had any power over them. From the beginning the Fillmores used the U.S. mails as their pulpit and relied wholly on voluntary contributions. Unlike Christian Science practitioners they made no charge for their healings which were published as testimonials in their magazines.

Mr. and Mrs. Fillmore established Silent Unity which offers a round-the-clock prayer service for all who phone, wire, or write for such help. A corps of Unity employees is on duty at all times to answer these appeals for prayers and to accept love offerings. An average week brings 10,000 appeals.

Myrtle and Charles Fillmore are both dead but their sons carried on the work. Unity moved to the new headquarters, eighteen miles from downtown Kansas City, in 1949. The property now includes an administration building, a 170-foot tower, a 22-acre artificial lake, training school, Unity Inn (vegetarian menu), the printing plant, swimming pool, golf course, picnic areas, and amphitheater. More than 500 Unity workers are employed at Lee's Summit.

People of widely varying religions subscribe to their literature, listen to the radio programs, watch the TV series called "Daily Word," and write to Silent Unity. However, there is a ministerial school which offers a three-year resident program and a summer school for teachers and counselors. These departments train leadership to serve some 265 local congregations known as Unity centers or churches which sponsor worship services, healing services, Sunday Schools, and offer classwork in counseling.

Unity converts are not required to sever connections with their former churches as is demanded of Christian Scientists. Many find the Christianity of their own churches prosaic compared to the esoteric teachings of Unity; they are likely to rely more and more on Unity Centers and Unity ministers for their spiritual needs.

Unity students interpret much of the Bible and many of the Christian doctrines allegorically or "metaphysically," as they would prefer to call it. A Hindu or Jew would find little to upset his religious sensibilities in Unity literature. In fact, the Hindu might feel more at home perusing Unity books than the Christian since the sect teaches that the soul passes through various reincarnations "till we all come into Unity." Unity sponsors no social welfare programs, hospitals, orphanages, or homes for the aged.

For all practical purposes Unity has become another sect and its claims to be nothing but a school of Christianity and nonsectarian are misleading. Its well-printed publications no doubt offer some comfort and inspiration to many millions who do not care about the cult's basic philosophy. Certainly, few Unity readers subscribe to Unity's belief in reincarnation. Were they to dig deeper into Unity they would find a school not of practical but of gnostic Christianity.

The New Thoughters

A variety of religious groups carry on the work begun in the mid-nineteenth century by the Portland, Maine, healer, Phineas P. Quimby. Some are tiny fellowships meeting in rented hotel rooms or private homes while others such as the Church of Divine Science and the Church of Religious Science have become substantial denominations with scores of local congregations.

New Thought covers a wide spectrum but all groups which can be identified by this term insist that man need not believe in sickness, evil, or poverty. They prefer not to draw a sharp line between God and man and their philosophies often verge on pantheism. New Thought teaches that man can always apply a spiritual solution to his problems; in this way he can achieve health, wealth, and happiness.

Most but not all such groups belong to the International New Thought Alliance; one of the larger holdouts is the Unity School. The *Yearbook of American Churches* fails to catalog most New Thought churches even though they influence millions of people through their publications and lectures. The Yellow pages of a metropolitan telephone book or the church ads in the newspaper list many New Thought groups.

Phineas P. Quimby, born in New Hampshire in 1802, opened an office in Portland in 1859 and began to treat a stream of patients. He himself said he had been cured of tuberculosis. At one stage of his healing career he practiced hypnotism but later he relied exclusively on mental healing. Quimby was critical of orthodox Christianity but nevertheless believed that Jesus had discovered the principles of spiritual healing. Among his many clients was a Mrs. Patterson known later as Mary Baker Eddy, founder of Christian Science.

Horatio Dresser edited Quimby's voluminous writings in

1921; the original manuscript in the Library of Congress runs to 2,100 pages in 12 journals. Charles Braden declares: "Carefully dated, they revealed beyond question to any but the most convinced Eddy disciples that Quimby had held the basic ideas of mental healing years before Mrs. Eddy sought healing at his hands in 1862." (*Spirits in Rebellion*, p. 57)

Warren Felt Evans left the Methodist ministry to become a Swedenborgian and later gave Quimby's ideas literary form. Quimby and the New Thoughters drew upon Transcendentalism, Swedenborgianism, mesmerism, Hinduism, Spiritualism, and other systems. New Thought rejected the Calvinism of American Protestantism and proposed an optimistic, empirical faith.

Most New Thoughters believe in the divinity of man and the impersonality of God. They admire the moral teachings of Jesus but repudiate the dogmas of orthodox Christianity such as those of original sin, the Trinity, the atonement.

Quimby died in 1866 and founded no church. New Thought groups began to be organized in the 1890s and often gained initial strength by absorbing disaffected Christian Scientists. New Thought is more syncretic, less authoritarian, and less monolithic than Christian Science. The cultists prefer spiritual healing but express less opposition to medicine than do the followers of Mrs. Eddy. Unlike Christian Science the New Thought cults do not insist that devotees cut all ties with other and more traditional churches.

New Thought ideas have been popularized by such authors as Ralph Waldo Trine whose *In Tune With the Infinite* has sold more than a million copies. The books of Emmet Fox, a former Roman Catholic, have introduced thousands of Americans to New Thought. For years Dr. Fox preached to the largest congregation in New York City, first in the Hippodrome and then in Carnegie Hall.

Four ladies participated in the founding of the *Church of Divine Science* in Denver in 1898. This church teaches that God is Spirit, Mind, Principle, Love, Truth, Substance, Soul, Intelligence, Being, Omniscience, Omnipotence, and Omnipresence. Ministers trained at the College of Divine Science staff several dozen autonomous churches.

Dr. Ernest Holmes started the *Church of Religious Science* in 1952; previously he had founded the Institute of Religious Science and Philosophy in 1927. He wrote the textbook of the movement: *Science of Mind*. This movement has split into two branches: about 30 churches form the International Association of Religious Science Churches and 70 belong to the Affiliated Churches of the Church of Religious Science. More than half of these congregations are found in California.

Other groups which fall into the New Thought category can usually be identified by such names as Metaphysical Science, Mental Science, Home of Truth. The importance of New Thought lies not in the number of adherents, although these number in the tens of thousands, but in its influence on those who never set foot in a New Thought church. William James once wrote that New Thought "together with Christian Science, constitutes a spiritual movement as significant for our day as the Reformation was for its time."

Further Reading

Swedenborgians

Swedenborg, Emanuel, *The True Christian Religion* (New York, E. P. Dutton, 1936).

Trowbridge, George, *Swedenborg: Life and Teaching* (New York, Swedenborg Foundation, 1944).

Spiritualists

Barbanell, Maurice, *Spiritualism Today* (London, Herbert Jenkins, 1969).

Ford, Arthur, *Unknown but Known* (London, Psychic Press, 1969).

Liljencrants, Johan, *Spiritism and Religion* (New York, Devin-Adair, 1918).

Pike, James *The Other Side* (Garden City, N.Y., Doubleday, 1968).

Thurston, Herbert, *The Church and Spiritualism* (Milwaukee, Bruce, 1933).

Unity School of Christianity

Bach, Marcus, *The Unity of Life* (Englewood Cliffs, N.J., Prentice Hall, 1962).

Cady, H. Emilie, *Lessons in Truth* (Lee's Summit, Mo., Unity School of Christianity, 1954).

Freeman, James Dillet, *The Story of Unity* (Lee's Summit, Mo., Unity School of Christianity, 1954).

New Thoughters

Braden, Charles S., *Spirits in Rebellion* (Dallas, Southern Methodist University Press, 1963).

Judah, J. Stillson, *The History and Philosophy of the Metaphysical Movements in America* ((Philadelphia, Westminster, 1967).

Chapter XVI

THE MORMONS

'What Man Is Now God Once Was;
What God Is Now Man May Become'

MORE than three million people, mostly Americans, who claim the name Christian believe:

That Christ preached to the American Indians after His ascension and founded a church among them for the Western hemisphere;

That an angel revealed the history of these people on golden plates to a young man in New York in 1827 and furnished magic spectacles to enable him to translate the record;

That this youth re-established the church of Christ which had been wiped out in the Americas and had apostatized elsewhere;

That there is not one God but many gods for many worlds;

That man lived with God in a previous existence and that after death he may become a god for his own planet;

That polygamy is the divine pattern of marriage.

These people are "Mormons" or, properly speaking, members of the *Church of Jesus Christ of Latter-day Saints*. Preponderant in Utah and strong in Idaho, Arizona, California, and other Western states, Mormonism can boast a tripled membership in 25 years. An unusually high birth rate, low death rate, and aggressive missionary program account for the growth of this sect into one of the leading denominations in the United States (1,930,000 members).

Four Mormons serve as U.S. Senators and five as Representatives. Mormons now direct such major corporations as Anaconda, National Biscuit, and F. W. Woolworth. Most Mormons live in the U.S. but there are growing communities in Canada, Mexico, England, West Germany, Scandinavia, South America, and the Pacific islands. Over 700,000 live in Utah.

The Mormon Church has become the dominant financial institution in the Rocky Mountain area. Its daily income from tithes and business investments is estimated at $1,000,000. The Church owns hotels and motels, a daily newspaper, 360,000 acres of Florida cattle land, two insurance companies, a mortuary, scores of farms, factories, and office buildings, Salt Lake City's largest department store, a publishing house, sugar refineries and a sugar plantation in Hawaii, and a short wave broadcasting company. The extent of its ownership of publicly held corporations such as the Union Pacific railroad cannot be easily ascertained.

The Church operates what has become the largest church-related university in the nation: Brigham Young University in Provo, Utah. It enrolls three times as many students as Notre Dame and 97 percent of its 26,000 students are Latter-day Saints. Because of a substantial subsidy from the Church, Brigham Young charges its LDS students a tuition of only $500 a year. The Mormon Church also claims to enroll a higher percentage of its young people in colleges and universities than any other major denomination.

Once confined mainly to the intermountain states, especially Utah, the Mormon Church is busy establishing new wards (parishes) in Eastern, Midwestern, and Southern states. Utah remains 60 percent Mormon but in Salt Lake City itself, the capital of Mormonism, the Latter-day Saints are now outnumbered by the non-Mormon "Gentiles."

Things have changed for the Mormon Church whose members were once massacred and driven out of Missouri and whose founder and first prophet was murdered in the Carthage, Illinois, jail by an enraged mob. Now noted for their sobriety, honesty, and industriousness, the Mormons were once branded from pulpits and political platforms as barbarians and lechers. After the Civil War the Federal government turned from the fight against slavery to the fight against polygamy and eventually forced the Mormon Church to suspend the practice of plural marriage.

A Federal army once entered Utah and threatened to depose Brigham Young but the Mormons vowed to burn their cities to the ground if the troops entered Salt Lake City. A compromise prevented a tragedy comparable to the burning of Moscow before Napoleon. For years American audiences were regaled by the stories of Mormon polygamy and alleged treason; one of the most popular lecturers was Young's 27th wife who had divorced him and joined forces with Gentile critics.

One basic reason for this persecution was the Mormon insistence that it was not a Christian Church but *the* one and only Christian Church. This claim infuriated frontier Protestants. The Mormon position has not changed much today. Mormonism teaches that all other Christian bodies lack any authority from God to teach or baptize and this includes all Catholic, Protestant, and Orthodox churches. Without exception these churches are considered apostate and counterfeit.

Mormonism claims to be a restored rather than a reformed Church. Founder Joseph Smith maintained that the Christian Church fell into apostasy shortly after the death of the last apostle. But he maintained that God the Father and Jesus Christ had appeared to him in person and restored the true Church and the authority of the priesthood in 1829. Acceptance of the claims of Smith and of the authenticity of the Book of Mormon and other Mormon scriptures is demanded of all members.

Mormondom is split into two main branches and a handful of tiny schismatic bodies. The main branch in Utah represents the majority of early Saints who followed Brigham Young westward after the Prophet's assassination. The other significant body of Mormons, the *Reorganized Church of Jesus Christ of Latter Day Saints,* objected to Young's leadership and eventually rallied around Joseph Smith's son. Its 200,000 U.S. members look to Independence, Missouri, as their Mecca. Except where noted our comments will apply to the larger Utah or Brighamite group rather than the so-called Josephites.

Smith, a Vermonter by birth, was a visionary, good natured young blood who passed his time hunting buried treasure by means of "peep stones." According to his own account and official Mormon history he was visited by a number of angels from the time he reached 14. One such angel, Moroni, informed him that all existing churches were in error, corrupt and apostate. His mission was to reestablish the true church and priesthood. Finally the angel gave him permission to dig near the top of the Hill Cumorah, near Palmyra, New York. There he unearthed a box of golden plates inscribed in "Reformed Egyptian." The obliging angel also supplied him with a pair of magic spectacles called the Urim and Thummim which enabled him to decipher the hieroglyphics.

The 22-year-old Smith employed various amanuenses, including Oliver Cowdery, an unemployed school-teacher. Sitting behind a blanket he dictated the *Book of Mormon*, the supposed history of the original inhabitants of this continent from 600 B.C. to A.D. 421.

According to this book North and South America were peopled by Jews who came by ship from Palestine. Two nations arose, the Lamanites and the Nephites. Essentially Mormonism is based on a version of the lost tribes of Israel legend; Cotton Mather, Roger Williams, and William Penn also speculated that the American Indians were Jews. Other variations of the lost tribes legend place the Israelites in Ireland, Japan, England (Anglo-Israel cult), and the lost continent of Atlantis.

The Mormon Bible relates that Christ appeared among the Nephites, chose 12 Indian apostles and set up a church which was a counterpart of the church he had established in Jerusalem. Eventually the dissolute Lamanites destroyed the virtuous Nephites in a battle near Palmyra in A.D. 421. Moroni, son of the vanquished Nephite general Mormon, buried the golden plates which recounted the history of his race. The plates also recorded the history of the Jaredites who were supposed to have come to America after the Tower of Babel.

After translating the Reformed Egyptian, Smith delivered

the plates and goggles to the angel and they have not been seen since. Linguists know nothing about a language called Reformed Egyptian and some of Smith's early disciples urged him to submit a specimen to a scholar in order to confound the skeptics. He copied down what he called some "caractors" and presented them to Prof. Charles Anthon of Columbia College. Anthon declared the sample consisted of "all kinds of crooked characters, disposed in columns . . . evidently prepared by some person who had before him at the time a book containing various alphabets." He repeatedly denied the Mormon claim that had declared the markings to be genuine "Reformed Egyptian."

The original edition listed Joseph Smith, Junior. as "Author and Proprietor." Of the 11 witnesses who testified to having seen the plates none ever admitted he had been duped or had perjured himself. Martin Harris, a farmer who mortgaged his land to pay the printer, testified in court years later that he had seen the plates "with the eyes of faith . . . though at the time they were covered over with a cloth." Five of the witnesses were Whitmers and three were Smiths including the Prophet's father. Harris, Cowdery, and David Whitmer eventually apostatized; the latter pair were driven out of Missouri by 80 Mormons who signed a complaint that they were thieves and counterfeiters.

Lengthy passages from the New Testament were included verbatim in the Book of Mormon and the entire book, supposedly written before A.D. 421, is phrased in King James idioms. It abounds in anachronisms, contradictions, and stock Campbellite answers to the theological questions of the early nineteenth century. At times its hindsight prophecy becomes entangled in such statements as "the Son of God shall be born of Mary at *Jerusalem*." Shakespearean students will be surprised to find the phrase "the undiscovered country from whose bourne no traveller returns" in a passage written 2200 years before the Bard.

Smith relates that John the Baptist appeared to Cowdery and himself in 1829 and ordained them into the Aaronic priesthood. The two baptized each other in the Susquehanna River. Later the Apostles Peter, James, and John conferred the higher priesthood of Melchizedek.

The tiny church, organized at Fayette, New York, the next

year, moved to Kirtland, Ohio, where Sidney Rigdon was pastor of a church. Here they found a ready welcome, built their first temple, chose 12 apostles to assist President Smith, and attempted to establish a communist order. Another band of Mormons continued to Missouri and the two Mormon settlements continued for some years 1000 miles apart.

Smith went to Missouri on a scouting expedition in 1831 and dedicated 63 acres in Jackson County which was proclaimed the exact site of the Temple of Zion where Christ would live and rule after His Second Coming. Today a tiny splinter group of Mormons owns the holy ground but has no funds to build the Temple. The schismatics say they have refused an offer of $5 million from the Utah Mormons for the property.

With the failure of a wildcat bank and impending indictment, Smith and Sidney Rigdon fled Kirtland by night and headed for the Missouri colony. Here the strange beliefs of the Mormon settlers and their suspected anti-slavery attitudes had antagonized the Missourians. Riots and incessant squabbles between Saints and Gentiles prompted the governor to call out the militia and the Mormons were expelled from the state in midwinter 1838-1839. Smith had been imprisoned for four and one-half months as a hostage and when he escaped he rejoined the Saints in neighboring Illinois.

Purchasing swampland on the Mississippi River, the Saints began to build their city of Nauvoo, which Smith maintained was a Hebrew word meaning "the beautiful." Its 20,000 citizens made it the largest city in the state and it received a liberal municipal charter. Thousands of English converts followed the exhortations of the Mormon missionaries to gather in Zion. To this day both Utah and Missouri Mormons look for the establishment of Zion at the Second Coming at Independence, Missouri (also reputed to be the site of the Garden of Eden).

The industrious Saints built a handsome temple at Nauvoo, laid out broad streets, built substantial homes and factories. Smith recruited a private army, the Nauvoo Legion, and designated himself as lieutenant general.

Rumors of polygamy, envy of Mormon prosperity, fear of the Saints' political power and dominance stirred the Gentiles to provocative actions. Smith contributed to the unrest when he announced himself a candidate for the presidency of the United States on a three-plank platform of abolition, nationalization of the banks, and prison reform. Rigdon ran for vice-president and Mormon missionaries were pressed into service as campaign spokesmen.

Disgruntled ex-Saints attempted to publish an anti-Smith newspaper in Nauvoo but Smith ordered his henchmen to pi the type and smash the presses. When the governor of Illinois promised Smith protection and safe conduct, he agreed to appear in Carthage to face charges of immorality, counterfeiting, sheltering criminals, and treason. But a mob of 200 men with blackened faces stormed the Carthage jail and shot the Prophet and his brother Hyrum to death. The Mormon prophet was dead at 39.

In stricken Nauvoo rivals vied for positions of leadership. The murder of Smith and his brother, the heir apparent, left the community in an unforeseen quandary. When Brigham Young returned from a mission in New England he managed to win the confidence of most of the bewildered Saints. Rigdon was banished. Many abandoned the Prophetless church and a minority which insisted that the leader should be a lineal descendant of the Prophet formed the nucleus of the Reorganized faction. Smith's widow Emma married a Nauvoo tavernkeeper, raised her family in the deserted city of Nauvoo, and eventually joined the Reorganized Church.

The demoralized Saints found an outstanding leader in Young. An ex-Methodist and fellow Vermonter, Young had joined the Prophet in Kirtland and never seemed to doubt Smith's extravagant claims. Although he had the benefit of only 11 days of formal schooling, this determined carpenter would build a theocratic empire in the West.

Realizing the precarious situation of the Saints in Nauvoo Brigham Young set about organizing the epic march to the West. To all who asked why he was leading the Saints out of Illinois he had one answer: "To get away from Christians and out of the United States." The first party left the state in the middle of winter, 1846. By April the last of the Saints had bidden farewell to their homes, factories, fields and temple in Nauvoo. Thousands would never reach their destination.

"This is the place" declared Young on July 24, 1847, when his advance party reached the valley of the Great Salt Lake, then a part of Mexico. The Mormons made the desert bloom. They irrigated, built homes, and started work on a new temple.

After the Mexican War the Saints found themselves subject to the same United States government from which they had fled. Congress turned down their petition for statehood for the "State of Deseret" but Young was appointed first governor of the Utah territory. Polygamy was traded for statehood in 1896 when Utah became the 45th state in the union.

After 1853 polygamy was openly practiced and defended. The Utah Mormons claim that Smith received the revelation on plural marriage at Nauvoo in 1843 but the controversial doctrine was not published until the Saints were safely entrenched in their intermountain sanctuary. Obviously polygamy was an afterthought since the Book of Mormon plainly states: "Wherefore, my brethren, hear me, and hearken to the word of the Lord: For there shall not any man among you save it be one wife; and concubines he shall have none" (Jacob 2:26). In other passages in the Mormon scriptures polygamy is called an "abomination before the Lord" and in *Doctrine and Covenants,* published in 1835, we read: "Inasmuch as this Church of Christ has been reproached with the crime of fornication and polygamy, we declare that we believe that one man should have one wife, and one woman one husband, except in case of death, when either is at liberty to marry again" (Section 101).

Nevertheless, the revelation to the Prophet no longer speaks of the "crime" of polygamy: "If any man espouse a virgin, and desire to espouse another, and the first give her consent; and if he espouse the second, and they are virgins, and have vowed to no other man, then he is justified; he cannot commit adultery with that that belongeth unto him and to no one else. And if he have ten virgins given unto him by this law, he cannot commit adultery, for they belong to him, and they are given unto him, therefore he is justified" (Section 132).

Not all Saints welcomed this innovation and 4000 English

converts who balked at polygamy were summarily excommunicated. In Utah the leaders of the priesthood advised the wealthier Saints to take a second or additional wife. The cult found itself with a surplus of female Saints, a theology which deprecated celibacy, and a desert which needed people. When Young died in 1877 he left his $2,000,000 fortune to 12 widows (nine had already preceded him in death) and 47 children. Another leader of the Mormon hierarchy, Heber Kimball, supported 45 wives.

The church has never renounced its belief in polygamy which Mormons believe was revealed by God Himself. It has become a "suspended" doctrine since 1890 when President Woodruff yielded to federal law and declared: "Inasmuch as laws have been enacted by Congress, which laws have been pronounced constitutional by the court of last resort, I hereby declare my intention to submit to these laws, and to use my influence with the members of the church over which I preside to have them do likewise. And now I publicly declare that my advice to the Latter-day Saints is to refrain from contracting any marriage forbidden by the law of the land."

Opposition by the Federal Government to the practice of polygamy was registered as early as 1862 when President Lincoln signed a bill condemning polygamy in the Territories of the United States. In his inaugural address President Garfield stated: "The Mormon church not only offends the moral sense of mankind by sanctioning polygamy, but prevents the administration of justice through the ordinary instrumentalities of law." Finally, in 1890 the supreme court upheld the constitutionality of the Edmunds Law of 1882 which disfranchised any person who practiced plural marriage. When Utah finally won statehood it was on the condition that polygamy be forever prohibited in the territory.

If the Federal Government were to withdraw its opposition to plural marriages, the Saints would certainly resume the practice. They have always considered the laws against polygamy to be unjust and an infringement of religious freedom. Scores of Saints went into exile in Mexico or served prison sentenced rather than submit to the Federal Government. Several Utah congressmen were denied seats because they had more than one wife. Thousands of Mormon fundamentalists have never recognized the church's surrender on the matter of polygamy and continue its practice in secluded Western villages. Several times state officials have raided a settlement of 400 Mormon fundamentalists in Arizona who were following Joseph Smith's original revelation on polygamy.

Mormons accept four sources of doctrine: the Bible "insofar as correctly translated," *The Book of Mormon, Doctrine and Covenants,* and *The Pearl of Great Price.* Smith labored for months over his own translation of the Bible but the Utah Mormons continue to use the King James version.

Doctrine and Covenants consist of a collection of dated revelations from God to the Prophet and a single revelation to his successor, Young. One such divine revelation set the price of the Book of Mormon at $1.25 and another presented the godhead's advice on the financing of a boarding house at Nauvoo: "And they shall not receive less than fifty dollars for a share of stock in that house, and they shall be permitted to receive fifteen thousand dollars from any one man for stock in that house." This book also includes the Word of Wisdom which forbids alcohol, tobacco, and hot drinks which the Saints have taken to mean coffee and tea.

The Pearl of Great Price is a slim volume of three sections: the so-called Book of Moses in which certain visions are described, the Book of Abraham, and a potpourri entitled the "Writings of Joseph Smith." The Book of Moses discloses that Satan originated Freemasonry in order to ensnare mankind.

The background of the Book of Abraham is instructive. At Kirtland, a traveling carnival owner invited Smith to examine the papyrus accompanying his circus mummy. The Prophet solemnly declared the hieroglyphics to be the writings of Abraham and Joseph and proceeded to produce a translation. Egyptologists realized the hieroglyphics were part of the well-known Book of the Dead and bore no similarity to Smith's efforts. Years later in Illinois the Prophet studied six brass plates with mysterious scratchings and explained that they told the history of the descendants of Ham; the wags who perpetrated the hoax could not contain their amusement. When a Protestant minister sought to test Smith's knowledge of languages he handed him a Greek copy of the Psalter. "It ain't Greek at all, except a few words. What ain't Greek is Egyptian and what ain't Egyptian is Greek. Them characters are like the letters that were engraven on the Golden Plates," explained the Prophet.

Mormon theology teaches that the god of this world is a man (probably Adam), a physical being, a polygamist. God did not create matter, which existed eternally (he "organized" it), but he did create a tremendous number of spirits or souls. All humans have entered a pact with the god of this world to erase the memory of their former existence if he would send them to earth. If they faithfully follow Mormon precepts and obey the priesthood they may be given charge of a planet of their own after death. Their leading theologian states simply, "All men are potential gods," and Young himself phrased the Mormon aphorism, "What God was once, we are now; what God is now, we shall be."

They believe in a practical universalism. Of the billions of souls who have inhabited the earth only murderers and apostates, sons of perdition, will go to hell. The afterlife for all others will be spent in a graded heaven: the celestial, terrestrial, and telestial. The celestial is reserved for Mormons who are married in the mystic temple rites. Lower grade Mormons and exceptional Gentiles may attain the terrestrial heaven which is presided over by Christ. Run-of-the-mill Gentiles may expect to spend eternity in the telestial plane and fraternize neither with God nor Christ but with angels. Their conception of heaven comes closer to the Moslem paradise than the Christian beatific vision.

The distinctive Protestant doctrine of justification by faith alone receives a thoroughgoing criticism by the cult which demands ethical, ceremonial, and moral works besides faith. Of course, the sole sufficiency of the Bible, another Reformation principle, is automatically denied.

The dead may receive Mormon baptism by proxy which enables them to advance to a higher plane in the afterlife. A Saint may be baptized for his ancestors as many as 30 times in an afternoon; President Woodruff was baptized for the signers of the Declaration of Independence, John Wesley, and others. The Saints specialize in genealogical studies so that they can trace all their ancestors. Some Mormons claim to be able to identify members of their family tree to A.D. 500. These proxy baptisms for the dead are performed only in the temples. Ordinarily Mormons are baptized by immersion at the age of 8.

Mormonism is Jim Crow. No Negro may enter the priesthood and blacks are not encouraged to join the church. This exclusion from the priesthood is quite significant in Mormonism since nine out of ten adult Mormon males hold some office of the priesthood. Brigham Young explained, "Why are so many inhabitants of the earth cursed with a skin of blackness? It comes in consequence of their fathers rejecting the power of the Holy Priesthood, and the Law of God." The cult considers all Negroes to be descendants of Cain, cursed by a dark skin or, as the Book of Mormon puts, "the Lord did cause a skin of blackness to come upon them." At another time Young told Horace Greeley, "We consider slavery of divine institution and not to be abolished until the curse pronounced on Ham shall have been removed from his descendants." This Mormon position is often softpedaled in missionary work, at least in the North.

The Big Fifteen who control the church consist of a "President, Prophet, Seer, Revelator, and Trustee in Trust," a First and Second Counselor, and the 12 Apostles, a self-perpetuating body which selects the President for a life term.

A bishop and two counselors supervise the ward, which corresponds to a parish. The wards are gathered into stakes of Zion similar to dioceses. All but a few dozen of the church's personnel serve without pay and carry on daytime secular occupations.

A Mormon lad advances in the lesser Aaronic priesthood from deacon to teacher to priest. As a priest he may baptize, administer the sacrament, and ordain other priests. A priest enters the Melchizedek priesthood and may continue his advance as an elder, seventy, high priest, patriarch (hereditary in the Smith family), apostle, and president.

The cult exaggerates the importance of sex and the family. Celibacy is regarded as an inferior state and virgins have no chance of attaining the celestial plane in heaven. To remain single is considered contrary to the Word of God and those who do not marry at a fairly early age are urged to do so by the priesthood.

Large families are encouraged; birth control is condemned; family solidarity is fostered by the regular recreational "Home Evenings"; divorces in temple marriages are rare. The Young Men's and Young Women's Mutual Improvement Associations enroll thousands and the cult sponsors Boy Scout programs.

Mormon temples are closed to Gentiles and to Mormons who do not tithe, observe the Word of Wisdom, and attend church regularly. Visitors may enter the 8000-seat Salt Lake City Tabernacle and attend services at ward chapels. Three main rites are performed in the 13 Mormon temples: proxy baptism of the dead, marriage for time and eternity, and the endowment.

Mormons classify marriages as those for time and those for time and eternity. The latter can be solemnized only in one of the temples. Christians usually marry with the formula "until death do us part" but Mormons (and Swedenborgians) consider marriage an eternal contract if performed by two Mormons in the temple rites. Saints who are unable to travel to a temple or who contract a marriage with a Gentile or who fail to meet temple entrance requirements are married "for time" in a ward chapel. Later they may undergo a second ceremony of "sealing" in the temple—if their circumstances change. Children born in a temporal marriage may also be sealed to parents in the temple.

In the day-long endowment rites young Mormons are initiated into the esoteric aspects of the cult. The endowment ceremony usually precedes the marriage rites. Participants enter the temple with their temple vestments of white shirt and trousers, white robe and girdle, cloth cap, moccasins, and a Masonic-type green apron with fig leaf design.

They first bathe and are anointed with oil. After this they don their long white underwear (LDS Approved Garments as they are known in Utah haberdasheries) which they will wear throughout life as believing Mormons. Three symbols stitched in the garment signify that if the initiate should reveal temple secrets he will allow his legs to be amputated, his intestines disemboweled, and his heart cut out. Mormons are buried in their endowment garb.

The initiate then receives a new secret name and secret grips. They pass from one room to another to watch a continuing playlet which includes scenes wherein Catholic and Protestant clergymen are ridiculed for their inadequate religious beliefs. The Five Rooms of the temple are called the Creation Room, Garden of Eden, World Room, Terrestrial Kingdom, and Celestial Kingdom.

Masonic influence is apparent in Mormon temple rites which is not surprising since both Smith and Young were Freemasons in Illinois but were expelled from the lodge. Utah Mormons are forbidden to join the Masonic lodge.

The regular Sunday afternoon worship service includes a simple observance of the Lord's Supper. Water is used in place of wine lest the Word of Wisdom be violated. The Saints believe their church possesses all spiritual gifts such as healing, speaking in tongues, communication with spirits, and prophecy.

At one time the doctrine of blood atonement embarrassed Mormon proponents but this vicious doctrine has gradually been forgotten by Gentile critics and young Mormons alike. Early Mormon theologians argued that some sins could only be forgiven by the shedding of the sinner's blood. As Young explained: "Cutting people off from this earth . . . is to save them, not to destroy them." The Danites were a band of avenging Saints who liquidated apostates and Gentiles for their own good.

The greatest scandal in Latter-day Saint history is the famous Mountain Meadow massacre of 1857. A party of 120 people on their way to the California gold fields passed through Utah and were promised safe passage and protection from the Indians if they would surrender their weapons to Mormon Bishop John D. Lee and his men. They agreed to this arrangement but at a signal from Bishop Lee ("Do your duty, men!") the Mormons murdered the men, hacked the women to death, and kidnaped the children. Twenty years later, Lee, a Catholic in his youth, was convicted and executed; the role of Young in this affair has never been ascertained. That this was a case of blood atonement rather than simple cold-blooded murder has been suggested by some Gentile historians.

Mormonism is the largest sect in the country to insist on tithing. A member who does not contribute 10 per cent of his income to the church does not qualify as a Mormon in good standing. This source of income provides the cult with huge sums for missionary activities, relief, educational programs, building, and other enterprises. The canny Mormon business-men undertake their major church construction projects during economic depressions, getting materials at lower prices and providing work for unemployed church members. Mormons also refrain from two meals on the first Sunday of each month and donate the proceeds to church welfare funds. The church maintains more than 100 warehouses for food and clothing for those in need.

All young men are expected to spend a year or two as un-paid missionaries and each year 4000 leave Utah in pairs to spread the message of the Prophet around the globe. All are members of the priesthood and graduates of a short course in missiology. They average 21 years of age and have memorized a sales talk, Bible proof texts, and stock answers to Gentile ob-jections. They direct their efforts at members of other denomi-nations rather than the unchurched and in one recent year claimed 100,000 baptized converts. Strangely the Mormon church has had little success in converting Gentiles in predominantly Mormon communities.

Rather than operate its own high schools as it once did, the church now supports 150 seminaries which supplement the sec-ular secondary school curriculum with Mormon theology. Insti-tutes of Religion provide a similar service for Mormon students on college campuses. Besides Brigham Young University the church operates colleges in Idaho and Hawaii.

Somewhat closer to traditional Christianity, the Reorganized church denies polygamy, blood atonement, and the Adam-god doctrine of their Utah cousins. They flatly deny Young's assertion: "When our father Adam came into the Garden of Eden, he came into it with a celestial body, and brought Eve, one of his wives with him. . . . He is our father and our God, and the only God with whom we have to do." This branch of Mormondom was organized at Beloit, Wisconsin, in 1852 and was headed by Joseph Smith III from 1860 to 1914.

Smaller groups which accept the authenticity of the Book of Mormon and the prophetic role of Joseph Smith include the *Church of Christ (Temple Lot), the Church of Jesus Christ* or Bickertonites, the *Church of the First Born of the Fullness of Time* which reportedly tolerates polygamy.

The 1906 religious census indicated a Mormon Church membership of only 215,000 in the U.S. The tenfold increase in the years since then has propelled this denomination into the ranks of the larger American churches. The high birth rate and successful missionary programs seem to guarantee continued growth of this American-born religion which proclaims itself the only true Christian Church on earth.

Further Reading

Brodie, Fawn M., *No Man Knows My History* (New York, Knopf, 1945).

Hirshon, Stanley P., *The Lion of the Lord, A Biography of Brigham Young* (New York, Knopf, 1969).

Mullen, Robert *The Latter-day Saints: The Mormons Yesterday and Today* (Garden City, N.Y., Doubleday, 1966).

O'Dea, Thomas F., *The Mormons* (Chicago, University of Chicago Press, 1957).

Turner, Wallace, *The Mormon Establishment* (Boston, Houghton Mifflin, 1966).

Whalen, William J., *The Latter-day Saints in the Modern Day World,* rev. ed. (Notre Dame, Ind., University of Notre Dame Press, 1967).

Chapter XVII

THE JEHOVAH'S WITNESSES

They Expect Final Battle
of Armageddon to Start Any Day

EVERY household in the United States has probably been visited by a Fuller Brush salesman, a tax assessor, and a Jehovah's Witness "minister." Once upon a time these door-to-door proselytizers toted phonographs and subjected citizens to transcribed sermons by their spokesman, "Judge" Rutherford. Nowadays most diligent Witnesses have undergone a speech training program and manage to deliver their own sales talks.

Such aggressive missionary tactics have brought impressive harvests. Jehovah's Witnesses are undoubtedly one of the fastest growing body of cultists in the world. From 129,000 members in 1945 their numbers have ballooned to 1,483,000, in 206 nations. Of these 401,000 reside in this country. And they are still growing. Fellow travelers and subscribers to their magazines must be numbered in the millions.

A public relations face lifting, a series of successful legal battles, and shrewd leadership have pushed this fanatical eschatological sect into the forefront of modern religious movements. Most of this progress and growth has been achieved since the death of the cantankerous Rutherford in 1942 and the ascendancy of Nathan Knorr.

Compared to Jehovah's Witnesses, Calvin Coolidge's minister who declared himself against sin was a piker. The Witnesses oppose blood transfusions, business, Catholics, Christmas trees, communism, civic enterprises, the doctrines of hell and immortality, evolution, flag saluting, higher education, liquor, lodges, Protestants, priests, the pope, public office, military service, movies, Mother's Day, religion, Sunday Schools, the Trinity, tobacco, the United Nations, voting, the Y.M.C.A., Wall Street, and women's rights. This list does not pretend to be complete.

The Witnesses want no inactive or "associate" members. Everyone save the lame and the blind is expected to devote many hours a month to door-to-door preaching. In recent years this has averaged about 11 hours and is in addition to attendance at five meetings a week at Kingdom Hall.

A growing full time body of nearly 88,000 Pioneers work 150 hours a month supervising congregations, handling administrative details, and distributing publications. All contributions for their books and magazines are forwarded to Brooklyn headquarters while the Pioneer lives on a small expense account and boards with sect members.

More than 17,000,000 books and booklets are sold or given away each year, most of them printed at the cult's modern printing plant. *Let God Be True*, a 320-page doctrinal exposition, has gone through several reprints and the latest count reveals 16,000,000 copies have been printed. It is hard bound and sells for only fifty cents.

The Witnesses specialize in conventions. Their 1958 Divine Will International Assembly in New York City, attracted 253,-000 Witnesses. Thirteen "Triumphant Kingdom" assemblies were staged in 1955 with a total attendance of 403,000 in Chicago, Vancouver, Los Angeles, Dallas, New York, London, Paris, Rome, Nuremberg, Berlin, Stockholm, The Hague, and Helsinki.

Charles Taze Russell, son of a Pennsylvania haberdasher, adopted adventist views after a Congregational boyhood and temporary loss of faith. He became distressed at the thought of hell and his Bible searching convinced him that the Hebrew word *sheol* should invariably be translated "grave" instead of "hell." He began his preaching activities in 1872 and many people found comfort in his flat denial of everlasting punishment.

"Pastor" Russell toured the nation preaching his novel Biblical interpretations on an average of six to eight hours a day. But two scandals rocked his new movement. His wife sued him for divorce charging him with infidelity and cruelty and the court declared that "his course of conduct towards his wife evidences such insistent egotism and extravagant self-praise that it would be manifest to the jury that it would necessarily render the life of any sensitive Christian woman an intolerable burden." Russell contested the divorce five times without success and eventually attempted to avoid alimony payments by transferring his property to corporations which he controlled. The cult leader's involvement in a phony $60 a bushel Miracle Wheat disillusioned other converts. He also promoted a "cancer cure" which consisted of a caustic paste of chloride of zinc, a wonderful Millennial Bean, and a fantastic cotton seed.

Russell died in 1916 on a Sante Fe Pullman after requesting an associate to fashion him a Roman toga whereupon he "drew up his feet like Jacob of old" and passed away. His successor, Joseph F. Rutherford, was a small town Missouri lawyer who preferred writing to preaching. He consolidated Russellism, quietly supplanted the founder in the memory of the devotees. His scripture-heavy polemics soon formed the bulk of the sect's printed propaganda. Later he recorded the short talks which Witnesses played for householders on their portable phonographs.

He also shrugged off Russell's pyramidism, a system by which the founder claimed to be able to foretell history by measuring the rooms of the Great Pyramid in Egypt. Several schisms erupted when old-timers objected to the mild debunking of the late "Pastor" Russell.

During World War I Rutherford and other officers of the cult were imprisoned for nine months on charges of sedition. Shortly after his release from Atlanta federal prison the "Judge" coined the slogan "Millions Now Living Will Never Die" which expressed the urgently adventist hopes of the movement and soon blossomed on road signs, handbills, and posters.

Rutherford's followers were known variously as Russellites, International Bible Students, Millennial Dawnists, Rutherfordites, Watchtower Bible and Tract People. This untidy situation was cleared up in 1931 when Rutherford disclosed that their new name would be "Jehovah's Witnesses." This proved a happy choice since any mention of "witness" in the Old or New Testament could now be adduced as evidence of the antiquity of the cult.

When not at his Brooklyn Vatican "Judge" Rutherford resided in a mansion near San Diego, California, whose deed was made out to Abel, Noah, and Abraham. This estate was kept in readiness for any Old Testament princes who returned to life before the Battle of Armageddon. Meanwhile, it served as Western headquarters. The "Judge" was not among the millions now living who will never die. He died in 1942 after dictating the affairs of the cult for more than 25 years.

The self-perpetuating hierarchy of 402 men chose the 36-year-old Knorr to succeed Rutherford. The present head left the Reformed church while in high school and was employed in various business capacities in the cult until his election to the top position. He holds office for life but is technically re-elected each year. Like all full-time workers he receives room, board, and $14 a month; insinuations that the leaders have enriched themselves on book profits seem unwarranted.

Many basic teachings of Jehovah's Witnesses resemble those of Seventh-day Adventism through whom Russell was introduced to millennial doctrines. Mankind lives in the latter days. The great battle between Satan and Christ, Armageddon, may occur any day now. Prepare. The Witnesses have learned by experience not to specify dates but all members confidently expect to see these events in their lifetimes, at least before 1984.

Satan was cast out of heaven and now rules the world; however, Jesus Christ returned to earth invisibly in 1914. We have already entered the early days of the millennium which will terminate in A.D. 2914 but only a few people recognize the theocracy. These few include Jehovah's Witnesses.

Satan is marshaling his forces for the battle of Armageddon. He finds his principal allies in an evil triumvirate: organized religion, the commercial world, and political organizations. During the course of the battle the faithful few will sit on a mountainside and watch Jesus and His angels defeat Satan and his cohorts. After the great battle Satan will be bound and cast into an abyss. The righteous survivors will marry and repopulate the earth during the remainder of the 1000-year reign. The dead will remain in their graves until the resurrection but the wicked will be annihilated. Those who have died without a chance to know the Lord will be resurrected and given a second chance. If they persist in their disbelief, they too will be totally destroyed.

At the end of the 1000 years Satan will be loosed and he will try one last time to seduce mankind. A few men will succumb to his temptations and with Satan will be annihilated. The billions who have repopulated the earth and been resurrected from the dead will continue to dwell on earth forever.

Only a fraction of Jehovah's Witnesses can be members of the invisible church since they believe its number has been set at 144,000, no more, no less. This quota has been filling up since Pentecost and few places remain. Today about one Witness out of 130 claims to belong to this select "bride's class" and only these few can entertain hopes of reaching heaven. They are the only ones who partake of the annual spring observance of the Lord's Supper in local Kingdom Halls.

. The best that other Witnesses can hope for is to be counted among the Jonadabs or "other sheep" who will protect and assist the "bride's class" from their earthly habitation. To summarize the final disposition of mankind according to Russell-Rutherford-and-Knorr: 144,000 will attain heaven and reign with Christ, the wicked will be annihilated, the righteous will live on earth forever.

Witnesses reject many fundamental Christian beliefs such as original sin, the divinity of Christ, His resurrection, immortality, and the Trinity. Christ was originally Michael the Archangel, lived and died a man, and is now an exalted being. He was not God. And besides, say the Witnesses, he was born on October 1, 2 B.C. rather than December 25 which just goes to show how heathenish Christendom has become. The authoritative text *Let God Be True* explains the Jehovah's Witness views on Christ:

"Prior to coming to earth, this only-begotten Son of God did not think himself to be co-equal with Jehovah God; he did not view himself as "equal in power and glory" with Almighty God; he did not follow the course of the Devil and plot and scheme to make himself like or equal to the Most High God and to rob God or usurp God's place. On the contrary, he showed his subjection to God as his Superior by humbling himself under God's almighty hand, even to the most extreme degree, which means to a most disgraceful death on a torture stake."[1]

They agree with the Seventh-day Adventists on immortality: "Immortality is a reward for faithfulness. It does not come automatically to a human at birth."[2]

The Christian doctrine of the Trinity is ridiculed in the following passage from the same textbook:

"When the clergy are asked by their followers as to how such a combination of three in one can possibly exist, they are obliged to answer, "That is a mystery." Some will try to illustrate it by using triangle, trefoils, or images with three heads on one neck. Nevertheless, sincere persons who want to know the true God and serve him find it a bit difficult to love and worship a complicated, freakish-looking, three-headed God. The clergy who inject such ideas will contradict themselves in the very next breath by stating that God made man in his own image; for certainly no one has ever seen a three-headed human creature."[3]

The Witnesses consider all religious bodies, Catholic and Protestant, to be tools of Satan and deceivers but they reserve a special hatred for Roman Catholicism. Their literature offers kind words for Arius, Waldo, Wycliffe, Huss, and the early Anabaptists but they lament that the Reformation never really got off the ground.

Some Protestant churches ask no more of a prospective member than that he sign the register, attend church with some regularity, promise to read the Bible, and contribute to the support of the church. Not so with Jehovah's Witnesses. Anyone who conscientiously meets the demands of the cult finds little time

---

[1]*Let God Be True*, 2nd ed. (Brooklyn: Watch Tower Bible and Tract Society, 1946, p. 34.

[2]*Ibid.*, p. 74.

[3]*Ibid.*, p. 102.

for anything else. A convert completes courses in the Bible, speech, salesmanship, and missionary techniques before being assigned to ring doorbells with an experienced Witness. Most members hold regular jobs and attempt to get in their required hours evenings and week ends.

A Witness may be a farmer or laborer or professional man but he cannot be a salesman or shopkeeper since these people are involved in Satan's commercial enterprises. He is encouraged to live and eat decently but invited to turn over any surplus wealth or income to the cult. Witnesses neither tithe their incomes (like Mormons and Adventists) nor pass the collection plate; members drop their contributions in a box at the rear of each local Kingdom Hall.

Mass baptisms by immersion are scheduled at the conventions and more than 4000 converts were baptized in swimming pools at the New York meeting. The baptism service, like the Lord's Supper, is more of a dedicatory than a sacramental rite.

Witnesses do not vote in local or national elections, hold public office, salute the flag, or enter military service since they consider the United States government and every other government an instrument of the devil. On this score one government is about as wicked as another be it democratic, fascist, or communist. To cast a vote or accept a public office would be supporting Satan's political ally. Oddly enough, they have never objected to paying taxes. At one time the sect discouraged marriage and the begetting of children since the theocracy was just around the corner, but this prohibition has been relaxed.

Some 700 Witnesses live a community life at Bethel House, a nine-story apartment building in Brooklyn. These members run the presses, set the type, bind the books, handle the mail and other chores at national headquarters. The Bethel residents eat in a common refectory whose food is supplied by several Witness-operated farms. Bells arouse the workers at 7 a.m. and signal lights out at 10:30 p.m. All get the same recompense from Knorr to janitor: room, board, and $14 a month.

The local congregation or "company" meets in a Kingdom Hall, usually a rented store or small building. Sixteen thousand such companies are grouped in 1000 circuits; a circuit servant visits each company once every six months. Sunday and Thursday evening meetings resemble discussion groups more than worship services. Prayer, study of scripture and Watchtower publications, reports of activities, and business comprise the meetings. Hymn singing has been considered a waste of time and music has played a minor role in Witness assemblies. A full-time Pioneer, known as the company servant, may conduct the meeting.

In recent years under the Knorr administration Witnesses have learned how to smile, to treat householders with some courtesy and tact, to inquire about the children and pet the dog. The old-fashioned belligerency and "hear me or be damned" approach antagonized most prospects. To many bibliolaters the scriptural gymnastics of a trained Witness is a sure sign of godliness. What matter if this "minister" never finished high school, knows no Biblical languages, chooses to quote out of context? As a matter of fact anyone who itches to engage an experienced Witness in a Biblical duel had better make sure he has spent as much time memorizing proof passages and persuading doubters as his opponent.

The Watchtower Bible School of Gilead at Brooklyn, N. Y., trains about 200 Pioneers a year for full-time missionary work. Many thousands have completed the course since the school opened its doors in 1943. Only Witnesses who have spent two years in the field are admitted.

The cult has found fertile missionary fields in West Germany, England, Canada, Nigeria, Brazil, France, Zambia, Mexico, and the Philippines. They enjoy high prestige in Germany since some 10,000 Witnesses were sent to Nazi concentration camps and 2000 perished. The Communists have forbidden Witness activity behind the Iron Curtain. More than 3000 missionaries are laboring in South America.

Few college graduates join the movement. Knorr himself never studied in an accredited college. Few younger members in the cult are encouraged to extend their formal education beyond high school. The main appeal has been to the socially, economically, and intellectually disinherited. The sect promises that the rich and powerful will soon get their comeuppance. About 20 per cent are Negroes and the sect makes a special effort to win Puerto Ricans and Mexican-Americans. Racial equality has been one of the long-time policies of the cult, but no Negro has ever held a top administrative office. Naturally the sect counts no representatives of the commercial, military, political, or academic worlds.

Evidently to many people the advantages of cult membership outweigh the burdens. Without spending years in college and seminary they can become "ministers." They can sit in other people's living rooms and command respect as they spin their peculiar doctrines and impress their listeners with heavy doses of proof texts. As "ministers" they can claim exemption from the draft, ride the railroads for half fare, preach, and baptize.

Witnesses have been stoned, imprisoned, fined, sent to concentration camps, tarred and feathered. They have become involved in dozens of law suits over their refusal to salute the flag, their peddling books without a license, their slandering of religious groups, their denial of blood transfusions to their sick children. Between 1940-45 almost 2000 were sent to federal prisons as draft dodgers although all claimed to be ministers of the gospel. They have won about two thirds of the 40 cases which have reached the Supreme Court. In most instances they were supported by the American Civil Liberties Union and in Witness gratitude they have branded the A.C.L.U. an agent of the devil.

A passage in Leviticus condemning the eating of blood is taken to refer to blood transfusions although the practice condemned was obviously a primitive tribal rite rather than a medical technique. Christmas trees are pagan-inspired since the Witnesses quote Jeremiah: "The customs of the people are vanity; for one cutteth a tree out of the forest, the work of the hands of the workman with an axe. They deck it with silver and gold."

Only unsigned articles now appear in their two magazines: *Watchtower* and *Awake!* The former is published semimonthly in 73 languages and has reached a circulation of 7,000,000 at five cents a copy. *Awake!* boasts a circulation of 6,750,000 in 27 languages. A 13-story magazine publishing plant has been built to supplement the Brooklyn factory. All books are now published anonymously and neither Russell's nor Rutherford's works are being reprinted. Even correspondence from the Society is anonymous and signed with a rubber stamp.

How the Witnesses can sell a 320-page book printed in two colors and hard bound for 75 cents can be explained. They pay no author's royalties, bookseller's commissions (usually 40 per cent), profits, union printing wages. They also print these books in such tremendous quantities that the unit cost can be cut to a minimum.

Witness scholars have completed an interesting New World translation of the Hebrew scriptures. As might be expected, they substitute the "correct" word Jehovah for God in many passages. Two volumes have appeared and two more are promised. Their translation of the Lord's Prayer runs as follows:

Our Father in the heavens, let your name be sanctified. Let your kingdom come. Let your will come to pass, as in heaven, also upon earth. Give us today our bread for this day; and forgive us our debts, as we also have forgiven our debtors. And do not bring us into temptation, but deliver us from the wicked one.[4]

Already we can observe the beginning of a transition from sect to church. The full-time Pioneers are assuming more of the duties ordinarily assigned to ministers and priests. Witnesses encourage their children to enter Pioneer work as a career. Kingdom Halls move from rented quarters to modest Witness-owned buildings. Publications have dropped their lurid illustrations and Rutherford era vilification and a new look tempers their attitude toward the public. Anonymous leadership replaces the colorful Russell and the brooding Rutherford. The democratic congregational organization of the local company has been replaced since 1938 by the autocratic theocracy.

Far more people are influenced by this cult and may consider Kingdom Hall their "parish" than the worldwide 1,483,000 baptized membership figure indicates. In 1970 more than 3,225,000 people gathered in 26,000 halls for the annual Memorial service. (Of those attending only 10,500 partook of the bread

---

[4] *Ibid.*, p. 162.

and wine and therefore identified themselves as part of the 144,000.) We can see from the circulations of *Watchtower* and *Awake!* magazines that about three non-baptized subscribers receive it for every Jehovah's Witness. Hundreds of thousands are receiving instructions from Witnesses or attending Bible study classes without yet committing themselves to the cult.

All but a handful of Witnesses are converts, mostly recent converts. Whether they will pass on the same enthusiasm and crusading zeal to their children seems doubtful. All expect to see Armageddon in their lifetimes. Can the movement sustain itself with a continually postponed Armageddon?

Neither scandals nor persecution have stopped the growth of this American-born cult. In 1928 there were only 6040 Witnesses in the entire nation. We can expect their membership to continue to grow but not at the rate of the past few decades. A nation with millions of fundamentalists, depressed minorities, and people in search of a cause provides a happy hunting ground for a band of dedicated fanatics such as Jehovah's Witnesses.

Further Reading

Gruss, Edmond Charles, *Apostles of Denial* (Nutley, N.J., Presbyterian and Reformed Publishing Co., 1970).

Martin, Walter R., and Norman H. Klann, *Jehovah of the Watch Tower*, 6th rev. ed. (Grand Rapids, Mich., Zondervan, 1963).

Pike, Royston, *Jehovah's Witnesses* (New York, Philosophical Library, 1954).

Stevenson, W. C., *The Inside Story of Jehovah's Witnesses* (New York, Hart, 1967).

Whalen, William J., *Armageddon Around the Corner* (New York, John Day, 1962).

Chapter XVIII

THE CHRISTIAN SCIENTISTS

'Man Is Incapable of Sin, Sickness and Death'
—*Mary Baker Eddy*

IN THIS age of antibiotics, revolutionary surgical techniques, the X-ray, and vaccinations for smallpox, diphtheria, and polio, we may forget that for religious reasons a substantial minority deprive themselves and their children of the benefits of medical science. They are following the teachings of an elderly New England matron, Mrs. Mary Baker Glover Patterson Eddy, discoverer of Christian Science.

For almost 100 years her loyal devotees have not only stubbornly denied the reality of disease but the reality of matter, of evil, and of death itself. Moreover, our Christian Science neighbors, numbering perhaps 450,000 in the United States, constitute a group of citizens of greater wealth and higher social standing and better education than most. Their ranks include college professors, an astronaut, a U.S. senator, movie stars, scientists, editors, financiers, lawyers, and artists.

With Mormonism and Jehovah's Witnesses, Christian Science stands as one of the three really successful home-grown religions. Excepting Madame Blavatsky's Theosophy it remains the only religion of consequence founded by a woman. Denying every fundamental Christian dogma, it presents itself to the public as a Christian denomination and appropriates a Christian vocabulary.

How a penniless woman of 50 carried through her plans to build a church to perpetuate her strange beliefs makes a fascinating story.

She compiled a book which, doctored and edited, has been given a place next to the Bible in many cultured homes.

Born Mary Baker on a New Hampshire farm in 1821 she spent a childhood plagued by sickness and "fits." In the space of a few decades early nineteenth-century New England would witness such enthusiasms as Shakerism, Mormonism, Spiritualism, and Transcendentalism. Mary Baker had to miss most formal schooling because of her delicate health. At the age of 17 she joined the Congregational church, of which she remained a nominal member for 40 years.

At 22 she married George Washington Glover, a bricklayer and small-time contractor. The newlyweds set up housekeeping in South Carolina but in six months Glover was dead of yellow fever. His young widow returned home and gave birth to her only child.

The tragedy aggravated her hysterical attacks and she dabbled in poetry, Mesmerism, and Spiritualism for some years. Eventually she married an itinerant dentist and philanderer by the name of Daniel Patterson. Her four-year-old son had been taken to Minnesota to be raised by foster parents and she would not see him again until he was 34. Dr. Patterson had the misfortune to visit a Civil War battlefield as an observer. He mistakenly crossed into Confederate territory and spent the duration of the war in a Southern prison.

Neither morphine nor Mesmerism seemed to help Mrs. Patterson's numerous physical complaints. But she happened to hear of a marvelous healer in Portland, Maine. To this day the healer with the Dickensian name of "Dr." Phineas P. Quimby remains the skeleton in Christian Science's closet.

Mrs. Patterson visited Quimby as a patient and student for three weeks in 1862 and again for three months in 1864. She received a copy of Quimby's writings on healing entitled *Questions and Answers* and expressed her appreciation for his help through letters to the press and quaint versicular testimonials. She would later explain these embarrassing tributes by commenting, "I might have written them twenty or thirty years ago, for I was under the Mesmeric treatment of Dr. Quimby from 1862 until his death" (*Boston Post*, 1883).

At any rate his death in 1866 evoked a eulogy by Mrs. Patterson entitled "Lines on the Death of Dr. P. P. Quimby, Who Healed With the Truth That Christ Taught in Contradistinction to All Isms." The founder and her followers have since then sought to ignore or minimize Quimby's contribution and to defend the complete originality of Mrs. Eddy's system.

Her P.O.W. husband meanwhile had returned and promptly announced that he had had enough and left home. She eventually obtained a divorce in 1873 on grounds of desertion. He left his profession, died a hermit in 1897, and was buried in a potter's field. The wife he abandoned left a fortune estimated at $3,000,000.

"The Fall at Lynn" is considered the first authentic Christian Science healing. Mrs. Glover (she had assumed her first husband's name) relates that she slipped on the ice returning from a ladies' aid meeting and suffered injuries which she (but not her doctor) pronounced incurable.

She could not appeal to the dead Quimby although she had dipped into Spiritualism. At this crisis she claims to have rediscovered the laws of healing which Christ had demonstrated in the New Testament and which had been lost through apostasy by the primitive Church. She began to read her Bible and came across the passage in St. Matthew in which Christ addressed the man sick with palsy: "Arise, take up thy bed." She now realized that death and sickness were illusions and within a few days she was walking around to the amazement of her few friends.

Her physician later signed an affidavit in which he declared, "I did not at any time declare, or believe, that there was no hope for Mrs. Patterson's recovery, or that she was in a critical condition."

Between the Fall in 1866 and 1870 she labored on her "textbook." Of *Science and Health With Key to the Scriptures* Mark Twain wrote, "Of all the strange and frantic and incomprehensible and uninterpretable books which the imagination of man has created, surely this one is the prize example." Despite the best efforts of editors and proofreaders *Science and Health* scares off most inquirers by its inconsistency, awkwardness, and abstruseness. The author shrugged off all criticisms and pointed out that "Learning was so illumined that grammar was eclipsed."

Christian Scientists considered the work inspired. "I should blush to write a *Science and Health With Key to the Scriptures* as I have, were it of human origin, and I, apart from God, its author; but as I was only a scribe echoing the harmonies of heaven in divine metaphysics, I cannot be super-modest in my estimate of the Christian Science textbook," declared Mrs. Eddy.

The first edition carried the following verse on the fly leaf *a la* Gertrude Stein:

> I, I, I, I, itself, I.
> The inside and the outside, the what and the why
> The when and the where, the low and the high.
> All I, I, I, I, I, itself, I.

This has since been deleted.

Revised and expanded many times, the book now includes chapters on Christian Science versus Spiritualism, Animal Magnetism Unmasked, Marriage, Physiology, etc. The Key to the Scriptures section was added in 1884 and consists of an allegorical interpretation of Genesis and the Apocalypse. The final edition concludes with a glossary and pages of "fruitage" or healing testimonials.

The book sold for $3 a copy when first offered in 1875 and this was mostly profit in those days. The original edition was advertised as "a book that affords an opportunity to acquire a profession by which you can accumulate a fortune." Church members and practitioners were forced to buy each new edition during the author's lifetime although the changes sometimes amounted to nothing more than a few words.

Shunted from one rooming house to another for nine years, the destitute grass widow decided to team up with a Richard Kennedy. Like the late Quimby he called himself "Dr." and advertised himself as a faith healer. She offered a series of lectures on her healing method, Christian Science. This series, originally 12 and then seven lectures, cost $300. She admits she hesitated to ask such a sum, half a year's wages for the Lynn, Massachusetts, shoe workers who comprised her early disciples, but a voice from heaven commanded it.

She taught a garbled pantheism which denies the reality of matter, evil, sickness, and death. These were not created by God and therefore constituted simply errors of mortal mind. Remove the erroneous conceptions and you remove the suffering and defeat the grave. Man's purpose in life is to free himself from these errors of mortal mind through application of the laws she had discovered. Once freed, he would find himself healthy, sinless, and immortal.

Her mechanical application of these mysterious laws forced her to conclude that if they could be employed to produce health they could be perverted to inflict sickness and death. This Yankee voodooism, a revival of New England witchcraft, she termed Malicious Animal Magnetism. In her later years she lived in terror of MAM, tormented by the malevolent forces of her enemies and critics. As protection she surrounded herself with a corps of devoted followers whose task was to ward off evil thoughts and forces. Christian Scientists who had been hexed told their troubles in a MAM column in the *Christian Science Journal*. Today this black magic aspect of the cult shares the closet with Phineas P. Quimby.

Her third venture into matrimony involved Asa Gilbert Eddy, a sewing machine agent whose name she would perpetuate. A few years later neither her healing laws nor the M.D.'s could prevent death. She disagreed with the post mortem (post mortems were later forbidden in her *Church Manual*) and maintained that her spouse had died of "arsenic mentally administered." She added emphatically: "My husband's death was caused by malicious animal magnetism. . . . I know it was poison that killed him, not material poison but mesmeric poison." Now she had all the more reason to dread the devils of MAM she had unleashed.

Kennedy was the first of a succession of co-workers and students who left to found cults of their own or who refused to turn over royalties to Mrs. Eddy for the use of her healing techniques. All were violently denounced; all were sinisterly accused of employing MAM to destroy the frail high priestess. She became embroiled in innumerable lawsuits to collect her 10 per cent royalty on students' healing fees.

A revolt of her students at Lynn finished her career in that community and at 61 she transferred her activities to Boston. Here she founded the First Church of Christ, Scientist. She had obtained a charter for the Massachusetts Metaphysical College of which she was the sole instructor. Between 1881 and its discontinuance in 1889, 4000 students each paid $300 tuition for the course. Later three advanced options were added including Metaphysical Obstetrics. Anyone taking the full course paid Mrs. Eddy $800. She probably collected $1,200,000 in the eight years the school functioned. Some charity cases were admitted.

In Lynn she had preached her new religion to factory workers. In Boston she managed to interest the wealthier classes for whom the cult would exert a perennial appeal. By now she had ordained herself and assumed the title "Reverend." Her organization prospered with practitioners, former students, and branch societies in the East and Middle West. She hired a retired minister to polish her textbook and by 1891 she would have sold 150,000 copies.

A 41-year-old physician, Dr. Foster, joined the college staff as instructor in obstetrics. At the age of 68 Mrs. Eddy legally adopted the doctor who changed his name to Ebenezer J. Foster Eddy. He played the role of crown prince in the cult until a falling out with his "mother" and subsequent exile.

Despite her successes, Mrs. Eddy was restless. MAM dogged her day and night; she knew her enemies were trying to poison her just as they had murdered her husband. She decided to leave Boston, close her profitable college, disband her present church structure.

A shrewd woman, Mrs. Eddy saw the need to forge stronger bonds between herself and her church. Defections and schisms were no novelty to her. A strong Boston organization with decentralized and wholly dependent branch churches seemed the answer. Now an elderly woman, she undertook a series of bold steps to insure her complete control of Christian Science not only during her lifetime but after her death.

She set up a single Christian Science church, the Mother Church in Boston. All others were and are simply branch churches of this one church—buildings where nonresident members of the Boston congregation and neophites could meet to study, sing hymns, and deliver testimonials. Only members of the Mother Church could teach Christian Science, receive the degrees C.S.B. and C.S.D., serve as Readers in branch churches. Only Mother Church members could qualify as practitioners. Those holding only branch membership had little standing in the cult.

District organizations and conferences were forbidden, which frustrated attempts at organized revolt. Next she deposed all pastors and substituted her textbook and the Bible as "pastors." First and Second Readers conducted the worship services but their terms were limited to five years. They were not allowed to elaborate on the *Science and Health* and Bible passages selected by Boston.

Mrs. Eddy encouraged each branch to sponsor an open lecture annually but all lecturers had to be approved by Boston. All lectures were submitted for censorship and no questions from the audience were tolerated. Only the Bible, the works of Mary Baker Eddy, and church periodicals could be sold in reading rooms operated by the branch societies.

A Committee on Publications set about correcting criticisms and misstatements about the cult in the press. Its boycott of the debunking Dakin book in 1930 backfired and turned, *Mrs. Eddy, the Biography of a Virginal Mind,* into a best seller. In recent years the Committee's methods of boycott and intimidation have managed to stifle nearly all published criticism of the cult.

After her reorganization of her church all decisions and power rested in Boston and Mrs. Eddy controlled Boston. She lived at her Concord estate 70 miles away. The Mother Church, dedicated in 1895, featured The Mother's Room. Pastor Emeritus Eddy is said to have spent one night in the shrine. A light has since burned before her portrait in the room.

The faithful undertook pilgrimages to Concord to get a glimpse of their Leader (a title which replaced Mother). Many vied for a chance to serve in her household. She fussed with her textbook, collecting royalties of $50,000 to $100,000 a year. She accused her foster son of practicing MAM and disowned another devotee who claimed to have experienced a virgin birth.

The old lady's health was failing but her followers could not be disillusioned. If the discoverer and founder of Christian Science could not apply its laws and defeat sickness and death, who could?

After 1900 her health declined rapidly. She had worn glasses and visited dentists for years. Now a doctor was called to administer regular doses of morphine. She was too ill to attend the ceremonies for the $2,000,000 addition to the Mother Church which was completed in 1906. Some 30,000 people jammed the edifice during six identical dedication services; retouched photographs of the Leader were distributed.

Her natural son reappeared but withdrew his suit to declare his wealthy mother mentally incompetent; he received $250,000 and Dr. Foster Eddy $50,000. When she excommunicated the popular Mrs. Augusta Stetson of the New York City branch she eliminated her last rival.

Two years before her death she founded the daily *Christian Science Monitor*. The *Monitor* ranks high in any appraisal of American journalism and its sponsorship by the cult has brought Christian Science considerable prestige. It has won 60 awards for excellence in journalism since 1915 and now reports 186,000 subscribers throughout the nation. It avoids sensationalism, observes the expected taboos on news of deaths, tragedies, epidemics, etc. No advertisements are accepted for coffee, tombstones, cemeteries, undertakers, dentists, oculists, or hearing aids. It never uses the word death but prefers the euphemism "passed away." The *Monitor* news story about the World War I battlefield littered with "passed on mules" is probably apocryphal. The official publication of the church, the *Christian Science Journal*, has been published since 1883. The Christian Science Publishing Society also publishes Mrs. Eddy's works and the three other official periodicals: *Christian Science Sentinel, Herald of Christian Science*, and *Christian Science Quarterly*. Authors must be members of the Mother Church.

Mrs. Eddy could make no real provision for her impending

death without compromising her religious principles. "Matter and death are mortal illusions" declares her textbook. Her associates grew alarmed but she was confident she had bequeathed a workable polity in her *Church Manual.*

Mary Baker Eddy died of pneumonia December 3, 1910, at the age of 89. Most of her fortune went to her church. Her cult had no provision for funeral rites. Probably 100,000 people called her Mother or Leader at the time of her final succumbing to error of mortal mind.

A self-perpetuating five-member Board of Governors ruled the church after her death. An article of her *Church Manual* asserts that nothing can be adopted, amended, or annulled without the written consent of the Leader which has been an impossibility since 1910. A struggle between the Board and the publications officers ended in two independent corporations, one for the church and another for the publications.

Another tenet forbids the tabulation of membership so we can only guess at the present strength of the movement. The more than 3100 branches of the Mother Church in the United States enroll an average of perhaps 150 members. Only 16 are needed to found a branch society. Christian Science is a cult for city ladies; perhaps three out of four Scientists are women. The church is strongest in California, Illinois, New York, Ohio, and Massachusetts. Few cults promise devotees a boost up the social ladder but Christian Science proves to be an exception.

A true Christian Scientist will take no medicine, consult no physician. Yet she will employ the services of an obstetrician, dentist, oculist, bone setter, and mortician. She will wear glasses and dentures but will vigorously oppose public health measures, compulsory vaccination or X-ray examinations, or flouridation of water supplies. Assured by her religion that matter is unreal, she ordinarily evinces the same interest in food, property, success, a home, and security as her Christian neighbors.

In many cases Christian Science seems to produce happy, serene, optimistic individuals. Perhaps some adjust to the make-believe world of childhood which knows no sin or death. The cult stresses self-mastery and Stoic courage.

Does Christian Science cure? Certainly. Recent research in

psychosomatic medicine confirms the belief in the close inter-action of mind and body. "A merry heart doeth good like a medicine" (Prov. 17:22). Any M.D. will testify that mental disturbances lie behind a large percentage of his patients' ills. Recognizing the role of mind in sickness and health is not the same thing as denying all sickness, sin, and death.

Christian Scientists are encouraged to treat themselves, but a class of professional healers, practitioners, tackle stubborn cases. Like doctors and dentists these practitioners hold regular office hours, bill their clients for their services (payments are deductible for income tax purposes). They attempt to convince the sufferer, who may or may not be a Christian Scientist, that she is in error in thinking she is sick or dying. They read from the Bible and textbook in the office or at the bedside. About 7000 registered practitioners, mostly women are listed in the *Journal* and several serve as chaplains in the armed forces. Authorized teachers of Christian Science are limited to 30 students a year.

The Christian Science church does not baptize members and observes only two spiritual communions a year; at these communion services there is no bread or wine but the worshippers spend a few moments in silent prayer. Mrs. Eddy prepared no ritual for marriage in her church; Christian Scientists seek the services of Protestant ministers or civil officials when they wish to be married. Of course, the church prescribes no burial ritual since this would imply the possibility of death.

Christian Scientists are urged to overcome any "depraved appetite" for alcoholic drinks, tobacco, tea, coffee, and opium.

The standardized Sunday morning service (identical in all branch churches) consists of Mrs. Eddy's version of the Lord's Prayer, alternate reading of the Bible, the Lesson-Sermon prepared by a committee in Boston, the collection, and the recital of the "scientific statement of being." Mrs. Eddy may have borrowed her term "Father-Mother God" from the Shakers, a defunct religious cult also founded by a woman, Ann Lee. The Shakers also called their main church the Mother Church.

Traditional Christian holidays such as Christmas and Easter are ignored but special services are held on Thanksgiving Day. Wednesday evening is devoted to oral testimonials of healing.

Scientists allot large sums for the erection of pretentious temples. Of course, they operate no hospitals, clinics, welfare agencies, or orphanages since this would entail coddling error. The Principia, a small Illinois college, is Christian Scientist in faculty and student body but is not owned by the church.

Practically all basic Christian beliefs, Catholic and Protestant, are flatly denied by the cult. Christian Science rejects the idea of a personal God, the Trinity, original and actual sin, the devil, the atonement, the resurrection, the divinity of Christ, judgment, heaven, and hell. Casual inquirers must be warned, however, not to assume that the use of common Christian terms in Christian Science literature supposes common meanings and interpretations.

Well-known Christian Scientists include Senator Charles Percy of Illinois, columnist Roscoe Drummond, party-giver Perle Mesta, comedian Milton Berle; Kay Kyser, who once led one of the nation's leading dance bands, has become a practitioner in North Carolina.

A number of Jews have embraced Christian Science and have found little incompatible with liberal Judaism. The cult is sometimes proposed as a happy compromise in a Jewish-Gentile marriage. We might say that this fashionable cult makes its chief appeal to Jew and genteel.

The cult inculcates an attitude toward life which nonmembers find impossibly inconsistent. In this it shares the difficulties of all systems of absolute idealism. The demands of faith it imposes on its members are enormous. Christian Science claims to offer much more than health to its faithful. It is advertised as the key to success in business, marriage, financial undertakings. The writer once heard a Scientist testify at a Wednesday evening meeting that he attributed his success in obtaining travel and hotel reservations to his application of Christian Science.

Mrs. Eddy was a shrewd, tenacious, and courageous woman. She seemed an utter failure before she discovered Christian Science in 1866; she died a millionairess.

Although Christian Science is only one of two score sects which feature faith healing, it has achieved a respectability, membership, and power which most have lacked. Its period of greatest growth may be seen between 1906 and 1926 and it seems to have reached its zenith. Its chance of becoming one of the great churches has gone.

For main agencies are employed in its widespread proselytizing program: the open lectures, the reading rooms maintained by each branch society, the *Monitor* and other church periodicals, and radio and TV programs. In each medium the healing testimonial is the basic selling point.

Its wealthy and educated devotees, impressive temples, and dignified publications make a good impression on the public. The Committee on Publications silences adverse publicity. But a taste of *Science and Health* disenchants many inquirers. Few can dissuade themselves from the common sense view of life and the world around them. The facts of measles and murder and mortuaries appear self-evident to most of mankind.

Mary Baker Eddy wrote her *Science and Health* when modern medicine was in its infancy. Quite possible many of her clients were better off reading her textbook than submitting to the bloodletting, leeches, and primitive surgery of the 19th century. Today the miracles of modern medicine are proof to most intelligent people that disease is real but can often be cured by drugs and surgery. Christian Science wins few converts and seems destined to remain a minority religion.

Further Reading

Beasley, Norman, *The Cross and the Crown* (New York, Duell, Sloan and Pearce, 1952).

Braden, Charles S., *Christian Science Today* (Dallas, Southern Methodist University Press, 1958).

Dakin, Edwin Franden, *Mrs. Eddy* (New York, Charles Scribner's Sons, 1929).

Eddy, Mary Baker, *Science and Health With Key to the Scriptures* (Boston, Christian Science Publishing Society).

Peel, Robert, *Mary Baker Eddy: The Years of Discovery* (New York, Holt, Rinehart and Winston, 1966).

The Christian Science Way of Life (Englewood Cliffs, N.J., Prentice-Hall, 1962).

Chapter XIX

THE UNITARIAN UNIVERSALISTS
Religious Liberals Challenge All Dogmas

THOMAS JEFFERSON predicted in 1822: "I trust that there is not a young man living in the United States who will not die a Unitarian." Our third President further believed that "the present generation will see Unitarianism become the general religion of the United States."

For all his great qualities Jefferson turned out to be a poor prophet. By 1971 the Unitarians (bolstered by a 1961 merger with the Universalists) claimed only 265,408 adult members in this country.

Yet an impressive case can be made for the proposition that no religious denomination has and does provide a greater number of national figures than the Unitarian Universalists. The last Unitarian who ran for the presidency—Adlai Stevenson—lost the election, but five presidents stand in the Unitarian tradition: John Adams, John Quincy Adams, Jefferson, Millard Fillmore, and William Howard Taft.

In the 90th Congress the Unitarian Universalists furnished 2.40 representatives in the House for 100,000 church membership. This is the highest representation of any religious group: the Presbyterians furnished 1.62 and the Episcopalians 1.59. Roman Catholics had only .21 representatives for each 100,000 Catholics. Three senators—Clark, Hruska, and Williams—and four representatives identify themselves as Unitarian Universalists.

Two Unitarians—Arthur Schlesinger, Jr. and Ted Sorenson —held top posts in the Kennedy administration. This tiny denomination has been the spiritual home of such people as novelist J. P. Marquand, architect Frank Lloyd Wright, diplomat Chester Bowles, composer Bela Bartok, historian Henry Steele Commager, social theorist David Riesman.

Unitarian figures in American literature include Oliver Wendell Holmes, Henry Wadsworth Longfellow, William Cullen Bryant, Edward Everett Hale, Ralph Waldo Emerson, James Russell Lowell, Nathaniel Hawthorne, Bret Harte, and Louisa May Alcott. Suffragette Susan B. Anthony, reformer Dorothea Dix, and Horace Mann are claimed by the Unitarians. Of 77 Olympians in the Hall of Fame, 17 were Unitarians.

Despite the small membership of the denomination, the influence of Unitarian Universalists must be reckoned as a major force in contemporary American life. What is more, millions of Americans hold views similar to Unitarianism but do not belong to a Unitarian Universalist church or fellowship. Some remain in mainline Protestant denominations.

All religious bodies evolve over a period of decades or centuries but few have changed as radically as Unitarianism and Universalism. Originally Unitarians affirmed the unity of God in contrast to the orthodox Christian doctrine of the Trinity. They revered Jesus as the unique exemplar of God's revelation, believed in his miracles as well as those of the Old Testament, relied on the Bible as the Word of God. The Unitarians of the 16th century held a heterodox but Christian theological position.

Today the majority of American Unitarians stand in the humanist tradition; almost all Unitarians in the Middle West and West can be classified as agnostics. Long ago they rejected the orthodox attitudes toward the Bible and miracles and few today profess belief in a personal God or in immortality. Jesus is considered one of many religious teachers and the Christian message takes its place alongside the teachings of Buddhism, Hinduism, Islam, etc.

Universalism began with an orthodox position on the Trinity but a belief that all souls will eventually be reconciled with God. The early Universalists simply denied that God would punish any soul for eternity. Someone has commented that classical Universalism believed that God was too good to damn any soul to hell while Unitarianism believed that man was too good to be damned.

A minority of American Unitarians represented by the Unitarian Christian Fellowship seeks to uphold the Christian witness in the denomination but the odds seem to be against this holding action. The growth of the denomination in recent years has been outside of New England which is where the Christian Unitarians preserve some strength.

Unitarians maintain that primitive Christianity was unitarian and only gradually changed to belief in the Trinity. At the Council of Nicea in 325 A. D. the Church declared that Jesus was the same essential substance as God the Father; the doctrine of the Trinity was further elaborated at the Council of Constantinople.

Early Unitarians might have been classified as Arians who believed that Jesus was not equal to God but was more than man. Their heroes were Arian, Origen, and Pelagius in early Church history.

With the orthodox doctrine of the Trinity firmly held by the Church little more is heard of Unitarian tendencies until the 16th century. About 14 years after Luther nailed his 95 theses to the church door, a Spaniard, Michael Servetus, challenged the doctrine of the Trinity. In a tract entitled "On the Errors of the Trinity" he sought to win the Reformers, especially Luther and Calvin, to his theological view. "Your Trinity is the product of subtlety and madness. The Gospel knows nothing of it," wrote the young Spanish rebel.

Far from accepting the anti-Trinitarianism of Servetus, the Reformers recoiled and condemned him as a blasphemer. He lived under an assumed name in France but reopened his correspondence with Calvin. Servetus was eventually arrested as he passed through Geneva, tried, and burned at the stake. Calvin thought this punishment was more than just.

Servetus attracted no followers and held doctrinal positions far from later Unitarianism. Unitarianism took root in two other areas: Transylvania and Poland. Two brothers, Faustus and Lelius Socinus, led the Unitarian movement in Poland. By 1618 there were 300 congregations of the Minor Reformed Church, the name of the Unitarian church in Poland. During the Counter-Reformation the Jesuits succeeded in eliminating Unitarianism in that country.

The kingdom of Transylvania maintained its independence from 1543 to 1691; it is now a part of Rumania. Here the leader was Francis David who was protected by the only Unitarian king in history, John Sigismund. By 1600 there were 425 Unitarian churches in the kingdom. Sigismund's successors did not share his religious views and persecuted the Unitarians. A few congregations in this area still meet for worship under the Communist government.

In England the first Unitarian service was held in an auction room in London in 1774. A former Anglican clergyman, Theophilus Lindsey, founded English Unitarianism. He was assisted by Joseph Priestley, best known as the scientist who discovered oxygen.

Although Unitarianism in England was not subjected to the severe persecution it endured on the Continent, it did antagonize many orthodox Christians. In 1791 a mob destroyed Priestley's home and laboratory as well as a Unitarian chapel in Birmingham. The scientist fled to London and a few years later to America. He founded the first church in America to bear the Unitarian name in Northumberland, Pa. James Martineau assumed leadership of the English Unitarians in the early 19th century.

In England the denomination suffered a sharp decline after 1900; attendance at Sunday service fell from 42,000 in that year to 13,500 just before World War II. Many Unitarian chapels were destroyed by German bombing during the war.

In America Unitarianism arose as a schism within New England Congregationalism. Unlike Calvinists the Unitarians affirmed that human nature was good, not depraved, that man was free rather than predestined, and that Jesus was a great moral teacher but not God. King's Chapel in Boston, the first Episcopal church in New England, adopted Unitarianism in 1787. All references to the Trinity were expunged from the ritual. The

Church of the Pilgrims at Plymouth joined the liberal camp in 1800.

The growing controversy between Calvinists and Unitarians was brought to a head by Jedidiah Morse, an orthodox Congregationalist and the father of the inventor of the telegraph. He launched a crusade to smoke out the heretics and found a perfect issue when Harvard picked Henry Ware, a theologian of Arian views, to fill the chair of divinity in 1805. In protest the orthodox founded Andover Theological Seminary. For 128 years Harvard saw a succession of Unitarian presidents.

The lines were now drawn. Most of the Congregational churches in the Boston area became Unitarian. By 1840, an estimated 135 of 544 Congregational churches had gone over to Unitarianism and many of these were the larger and more affluent parishes.

A group of Boston and New England ministers formed the American Unitarian Association in 1825. (The British association was founded in the same year.) Later the Western Unitarian Conference was organized to extend the free religion movement to the Middle West and West. Its orientation has always been more humanistic than that of the New England Unitarians. Western Unitarians were instrumental in the establishment of Washington University in St. Louis and Antioch College, but neither institution remained under church control.

Meanwhile the other partner in the 1961 merger—Universalism—was establishing roots in America. John Murray, a former Methodist, preached the first Universalist sermon in America in 1770. He taught that ultimately all souls would be reconciled to God. Although Universalism as a religious system predated Unitarianism in this country it did not formally organize until 1866.

Originally Universalism was Trinitarian but one influential preacher, Hosea Ballou, swung the theological direction of the denomination toward unitarianism. Ballou served a Boston church from 1817 to 1852.

The Universalists went on record in 1790 as opposing human slavery—the first religious body to take this stand. They were also the first denomination to sponsor women for the ministry. Universalists worked for prison reform and the parole system and fought capital punishment.

Universalism always found its greatest strength among rural New Englanders. It has not counted the distinguished roster of communicants which has been found in Unitarianism. Yet Benjamin Rush, a Universalist layman and physician, was a signer of the Declaration of Independence, and Clara Barton, founder of the American Red Cross, belonged to the Universalist Church. This church founded Tufts, Akron, and St. Lawrence universities.

Today the theological battle between theists and humanists is almost over and the humanists must be considered the victors. Here and there especially in New England, you will find individual Unitarians or congregations which still favor the Christian or theistic position, but they are dwindling.

The denomination published the results of a comprehensive survey of beliefs of adult Unitarian Universalists in 1967. Only 3 percent think of God as a supernatural being, although four out of ten think of God as love, evolution, or some other natural process. About 90 percent repudiate any belief in personal immortality and 64 percent declared that they seldom or never pray.

Most Unitarian Universalists are converts; 60 percent belonged to some other religion and 28 percent had no previous religious affiliation. Approximately 5 percent came from Jewish backgrounds while 20 percent said their parents were Protestant fundamentalists. Unitarian Universalists are normally wealthier and more active in community affairs than people in other churches; six out of ten are college graduates.

The Unitarian Universalist Association reports 104,000 pupils in its church schools. There are 681 churches and 447 Fellowships or mission churches served by 968 ministers. Isolated Unitarian Universalists may join the Church of the Larger Fellowship which provides a correspondence-type program. About 5,000 men and women belong to this church.

Ministers usually take training at Meadville affiliated with the University of Chicago, Harvard Divinity School, or Starr

King School for the Ministry, near the University of California.

Humanitarian activities are carried on throughout the world by the Unitarian Universalist Service Committee. This might take the form of civil rights work in Atlanta, social work training in Korea, community centers in Rhodesia, medical programs in Haiti, birth control clinics in Nigeria. The Committee was organized in 1940 to aid refugees from Nazi tyranny. The Committee conducts its projects on a nonsectarian basis.

The Unitarian Universalist Association belongs to the International Association for Liberal Christianity and Religious Freedom which claims to represent some 1,500,000 Europeans. The American denomination also maintains friendly relations with the Universalist Church of the Philippines, the Philippine Unitarian Church, the Non-Subscribing Presbyterian Church of Ireland, and Unitarian churches in Hungary and Czechoslovakia.

Freedom is the characteristic theme of contemporary Unitarianism. No one in the Unitarian Universalist church expects any other member to hold any particular belief or subscribe to any creed. A member who believes in the unique mission of Jesus and the inspiration of the Bible may sit beside another Unitarian Universalist who denies the existence of God.

At the same time it is not difficult to predict Unitarian Universalist positions on given issues. A Unitarian Universalist will usually support civil rights, easier divorce laws, abortion, euthanasia, a strict interpretation of separation of church and state, birth control, sex education programs, prison reform, mental health, the United Nations, cremation or simple burials, urban renewal. They will oppose capital punishment, censorship, war, the John Birch society.

Sharing many Unitarian Universalist positions are such other groups as the Ethical Culture Societies, the American Humanist Association, the Hicksite Quakers, and Reform Jews. The New York Ethical Culture Society was founded in 1876 by Dr. Felix Adler. The 21 local branches seek "to assert the supreme importance of the ethical factor in all relations of life—personal, social, national and international—apart from any theological or metaphysical considerations." It has about 6,000 members. The Fellowship of Religious Humanists, founded in 1963 and affiliated with the American Humanist Association, promotes the cause of humanistic religious living and ethical religion. Some members of mainline Protestant denominations may also favor a unitarian theology.

Unitarian Universalism faces the future with confidence. The 1961 merger and the rapid growth of the Fellowships have given the denomination a much larger base than ever before. It has a well-educated ministry, a distinguished publishing program and an influence out of all proportion to its numbers.

Millions of Americans hold basic Unitarian Universalist positions but do not belong to the denomination. The Unitarian Universalists are making strong efforts to gain converts. It has even launched an advertising campaign to attract inquiries. But, the question is whether liberal religion can appeal to the liberal who works in a factory instead of a university, who reads *Life* instead of *Harper's* or *The Nation*, who holds a high school diploma instead of a college sheepskin or Ph.D.

Standing outside of the Christian family, the Unitarian Universalists do not stand outside of the pale of dialogue with Christians. Cardinal Cushing addressed the UUA's general assembly in 1965 and called for a continuing dialogue between Catholics and Unitarian Universalists as the "link between Christianity and secular humanism." He added that "both secular humanism and Christianity have a thirst for social justice and the discussion of this fact alone brings us closer to the theological postulates by which social justice can be demanded." The Boston cardinal noted that there are Unitarian Universalists "still oriented toward the insights of the Christian message" and others whose faith "is more profoundly based on man."

Unitarian Universalism, freed of all but vestigial Christian traditions, presents itself as a religion which can exert a strong appeal to secular humanists who do not wish to go it alone. These people can find fellowship, spiritual inspiration, counseling, organized outlets for humanitarian work through this denomination. In past years neither the Unitarians nor Universalists excelled at missionary work or organization. Both of these problem areas seem to be getting attention and we may expect to see Unitarian Universalism assume a larger role among American religions.

Further Reading

Mendelsohn, Jack, *Why I am a Unitarian Universalist* (Boston, Beacon, 1964).

Parke, David B., *The Epic of Unitarianism* (Boston, Starr King Press, 1967).

Chapter XX

THE OLD CATHOLICS

Who Are the Old,
Polish National, and Liberal Catholics?

REUNION of separated Christian churches and communions has been one of the major long-range goals of the Second Vatican Council and the ecumenical movement. It now appears that one of the most likely reunions will involve the Roman Catholic Church and the Old Catholic Churches. The latter began in protest against the doctrine of papal infallibility defined by the First Vatican Council.

On November 7, 1966, Bernard Cardinal Alfrink of Utrecht and Andreas Rinkel, Old Catholic archbishop of Utrecht, joined in a eucharistic service in St. Gertrude's Church. Both prelates extended a joint blessing at the common service on the feast of St. Willibrord, first bishop of Utrecht and patron saint of the Netherlands.

During the unprecedented rite it was revealed that Rome's insistence that Old Catholics assent to the bull *Unigenitus* prior to any theological dialogue had been abandoned. This bull condemned Jansenism in 1713. Rome's new position was clarified in a letter from Augustin Cardinal Bea, president of the Secretariat for Promoting Christian Unity.

A reunion of the Old Catholics and the Roman Catholics would affect about 150,000 Old Catholics in Holland, Germany,

Austria, Switzerland, Yugoslavia, and Czechoslovakia. Whether it would also extend to the Polish National Catholic Church (282,000 members) which traces its priestly orders through Old Catholicism is unknown.

Rome already recognizes as valid the ordination of Old Catholic priests and consecration of Old Catholic bishops. Those who organized the Old Catholic movement in 1870 presented one of their leaders for consecration by the Church of Utrecht which had been separated from Rome since 1724. The legitimacy of Utrecht's orders has never been questioned by Rome.

The history of Old Catholicism, especially in its American expressions, is complicated and often bewildering. Both saints and ecclesiastical adventures have called themselves Old Catholics. To get some idea of this movement we will examine four groups of churches which identify themselves as Old Catholic.

First, continental Old Catholic churches which subscribe to the Declaration of Utrecht of 1889. Second, the numerous small churches and sects, especially in the United States, which have taken the Old Catholic label but which enjoy no recognition from the original Old Catholic churches of Europe. Third, the Polish National Catholic Church whose membership in the United States, Canada, and Poland makes it the largest Old Catholic communion by far. Fourth, the amazing mixture of Old Catholicism and Theosophy known as the Liberal Catholic Church.

The dogma of papal infallibility proclaimed in 1870 aroused the lively opposition of thousands of Roman Catholics in Germany, Switzerland, and Austria. Some 1,400 Germans alone signed a statement declaring that the dogma was an innovation. Leader of the resistance was Dr. Ignaz von Dollinger, professor of theology at Munich. He declared: "As a Christian, as a theologian, as a historian, as a citizen, I cannot accept this doctrine."

In 1871 about 300 delegates met at the first Old Catholic congress in Munich. No Roman Catholic bishops joined the protesters but a number of priests allied themselves with the Old Catholics. Since the Old Catholics valued the apostolic succession and realized that they would be unable to ordain new priests or administer confirmation without a bishop, they sought consecration from the schismatic Church of Utrecht.

During the 17th century a number of Jansenists fled from France to predominantly Protestant Holland. They were received with hospitality by the Dutch Catholics but considered heretics by the Vatican. When the majority of Dutch bishops and priests refused to accept the bull against Jansenism in the early 18th century the Church of Utrecht went into schism.

For many decades this Church of Utrecht continued as a Roman Catholic but ostracized church. This Church dutifully informed the pope when it elected a new bishop and the popes regularly replied with decrees of excommunication. At the start of the schism three out of five Dutch Catholics sided with the schismatics but by 1815 the Utrecht Catholics numbered only 6000 while those in communion with Rome exceeded 1,000,000.

Originally the Church of Utrecht had no bishop. A French bishop traveling to his new post in Babylon by way of Amsterdam was prevailed upon to confirm 600 children at Utrecht. For this and other activities he was suspended by Rome and settled in Amsterdam. In 1724 he consecrated a priest of the Church of Utrecht who died the next year. The suspended bishop—Dominicus Marie Varlet—consecrated three other priests of Utrecht and it is through Petrus Johannes Meindaarts that Utrecht and the Old Catholics trace their orders.

It was to the remnant of the Church of Utrecht that the Old Catholics turned in 1873. Prof. Josef Reinkens of Bonn was elected first bishop of the Old Catholic Church and consecrated by the bishop of Deventer.

Dollinger himself respected the excommunication of the Roman Catholic church and ceased to perform spiritual functions as priest. He encouraged the Old Catholic movement but balked at the idea of organizing separate parishes and abolishing clerical celibacy. He died at the age of 91 and received the rites of the Old Catholic church.

In many areas the new Old Catholic churches sided with anti-clerical governments and received material support in return. The governments of Prussia, Baden and Hesse favored the Old Catholics who also sided with Bismarck in his *Kulturkampf*.

Over the years the Old Catholic churches introduced a number of changes into the religious life which their adherents had followed while Roman Catholics. In 1874 fasting and confession were made optional and the next year the Church removed the *Filioque* from the creed and eliminated the granting of indulgences. The Old Catholics adopted a vernacular liturgy in 1880. Pastors were elected by the people. Clerical celibacy was no longer required in Germany and Switzerland after 1878 although the Dutch Old Catholics insisted on celibacy until 1922.

Except for a small mission in South Africa the Old Catholics engage in no missionary work. They recognized the validity of Anglican orders in 1925 and signed an agreement at Bonn in 1931 to enter intercommunion with the Anglican churches. In 1965 the churches subscribing to the Declaration of Utrecht entered into full sacramental union with the Philippine Independent Church (the Aglipayans) which claims 1,500,000 members.

A representative of the Old Catholic churches attended the sessions of Vatican II and a Vatican observer attended the 19th International Congress of Old Catholics in 1965. This meeting, held in Vienna, brought together 400 Old Catholic delegates from 17 countries and included 22 bishops. Two Old Catholic bishops from Poland were denied travel permits.

At the present time there are about 40,000 Old Catholics in Germany, 40,000 in Austria, 28,000 in Switzerland, 12,000 in Holland, 5,000 in Czechoslovakia, and small communities in Poland and Yugoslavia.

No one would suggest that after almost a century of existence the Old Catholic churches have achieved the membership or influence that their founders anticipated. At the same time we can see certain changes in Roman Catholicism in such areas as the vernacular liturgy, fasting, the abolition of the Index, and the married diaconate which were foreshadowed by the Old Catholics.

The irrelevancy of the Jansenist controversy in the modern world, the willingness of Old Catholics to reexamine the role of the papacy and the concept of collegiality, and the renewal of Roman Catholicism have combined to encourage the Old Catholics and the Roman Catholics to investigate reunion possibilities.

Cardinal Bea wrote to the Old Catholics: "An encounter which is conducted in the spirit of faith and in Christian charity is the first step on the road toward the hoped for unity." Theological committees from both churches are meeting to discuss the issues which must be resolved to achieve reunion.

All the churches in the United States which use "Old Catholic" in their titles derive their orders from questionable sources and stand outside the fellowship of the legitimate Old Catholic churches of Europe. Only the Polish National Catholic Church is recognized by the Europeans and holds valid orders.

The chronicler of these independent Old Catholic churches, Peter Anson, estimates there are more than 150 such bodies in the United States, England, Australia and other countries. His definitive 593-page study of these fascinating sects, *Bishops at Large,* describes most of them in detail.

These sects pretend to some degree of legitimacy only because the Roman Catholic church follows the Augustinian theory of orders. This theory states that a validly consecrated bishop retains the power to transmit valid but irregular orders even though he separates himself from the rest of the Church. In practice, however, the Roman church ignores the orders received by apostates from schismatic bishops. If such individuals return to the Catholic church they may not say Mass nor are they bound to celibacy or to recitation of the divine office.

The establishment of these wildcat churches follows a familiar pattern. Someone, possibly a former Roman Catholic or Anglican priest, obtains what he believes to be valid consecration as a bishop. He founds his own "Old Catholic" church or outmaneuvers rival bishops in his home church. These bishops regularly excommunicate each other, make up, start new churches, return to Rome, or construct elaborate paper churches with few or no members.

These "Old Catholic" prelates put primary emphasis on valid orders and often tolerate the oddest theological teaching, even Theosophy. They enjoy the ritual of Catholicism and the titles which they assume: Catholicos, Hierarch, Mar, Metropolitan, Monsignor, Pontifex, Primate, Patriarch, etc. It seems the smaller the church following the more grandiose the titles and the larger the hierarchy. A tiny band of such "Old Catholics" may be served by a metropolitan, a couple of archbishops, and a group of bishops.

These assorted "Old Catholic" churches attract disaffected Roman Catholics and Anglicans. Some make frankly nationalistic appeals to Poles, Italians, and others who are dissatisfied with Roman Catholicism as they experience it in the United States. No one should take the membership claims of these U.S. "Old Catholic" groups too seriously. When they say thousands they mean hundreds of adherents.

Two former Roman Catholics provided orders to most of the groups in the United States and England claiming to be Old Catholic. One of these gentlemen—Joseph Rene Vilatte—was ordained by an Old Catholic bishop in Switzerland but was consecrated a bishop by a Jacobite bishop in Ceylon. The other —Arnold Harris Mathew—was ordained a Roman Catholic priest and consecrated by the Dutch Old Catholic bishops. About 20 churches each trace their orders to the Vilatte and Mathew successions.

Vilatte was born in Paris in 1854. His father, a butcher, belonged to a tiny schismatic sect called the *Petite Eglise* but Vilatte became a Roman Catholic and was educated by the Christian Brothers. After service in the French army during the Franco-Prussian war Vilatte emigrated to Canada. He left Canada for France and then Belgium and became a novice Christian Brother. This did not last long. Vilatte went back to Canada and began studies for the priesthood for the diocese of Montreal.

For a time he left the Church but soon afterwards he was found at the house of study of the Viatorian Fathers in Bourbonnais, Illinois. In Illinois he got in touch with Pastor Chiniquy, an apostate priest from Canada. Chiniquy advised Vilatte to leave the Roman church and labor as a Presbyterian missionary among the Belgians in Wisconsin.

Now Vilatte contacted the Episcopalian bishop of Fond du Lac and suggested that he be ordained an Old Catholic and coordinate his evangelistic efforts with the Anglicans. Bishop J. H. Hobart Brown believed Vilatte and the latter's estimate that 8,000 Belgians were "inclined to the principles of a pure and primitive

Catholicism" as preached by the former Catholic-Presbyterian. The bishop wrote to the Swiss Old Catholics: "Mr. Vilatte's character for piety, sobriety, purity, intelligence and prudence has been attested to the satisfaction of the authorities of this diocese." Vilatte sailed for Europe and was ordained by the Old Catholic Bishop Herzog in 1885.

Back in Wisconsin Fr. Vilatte opened several churches and missions in the Green Bay area. These were financed by the Episcopalians. His relationships to his benefactors were disrupted when Fr. Vilatte expressed a desire to be consecrated a bishop while refusing to allow the Episcopalian bishop to confirm his parishioners because he doubted the validity of Anglican orders.

A flirtation with the Russian Orthodox Church in Alaska did not last long. Meanwhile the Episcopalian bishop of Fond du Lac reported Fr. Vilatte's actions to the Old Catholics in Switzerland, which squelched any chance that they might raise him to the episcopacy.

Fr. Vilatte had heard about a small body of schismatic Catholics in Ceylon and South India. The priest who headed this Independent Catholic Church of Ceylon, Goa and India had been consecrated by a Jacobite bishop. He agreed to consecrate Vilatte in 1891. Vilatte now called himself the Archbishop of the Old Catholic Church of America.

The Episcopalian bishop of Fond du Lac lived to regret his sponsorship of Vilatte. Eventually he branded the wandering bishop as "morally rotten" and a "swindling adventurer."

Anson doubts if Vilatte ever had more than 500 followers in Wisconsin. When he left this state these people became Episcopalians, Roman Catholics, or spiritualists. One happy aftermath of the Vilatte episode was the arrival of the Norbertine Fathers who were sent to counteract his influence. Today the Norbertines number 174 priests and 14 Brothers and operate a college, several high schools, a radio-TV station, and parishes.

Calling himself Mar Timotheos, Vilatte traveled around England, the Continent, Canada and France. For a time he made Chicago his headquarters and started the American Catholic Church in 1915 and also the African Orthodox Church, largest surviving church claiming the Vilatte succession.

In 1925 Vilatte rejoined the Roman Catholic church and took up residence in a Cistercian monastery near Versailles. At first he refrained from exercising his orders but he succumbed on at least one occasion and raised a monk to the episcopacy. Rome never recognized the validity of his orders nor treated him like a bishop.

Mar Timotheos consecrated at least seven bishops during his career and no one knows how many priests were ordained by the colorful prelate. He died in 1929 and was buried in the monastery cemetery.

The American Catholic Church which he founded was taken over by a former Episcopalian minister, Frederick Ebenezer Floyd, in 1920. He consecrated a number of other bishops before his death in 1932. This church has been reduced to a few hundred members. Two other tiny American churches trace their lineage to Vilatte's work: the American Catholic Church (Syro-Antiochean) and the American Catholic Church (Archdiocese of New York).

Vilatte consecrated George Alexander McGuire, a Negro, in 1921. He was a former Episcopalian missionary in the West Indies and he soon surrounded himself with four other bishops. This Negro church was plagued by schisms after Bishop McGuires' death in 1934.

The other prolific church founder was Arnold Harris Mathew. Born in 1852 in France, he was baptized a Roman Catholic but rebaptized at the age of two in Anglican rites at his mother's insistence. He began studies for the ministry of the Church of England but reverted to Roman Catholicism. A bright student, he completed philosophy and theology studies in only 18 months and was ordained a priest in 1877. For a few months he tasted the life of the Dominican order but returned to the diocesan priesthood. In 1889 his parishioners received a notice that their pastor could no longer serve them since he had abandoned belief in the fundamental doctrines of Christianity and was attracted to Unitarianism.

The next year Mathew changed his name to Count Arnoldo Girolomo Povoleri. In 1892 he married and subsequently fathered three children. He announced that he again accepted the doctrines of the Church but remained a suspended priest. He spent about ten years as a lay Catholic author without revealing his clerical background.

Count Povoleri now became convinced that England was ripe for the Old Catholic message. He got in touch with the continental Old Catholics in 1907 and finally persuaded the Dutch Old Catholic bishops to consecrate him. When the conservative Dutch Old Catholics discovered that their episcopal candidate was married and had a family they backed away from the consecration but finally agreed to proceed with the plan. The count was raised to the episcopacy on April 28, 1908.

Mistaken in the reception which Old Catholicism would receive in the British Isles, Bishop Mathew went ahead with the consecration of two former Roman priests. This outraged the Dutch bishops since it violated the Declaration of Utrecht. The count declared his independence of the continental Old Catholics. Before long he raised four more priests to the episcopacy so that his church boasted seven bishops for about 100 faithful.

Among the men he consecrated was an Austrian nobleman, the Prince de Landas Berghes et de Rache, who would bring the Mathew succession to American shores. Mathew also consecrated the man who would lead the remnant of the English Old Catholic church into the wilds of Theosophy.

Mathew returned to the Roman Catholic Church briefly in 1915 but was soon back in the labyrinthine ways of Old Catholicism. He died in 1919 and was buried with Anglican rites.

Besides the Liberal Catholic Church, the Theosophical stepchild of English Old Catholicism, the Mathew succession is claimed by a variety of "Old Catholic" churches in England and the United States.

Prince de Landas Berghes consecrated two bishops in America before he returned to Roman Catholicism in 1919; he spent the rest of his life teaching at Villanova University. One of the men he consecrated founded the Old Catholic Church in America, also known as the Catholic Church of North America and the Orthodox Old Catholic Church in America. This bishop was William Henry Francis Brothers who once started a tiny Old Catholic monastery in Waukegan, Illinois. His church, reduced to a few priests and a handful of laity, was received into the Russian Orthodox Catholic Church in America in 1962. This is the smallest of the three Russian Orthodox bodies in this country. For 46 years Brothers had called himself archbishop and metropolitan but he had to submit to reordination when he joined the Russian Orthodox Church. His aim was to promote Western rite Orthodoxy.

One of Brothers' collaborators, Joseph Zielonka, parted company with him in 1940 and set up the rival Polish Old Catholic Church. He was succeeded in 1961 by a former Roman Catholic priest, Archbishop Peter A. Zurawetsky, who lives in Rahway, New Jersey. The name of this small church was changed to Christ Catholic Church. In 1970 it claimed 16 parishes and 5,500 members.

Another bishop consecrated by the prince was Carmel Henry Carfora, an ex-Franciscan priest. Born in Italy, Fr. Carfora had been sent to work among the Italian immigrants in Chicago. He left the Roman Catholic Church after disagreements with his superiors and started several schismatic parishes. With episcopal consecration he launched the North American Old Roman Catholic Church of which he was the "Most Illustrious Lord, the Supreme Primate."

Carfora enrolled disaffected Italians, Poles, Lithuanians, ex-Roman priests, West Indian Negroes, former Episcopalians, and Mexicans. He appointed five bishops for as many nationality groups. When the primate died in 1958 this church split into two factions: one is headed by Hubert A. Rogers and claims 18,500 adherents and the other, headed by Gerard George Shelley, claims 88,788. Both membership figures are highly exaggerated.

The Yearbook of American Churches also lists the Reformed Catholic Church (Utrecht Confession) which reports 2,217 members in 20 parishes. The source of this church's orders is uncertain. Its head, Archbishop W. W. Flynn, has criticized the Old Catholics of Europe for falling under Anglican domination.

By far the largest single component of worldwide Old Catholicism is the Polish National Catholic Church. This church also represents the only serious schism in the history of American Catholicism. It reports more than 282,000 members in 172 parishes in the United States, 18 in Canada, and others in Poland.

For the first time an American-born prelate heads this church. Bishop Thaddeus F. Zielinski, a native of Wilkes-Barre, Pa., was named in 1969 to succeed the late Prime Bishop Leon Grochowski. The new prime bishop has sought ways to retain the loyalty of second generation Poles whose knowledge of the language and customs is limited. He celebrated Mass in English rather than Polish in his Buffalo cathedral as long ago as 1961 and has translated and published the first English catechisms, prayerbook, ritual, and hymns for his church.

In externals a Polish National Catholic church looks much like a Roman Catholic church with altar, tabernacle, statues, stations of the cross, sanctuary lamp, holy water fonts, etc. At Mass Polish National Catholic priests wear vestments identical with those of the Latin rite.

In addition to most of the holy days observed by the Roman Catholic Church, the PNC Church has added a number of unique feast days such as the feasts of the Poor Shepherd, the Remembrance of the Dear Polish Fatherland, Brotherly Love, and the Christian Family. The church also holds special commemorations for Polish patriots and for heroes and reformers such as Huss, Savonarola, and Peter Waldo.

Although the Polish National Catholics believe in seven sacraments they have added a new sacrament, the Word of God; they combine Baptism and Confirmation into one sacrament. The faithful receive the sacrament of the Word of God by hearing the reading of the Scriptures. Young people must go to confession to the priest but after the age of 20 they may receive absolution in a general public confession at Mass which does not involve an enumeration of specific sins. If they wish, older members may also continue to avail themselves of private confession.

The sacramentals of the Polish National Catholic Church would be familiar to Roman Catholics: the sign of the cross, the Angelus, holy oils, holy water, candles, ashes, palms, incense, crucifixes, and images. Devotions to the Blessed Virgin play an important part in the religious life of Polish National Catholics.

Despite its strongly nationalistic appeal, it has been able to attract only about one out of 20 Polish Americans. The faithfulness of the Polish people to the Roman Catholic church in this country as well as in Poland is well known. Probably no ethnic group has a smaller percentage of defections from the Church. For example, the number of Poles in the United States who have embraced Protestantism does not exceed 6,000. An estimated 4,000,000 Americans claim Polish ancestry, most of whom reside in Massachusetts, Connecticut, New York, New Jersey, Pennsylvania, Ohio, Michigan, Illinois, and Wisconsin.

Sts. Cyril and Methodius brought the gospel to the Slavic people in the 9th century. In 965 the Poles accepted Catholicism. They rejected the new religious doctrines of the Hussites and Lutherans during the Reformation period and have remained stalwart defenders of the faith to the present day when the Catholic Church in Poland must carry on its mission in an officially Communist state.

Hundreds of thousands of Poles immigrated to the United States before World War I and brought with them their Catholic faith and ethnic customs. The parish served as a family and community center for these new Americans. They preserved their Polish Christmas carols, the Kolenda, and the Gorzkie Zale lamentations in memory of the passion of Christ. The Polish language was used in sermons, church periodicals, and parochial schools.

The Polish immigrants soon discovered, however, that the Church in the United States was not governed by Polish bishops but by bishops of Irish and German descent. Even though these bishops helped establish more than 850 predominantly Polish parishes some Polish nationalists objected to their treatment at the hands of non-Polish prelates. Sometimes it became necessary to appoint non-Polish priests as pastors of Polish parishes. These priests were usually unable to speak and preach in Polish and their appointments sometimes aroused hostile feelings.

Several groups of separated Poles emerged to form the present Polish National Catholic Church. In 1895 a curate in Chicago, the Reverend Antoni Koslowski, organized an independent parish, All Saints, for a group of Poles who objected to the way they were treated by the hierarchy. He was consecrated by a bishop of the Old Catholic Church in Switzerland in 1897 and proceeded to organize parishes in what he called the Polish Old Catholic Church. By the time of his death in 1907 he had started 23 such parishes.

A dispute over control of church property led to the formation of an independent parish in Buffalo, New York, called Our Lady of the Rosary, in 1895. The pastor, the Reverend Stanislaus Kaminski, was consecrated a bishop by an Old Catholic bishop in 1898. Bishop Kaminski died in 1911 and several years later his followers joined the previously organized Polish National Catholic Church.

Meanwhile in Pennsylvania a group of Poles, mainly miners and factory workers, demanded greater control of parish affairs of Sacred Heart parish in Scranton. They were admonished by their bishop, and the controversy continued until it resulted in a fist fight in front of the church which led to the arrest of 20 participants. The dissidents appealed for support to a former Scranton priest who had become pastor of a church in nearby Nanticoke. He was the Reverend Francis Hodur, a 30-year-old priest who had been born and ordained in Poland.

Fr. Hodur agreed to lead the 250 families who built a new church and named it St. Stanislaus. Their new pastor traveled to Rome to plead their case, saw two cardinals but obtained no satisfaction.

Hodur began publishing a weekly newspaper, *The Sentinel*, in which he outlined the three major principles of the new independence movement. These were: control by the Polish people of all churches built and maintained by them; the right of Polish Catholics to administer their own church property through a parish committee; and the right to choose their own pastors. These demands conflicted with the established forms of church property control drawn up by the Council of Baltimore.

Hodur was excommunicated in 1898 and burned the document of excommunication in the presence of his congregation. He celebrated the first Mass in the Polish language on Christmas eve in 1900.

Other independent congregations joined the Hodur group in the following years. A synod was held in Scranton in 1904 representing about 16,000 dissident Poles. The delegates elected Father Hodur to be their bishop but the Old Catholics hesitated to consecrate him as long as Bishop Koslowski was living. When he died the Old Catholics consecrated Hodur in St. Gertrude Church in Utrecht.

The 1904 synod also acted to translate all Latin service books into Polish, cooperate with Protestant denominations, and repudiate the claims of the Roman Catholic Church to be the one true church.

The Polish National Catholics set up the Polish National Union in America to provide insurance benefits for members who had left Roman Catholic fraternal societies. They established their own cemeteries when their deceased members were denied burial in Catholic cemeteries. Further changes were authorized in a synod in 1921. Over some opposition by lay delegates the synod approved marriage of the clergy. Bishop Hodur never married but most bishops and priests in recent years have been married; newly ordained priests must wait two years before marriage. The 1921 synod also authorized a mission to Poland and elected four more bishops who were consecrated in 1925 by Bishop Hodur.

One of these bishops served the Lithuanian National Catholic Church which had been organized by four parishes in 1914. Since his death the Lithuanian parishes have been visited by Polish National Catholic bishops. Membership in the Lithuanian branch has dropped from 5,672 in 1953 to fewer than 4,000 today.

For some years Bishop Hodur tutored those young men who wished to prepare for the Polish National Catholic priesthood but eventually the church opened a small seminary in Scranton. About a dozen students are enrolled in the practical three-year course in Savonarola Seminary. All instruction is in the Polish language; the students study no Latin, Greek or Hebrew. The six main courses are in scripture, philosophy, church history, Polish history, moral and doctrinal theology. The seminary admits high school graduates.

Hodur guided the destiny of the new church from 1897 until his death in 1953. He made 14 trips to Poland and during the last eight years of his life he was blind. In many ways Hodur's theological views on such questions as original sin, eternal punishment and the unique role of Christ were unorthodox. This does not mean that all of his views have become normative. Since his death the Polish National Catholic Church seems to have drawn closer to traditional Christian positions. A visit by the Old Catholic Archbishop of Utrecht has also helped steer the PNCC away from unitarianism.

Bishop Hodur emphatically denied the doctrine of eternal punishment. He declared that is would show a lack of confidence in the justice and mercy of God to believe in an eternal hell. "He would not deliver His creatures into the power of evil spirits, for them to torment or destroy," he wrote. A man's conduct on earth somehow determines his status after death but eventually all men will attain the goal of union with God, Hodur believed. The soul may undergo purification or cleansing after death but will never be lost.

He claimed to place a high value on apostolic succession and membership in the Holy Catholic Church which, he said, was composed of all baptised Christians. At the same time he would declare: "The leaders of the PNCC are of the opinion that before God and before America all beliefs, all sects, are equal. If God did not wish a certain sect to exist, He would not give it the necessary powers to exist and develop."

Although the PNCC baptizes infants, it denies the doctrine of original sin. The author of the church's catechism, Bishop Zielinski, explains:

"We do not teach original sin as in the Roman Catholic Church—that it comes down to us from the origin of the human race, and that we inherit it through our descent from Adam. We do not teach that man is born with a depraved nature.

"We do teach that man is born with an inclination to do evil; but that is not original sin in the Roman Catholic sense."

Accordingly the PNCC has changed the rite of baptism. Where the Roman ritual says: "Depart from him, thou unclean spirit, and give place to the Holy Spirit, the Comforter," the Polish National Catholic ritual says: "Receive the Holy Spirit, the Comforter, promised by Jesus Christ."

The Polish National Catholic Church recognizes only the first four ecumenical councils and its General Synods as authoritative. In contrast, the Eastern Orthodox acknowledge the authority of the first seven councils and the Catholic Church has held its 21st ecumenical council.

The second Prime Bishop of the Polish National Catholic Church was the Most Reverend Leon Grochowski. He was born in Poland in 1886 and ordained by Hodur in 1910. The Prime Bishop consecrates other bishops, examines candidates for the priesthood, directs Savonarola Seminary and other church institutions, and controls the church's publications program. Bishop Grochowski died in Poland in 1969 where he was organizing a meeting of bishops in Warsaw.

The PNCC forbids divorce and remarriage although the Prime Bishop may grant annulments. The church has taken no stand on artificial contraception; it leaves the use of various forms of birth control methods to the wishes of the couple. Polish National Catholics are free to join the Masonic lodges or any other organization which is not condemned by the state.

Authority in faith, morals, and discipline resides with the Prime Bishop and clergy while authority in social and economic matters is shared by the laity. The top administrative body is the General Synod; each parish is entitled to send one delegate for each 50 active members.

The church sent a bishop to Poland in 1925 to supervise missionary work in the homeland. He consecrated a native Polish bishop in 1930 but when the latter began to remarry divorced people contrary to church law he was deposed by Hodur. Another Polish bishop was consecrated in 1936; he survived the war but was imprisoned by the Communists and died in prison in 1951. Since then the National Church in Poland has cut all jurisdictional ties with the church in the United States.

The PNCC in Poland enrolls about 60,000 adherents. It maintains dioceses in Warsaw, Cracow, and Wroclaw.

The Polish National Catholic Church embraces four dioceses in the United States. The Central Diocese whose see city is Scranton includes eastern Pennsylvania, New York, New Jersey, and Maryland and is presided over by the Prime Bishop. The Eastern Diocese whose see is Springfield, Mass. includes all parishes in New England. The Northern Diocese includes western Pennsylvania and western New York and has its see in Buffalo. Chicago is the see of the Western Diocese which embraces Ohio and all points west.

This church maintains intercommunion with the Protestant Episcopal Church, the Old Catholic churches of Europe, and the Independent Church of the Philippines (Agilpayan). Prime Bishop Zielinski recently participated in the consecration of three bishops for the latter church. The PNCC belongs to the National Council of Churches of Christ and the World Council of Churches.

The Polish National Catholic Church signed an agreement of intercommunion with the Episcopalian Church in 1946. This was similar to the intercommunion agreement between the Anglican and Old Catholic churches in 1931. The agreement observed, "Intercommunion does not require from either Communion the acceptance of all doctrinal opinion, sacramental devotion, or liturgical practice characteristic of the other, but implies that each believes the other to hold all the essentials of the Christian faith." Since 1946 some Polish National Catholic bishops have participated in consecrations of Episcopalian bishops.

Growth of the Polish National Catholic Church since 1926 has been greater than the overall growth of the Polish American community but the great majority of Poles have remained loyal Roman Catholics. The fires of intense nationalism have banked in recent years and this has affected the Polish American community as well as other ethnic groups. Fewer Americans become fluent in a language other than English, limit marriage to members of their own ethnic group, and see themselves primarily as members of an ethnic minority.

Recently Bishop Grochowski told his church leaders that he had furnished information on the episcopal consecrations of Polish National Catholic bishops to Abbot Laurentius Klein, O.S.B., at the latter's request. Abbot Klein planned to forward this information to Cardinal Bea of the Secretariat for Christian Unity. Bishop Grochowski told the Supreme Council of his church that it is "willing to unite with any Church." He added, "We came to the conclusion that if we are really united with the Lord, as we should, then unity will come of itself."

For the first time in the history of the PNCC a Roman Catholic priest attended this church's general synod in 1967. Msgr. Eugene Clark represented the Roman Catholic bishop of Scranton at the meeting which was composed of 120 clerical and 430 lay delegates.

Bishop Zielinski told the general synod: "Christians must face the world with a single front, a single voice, and a single faith."

By Liberal Catholic in the context of this study we do not mean a Roman Catholic who reads *Commonweal* and questions *Humanae Vitae* or clerical celibacy. The Liberal Catholic Church derives its orders from the Mathew succession but receives no recognition from continental Old Catholics—for good reason. The mixture of Catholicism and occultism found in Liberal Catholicism can only be described as weird.

By 1915 most of the clergy of Archbishop Mathew's Church had become Theosophists. This occult religion was founded by an eccentric Russian noblewoman, Madame Helena Blavatsky, and propagated by Annie Besant. Madame Blavatsky claimed to receive mysterious spiritual instruction from invisible Masters. Her religion combined elements of Hinduism, pantheism, Christianity, spiritualism, Freemasonry, Buddhism, and other Eastern cults.

Archbishop Mathew consecrated a former Anglican clergyman, Frederick Samuel Willoughby, who was a convinced Theosophist. He in turn consecrated another Theosophist, James Wedgwood. Mathew lost control of the situation and the Theosophists took over the apparatus of his church and renamed it the Liberal Catholic Church (Old Catholic). The new management promised stately ritual and valid orders but the greatest freedom of religious thought. In a few years the Liberal Catholics started missions in Australia and the United States.

The Liberal Catholics deny communion to no one who approaches their altars. They introduced the dialogue Mass in 1934, several decades before Rome gave her approval. They allow no crucifixes or images of the dead Christ in their churches.

As Theosophists the Liberal Catholics believe that the Christ principle has appeared many times in history. Jesus was only one manifestation of this principle. Not only Christianity but many other world religions are divinely inspired and therefore the Liberal Catholics do not proselytize.

Reincarnation is a basic belief. Man dies and is reborn in a long cycle of death and life. Purgatory is simply the time and place between reincarnations; there is no hell.

Priests of this church do not accept salaries or stipends and support themselves at secular jobs. Their congregations are usually small. Liberal Catholic priests often use the parlors of their homes as chapels which seat perhaps 25 worshippers.

In 1947 the Liberal Catholics in this country, who never numbered more than 4,000, suffered a schism. Now the strict Theosophists recognize a bishop who resides in Minneapolis while the smaller body, leaning more to orthodox Christianity, has its headquarters in Los Angeles.

The Theosophists acknowledge the spiritual authority of an English bishop as presiding bishop of the church. He is the Rt. Rev. Sir Hugh Sykes of London. Bishop Sykes in active in the Theosophical Society and in Co-Masonry, a form of Freemasonry which admits both men and women. In secular life the bishop works for the firm which publishes the London telephone directory.

There are regionary bishops for dioceses in Austria, Germany, Switzerland, France, French Africa, Belgium and Holland, the Scandinavian countries, Australia, New Zealand, Great Britain and Ireland, and the United States. The sect has recently established missions in Latin America.

Considering the occult orientation of Liberal Catholicism and the type of personality often drawn to such esoteric movements, the wonder is that this church has maintained relative stability for more than 50 years. Rome would probably take a negative position regarding the orders of Liberal Catholicism since the Liberal Catholics are not schismatic Christians but devotees of a non-Christian cult, Theosophy.

Whenever reunion is discussed, Roman Catholics must distinguish clearly between the Old Catholics who are bound by the Declaration of Utrecht and the numberless sects which call themselves "Old Catholic." The possibility of reunion with the continental Old Catholics is genuine, especially since each church recognizes the validity of the other's orders. Attempts to engage in serious dialogue with the adventurous, ambitious, and romantic personalities who populate the "Old Catholic" world would have slim chance of success.

Further Reading

Andrews, Theodore, *The Polish National Catholic Church in America and Poland* (London, S.P.C.K., 1953).

Anson, Peter, *Bishops at Large* (London, Faber and Faber, 1964).

Moss, C.B., *The Old Catholic Movement* (London, S.P.C.K., 1948)

Chapter XXI

THE EASTERN ORTHODOX

Churches of East and West Divided Since 11th-Century

WHEN Pope Paul VI and Patriarch Athenagoras I lifted the mutual excommunications in 1965 which had precipitated the division of the Christian community into Eastern and Western churches, they took an important step in reconciliation. The ecumenical patriarch holds the position of spiritual leader of the estimated 125 million Eastern Orthodox.

Almost 90 percent of all Orthodox Christians now live in Communist countries but Orthodoxy remains the main Christian denomination in Eastern Europe and the Middle East. Almost all Greeks and Eastern Slavs who profess Christianity follow the Orthodox faith.

Since 1054 the Roman Catholic and Orthodox churches have gone their separate ways although several attempts at reunion have been made. Each church recognizes the other's bishops as standing in the apostolic succession, admits the validity of priestly ordinations, confers seven sacraments, venerates the Blessed Virgin and the saints, fosters monasticism, and adheres to basically the same theology. Yet theological and cultural differences have kept the two Churches of the East and the West apart for 900 years.

Orthodoxy means "right belief" and identifies the various national churches which make up Eastern Orthodoxy. These churches are known as autocephalous; they elect their own bishops who form a Synod and are led by a patriarch, metropolitan, or archbishop.

The ecumenical patriarch of Constantinople holds a primacy of honor among Orthodox prelates. For centuries the number of faithful directly under the ancient patriarches of Constantinople, Alexandria, Antioch, and Jerusalem have been relatively small; at present they total only about 1 million.

The strength of Orthodoxy lies in the autocephalous churches of Russia, Greece, Yugoslavia, Bulgaria, Cyprus, Rumania, and Georgia. There are also semi-independent churches in such countries as Poland and Finland; Orthodox missionary churches are found in Japan, Uganda, Tanzania. All legitimate Orthodox bodies acknowledge the jurisdiction of one of the patriarchs or autocephalous churches. In theology they adhere to the decisions of the seven ecumenical councils held between A.D. 325 and 787.

To Orthodox Christians their church is the "One, Holy, Catholic, and Apostolic" church which was founded by Jesus Christ and which had preserved the faith intact. A contemporary statement of the Greek Orthodox church in the United States maintains that Orthodoxy is the "authentic and infallible interpreter of the faith in dogmas as contained in the Symbol of Faith (or Nicene Creed) in an unbreakable continuity."

This conviction that Orthodoxy is the one true church has not kept the Orthodox aloof from the ecumenical movement. All the major Orthodox churches, except those of Serbia and Albania, belong to the World Council of Churches; Archbishop Iakovos of the Greek Archdiocese of North and South America serves as one of the five WCC presidents. Most Orthodox churches also hold membership in the National Council of Churches. Relations between Roman Catholics and Eastern Orthodox have not been more cordial in many centuries.

Another name for the Eastern Orthodox is Greek Orthodox. This does not mean that most Orthodox are Greeks anymore than Roman Catholic means most Catholics are Romans. But early Christianity was propagated through the Greek language. The New Testament was written in Greek as were the works of the

Fathers of the church. Greek was the language even of the Latin church until the 3rd century.

Christianity naturally took on some of the characteristics of the East and the West as it matured. The first serious trouble took place in 862 when Pope Nicholas refused to recognize the election of Photius as patriarch of Constantinople. This dispute was finally settled but the seeds of separation were sown.

When a papal legate excommunicated the patriarch in 1054 and the patriarch excommunicated the pope the break was complete. The savagery of the crusaders who sacked Constantiople and the Church of Holy Wisdom in 1204 further estranged the Byzantines from Rome.

Meanwhile the Orthodox brought the Christian gospel to the Slavs and to the descendants of Roman settlers known as Rumanians. With the baptism of Vladimir Russia accepted Orthodoxy in 988. After the fall of Constantinople in 1453 to the Ottoman Turks Russia assumed the leadership of world Orthodoxy. For 400 years the non-Russian Orthodox lived under the rule of the Turks. The ecumenical patriarch still resides in Istanbul, Turkey.

In 1589 the archbishop of Russia was elevated to the position of patriarch. Church and state were closely allied until the Russian Revolution when an atheist government sought to eradicate religion from the lives of the people. The effort has not been wholly successful. A few years ago when the Russian Orthodox church applied for membership in the World Council of Churches it reported between 30 and 90 million members, 73 bishops, 30,000 priests, 20,000 parishes, 40 monasteries and eight seminaries.

The Church of Greece remains the only Orthodox body which is a state church. Until 1852 it was under the jurisdiction of the ecumenical patriarch. Until recently this branch of Orthodoxy has been ultraconservative and has looked with disfavor on closer relations with Roman Catholics and Protestants. Such movements as the ZOE brotherhood of theologians and upgrading of seminary training have injected new life into the 8,500,000-member Church of Greece.

Americans of Greek and Slav descent make up the 4 million Eastern Orthodox in the United States. Since parish membership is often determined by the number of men over 21, some Orthodox scholars suggest that the total Orthodox constituency in the United States may be closer to 5 million. They are concentrated in the larger cities of the East, Middle West, and West coast.

Eight Russian monks founded a mission on Kodiak Island in 1794 when Alaska was still owned by Russia. Within two years they had baptized 12,000 natives. About 80 years later the Russian Orthodox bishop of Alaska moved his see to San Francisco. When Russian immigration began to snowball he moved again to New York City in 1905.

Most Greeks came to these shores after 1880 and built Greek Orthodox churches where they settled. So did Ukranians, Serbians, Rumanians, Bulgarians, Syrians and others. Before World War I the Russian Orthodox diocese and bishops served Orthodox of all nationalities. They encouraged the introduction of English in liturgy and were moving toward formation of an American Orthodox Church but the events of the Russian Revolution disrupted these plans.

Suspicious of the influence of Communism on Russian church officials the various national groups organized separate Orthodox bodies in the United States. Recent years have seen a renewed interest in a federation of all Orthodox groups in this country. Orthodox young people seem to prefer an English liturgy and development of a single Orthodox church. Formation of a Standing Committee of Orthodox Bishops in 1960 may speed the day when such unification may become a reality.

The *Greek Archdiocese of North and South America* was not organized until 1922 but now claims the largest Orthodox membership: about 1,875,000. It maintains 470 churches, 250 parochial schools, and a seminary in Brookline, Massachusetts. Patriarch Athenagoras served as archbishop of the archdiocese from 1930 to 1948 before his election as ecumenical patriarch.

The majority of Russian Orthodox reject any jurisdiction by the Patriarch of Moscow. The *Russian Orthodox Greek Catholic Church of America* claims 1 million adherents under the spiritual rule of nine archbishops and bishops. A second group, the

Russian Orthodox Church Outside Russia maintains that the Moscow patriarchate is no longer even a true Orthodox church because of its relationship to an atheist regime. It claims 55,000 members.

A Russian bishop arrived in New York City in 1926 and seized St. Nicholas cathedral but only two parishes accepted his authority. Those who did formed the *Russian Orthodox Catholic Church in America, Patriarchal Exarchate*. This body launched a Western rite in 1962 and engages in missionary work in Puerto Rico and among Spanish-speaking Americans.

The Syrian Orthodox in this country accept the jurisdiction of the patriarch of Antioch and number about 160,000. A group of immigrants from the mountain region of eastern Czechoslovakia had been members of the Uniate church in their homeland; they preserved Byzantine customs and liturgy but recognized the primacy of the pope. Some of these Uniates left the Catholic church and set up the *American Carpatho-Russian Orthodox Greek Catholic Church* in 1938. They have 104,000 members in 69 churches including a cathedral in Johnstown, Pennsylvania. Other national bodies of Orthodox include the Serbians (65,000), Ukranians (127,000), Bulgarians (86,000), Rumanians (50,000), and Albanians (17,000).

In recent years the Orthodox have pressed for recognition as the fourth major faith along with Protestantism, Catholicism, and Judaism. More than half the states have officially granted such recognition. Orthodox prelates offered invocations at several presidential inaugurations. GIs can request a dog tag marked "EO" to identify their religious faith. Orthodox priests serve as chaplains in the armed forces. Orthodox students on college campuses join a single Orthodox student foundation. Candidates for the priesthood from the various national churches study at the six Orthodox seminaries; the two main ones are the Greek seminary at Brookline and the Russian Orthodoxy seminary in Crestwood, New York.

Americans of Greek and Slav backgrounds, generally late arrivals in the wave of immigration, are gaining prominence. Some have entered political life such as Vice President Spiro Agnew (an Episcopalian) and former Mayor George Christopher of San Francisco. Others have won fame in other fields such as aircraft manufacturer Igor Sikorsky and movie magnate Spyros Skouras.

The religious life of the Orthodox Christian is sustained by the seven Mysteries or sacraments. Infants are baptized by triple immersion. Chrismation or confirmation is usually administered immediately after baptism by the priest. Orthodox are expected to receive holy communion at least once a year; the trend is toward more frequent, even weekly, communion. Communicants receive both bread and wine. Sins are forgiven in the sacrament of repentance and confession.

Orthodoxy considers Christians united in the sacrament of matrimony to be partners in an indissoluble union but unlike Roman Catholicism Orthodoxy allows divorce and remarriage in certain situations. For example, the church will grant a divorce for adultery or other immoral conduct, impotence prior to marriage and continuing for two years, desertion for more than two years, apostasy or heresy, long-term insanity. It strongly discourages mixed marriages. The church equates abortion with murder and generally condemns birth control.

The ministry of the Orthodox church includes bishops, priests, and deacons. Parish priests are almost always married men but bishops are chosen from the ranks of celibate monks or widowers. Married men may be ordained priests but priests may not marry. This means a priest may not remarry if his wife dies.

The seventh sacrament, Holy Unction, is administered for the restoration of health of body and soul. The priest anoints the body with oil and prays for the welfare of the recipient.

The Divine Liturgy or Mass is the highest act of Orthodox worship. The Orthodox tradition has been to celebrate the liturgy in the language of the people while the Western church retained Latin until a few years ago. In the United States the Greek Orthodox allow English only for the sermon but Russian and other Orthodox bodies regularly employ the vernacular in the liturgy. The Divine Liturgy takes from one to three hours and is always sung.

An icon screen or iconostasis divides the worshippers in the nave from the altar in an Orthodox church. Icons are two-dimensional images of Christ, the Blessed Virgin, and the saints and have always been objects of deep devotion in the Eastern church.

Orthodox monks live according to a rule drawn up by St. Basil in the 4th century. In this respect the Eastern church differs from the Roman church which embraces many different religious orders such as Franciscans, Jesuits, Dominicans, etc. By far the most famous Orthodox monastery is Mt. Athos which was founded in 963. About 2,000 monks live in a cluster of 20 separate monasteries on Mt. Athos. There are also Orthodox nuns.

Although much closer to Roman Catholicism than is Protestantism Orthodoxy differs from Rome in several respects. For example, the Orthodox acknowledge the bishop of Rome, the pope, to be the patriarch of the West and will accord him a primacy of honor; they refuse to admit his supreme jurisdiction and infallibility. The Orthodox object to the word "filioque" in the Nicene creed, believe that the Virgin Mary was cleansed from original sin at the Annunciation rather than at her conception, do not define the dogma of the Assumption of Mary, do not believe in the system of indulgences.

The Eastern church also differs from the Roman church in its eschatology. It has no doctrine of purgatory. Orthodox believe that each individual undergoes a particular judgment immediately after death. The soul then enters an intermediate state between heaven and hell until the last judgment at the Second Coming. Orthodox offer prayers for the dead but do not believe that such prayers affect the condition of the dead.

Many Orthodox resent the existence of the Eastern rites of the Roman Catholic church. About 12 million Catholics including 700,000 in the United States follow the liturgy and customs of the Eastern church but acknowledge the primacy of the pope. They are directly subject to Eastern patriarchs in union with Rome.

Both East and West are attempting to heal the centuries-old separation. Patriarch Athenagoras declared recently: "Christians must realize that they have one church, one cross, one gospel." The Fathers of the Second Vatican Council rejected the idea that the differences between East and West are insurmountable. In the Decree on Ecumenism they declared: "With regard to the authentic theological traditions of the Orientals, we must recognize that they are rooted in an admirable way in Holy Scripture, fostered and given expression in liturgical life, and nourished by the living tradition of the Apostles and by the works of the Fathers and spiritual writers of the East; they are directed toward a right ordering of life, indeed, toward a full contemplation of Christian truth."

Further Reading

Benz, Ernest, *The Eastern Orthodox Church* (New York, Doubleday, 1963).

Constantelos, Demetrois J., *The Greek Orthodox Church* (New York, Seabury, 1967).

French, R.M., *The Eastern Orthodox Church* (London, Hutchinson University Library, 1951).

Meyendorff, John, *The Orthodox Church* (New York, Pantheon, 1962).

Chapter XXII

THE JEWS

God's Mystery People

WE CAN hardly imagine what the world would be like if it had not been decisively influenced by descendants of a small Semitic tribe which took form more than 3,000 years ago. From this people came the chief Western religions of Judaism, Christianity, and Islam. From them came such figures as Moses, Jesus, Karl Marx, Sigmund Freud, and Albert Einstein who reshaped human history. In a world of 3 billion Gentiles the 13 million Jews continue to uphold ancient beliefs and traditions.

Common sense would tell us that the Jews should have disappeared centuries ago. In the year 70 the Romans destroyed the Temple in Jerusalem and scattered the Jews throughout the world. Christians and Muslims tried to convert the Jews; many did accept the newer faiths but millions kept their Jewish identity. Hitler murdered 6 million Jews in what the Nazis called the "final solution" to the Jewish problem but the Jews remain.

Most Jews are Caucasians but there are also Chinese, Negro, and Indian Jews. If not by blood then by conversion all Jews claim to be children of Abraham. He was a nomad who traveled from Chaldea to the land of Canaan now known as Israel. His vision of God as one, loving, and merciful was passed on to his son, Isaac, and his grandson, Jacob. Jacob led the tribe to Egypt to escape a severe famine but there they were enslaved. Still they held fast to their belief in the one God and were led out of bondage by Moses about 1280 B.C. En route to their ancient homeland Moses underwent a transforming experience on Mount Sinai which led to the proclamation of the Ten Commandments.

Through a long history of prosperity and disaster, freedom and bondage, apostasy and religious fervor the Jews were called back to their simple creed: "Hear, O Israel, the Lord our God, the Lord is One." Calling the Jews back to their spiritual heritage and ideals were the prophets: Isaiah, Jeremiah, Ezekiel and others.

In their darkest hours the Jews looked for a Messiah who would usher in a new age for mankind. About 1900 years ago a rabbi called Jesus proclaimed himself that Messiah, gathered a band of followers, and was crucified. Most Jews rejected Jesus as the long-awaited Messiah but his disciples established a sect within Judaism. For a while the Christians continued to attend the synagogue, follow the Jewish laws, and submitted to circumcision but finally broke away from Judaism and carried the Christian message to the Gentiles. Paul became known as the apostle to the Gentiles. The Christians accepted Jesus not only as the Messiah but as God incarnate, the second person of a Trinity. They continued to use the Jewish scriptures but added a New Testament.

Six centuries later an Arabian teacher, Mohammed, also accepted the Old Testament and acknowledged the prophethood of Jesus but declared that Allah is God and Mohammed was his prophet. He founded Islam which became one of the major religions of Africa and Asia. Through Christianity and Islam the Jewish beliefs in monotheism, in revelation, and in the commandments would be carried to billions of Gentiles.

The first Jews to come to the New World came from Spain and Portugal. For centuries the Jews had lived in relative peace under the Moorish rulers of Iberia. Some Jews, the Marranos, accepted Christian baptism under duress but continued Jewish practices within the family. The Inquisition saw no possibility of uniting Spain unless the Jews were driven out. Ferdinand and Isabella signed the expulsion order in 1492 and many Jews eventually looked for haven in South America.

A party of 23 Jews came from Brazil to New Amsterdam in

1654. For a brief period they had enjoyed freedom in Brazil under the Dutch but faced renewed persecution when the Portuguese returned to power. If not welcomed by the Dutch they were at least tolerated. These Portuguese founded the first congregation in North America, Shearith Israel in New York City. Another group of Jews settled in Newport, Rhode Island and dedicated Touro synagogue in 1763; this building still stands and has been designated a national shrine. Another Jewish settlement was made in Savannah, Georgia.

Forbidden to own land in the Old World the Jews in the colonies tended to settle in the cities where they became merchants and traders. By the time of the American Revolution their number had risen to about 2,000. Almost all had come from Spain or Portugal. Jews served under Washington in the Revolution and favored the cause of the colonists.

After the defeat of Napoleon and again after the failure of the 1848 rebellion thousands of Jews from the ghettos of Germany came to the United States. Jewish peddlers carried goods from city to city and started many of America's department stores.

One Jew, Judah P. Benjamin, represented Louisiana in the U.S. Senate. At the outbreak of the Civil War he became Attorney General in the Confederate cabinet and then Secretary of War and Secretary of State. After the South's defeat Benjamin fled to England.

Starting in 1881 waves of Russian and Eastern European Jews sought refuge from the Czar's pogroms in America. For centuries the rulers of Russia had forbidden Jews to live in that country. But in 1654 the Czar took the Ukraine and inherited the Jews living there; later when Poland was partitioned the Czar gained an additional 1 million Jewish subjects. By law these Russian Jews were confined to shabby villages along the western border. The fierce persecutions directed by Alexander III drove the Jews to seek safety elsewhere. Between 1881 and 1924 more than 2 million came to this country.

The tenements of the lower East Side of New York City absorbed many of these immigrants. Like other Jews they brought not only their religious faith but their love of learning.

They spoke Yiddish, the daily language of East European Jewry; it was a German dialect written with Hebrew characters. Many Jews entered the garment industry and worked long hours in the sweatshops. Jews entered the labor movement and organized unions such as the International Ladies Garment Workers Union. Samuel Gompers became one of the founders of the AFL and served as its president for almost 40 years.

Several factors helped the Jews to achieve success in American society. They found a freedom denied them in the ghettos of Europe. They worked hard, provided the best possible education for their children, seldom wasted money on liquor or gambling, maintained a stable family life, helped one another. Today the Jewish community provides a disproportionate number of the nation's scientists, physicians, lawyers, writers, musicians, entertainers, college professors, artists.

Because of the virtual extinction of the European Jewish community the Jews in the United States have become the largest and most influential section of world Jewry. Of the 5,720,-000 Jews in the United States more than 1,800,000 live in New York City. There are also 500,000 Jews in the Los Angeles area, 265,000 in Chicago, 185,000 in Boston, and 100,000 in Miami. Jews comprise about 3 percent of the total population.

Worldwide there are an estimated 13,538,000 Jews of whom half live in North and South America. The state of Israel has provided a home for 2,344,000 Jews and the USSR counts 2,543,-000 Jews within its borders. Other large concentrations of Jews can be found in France (520,000), Argentina (450,000), Great Britain (450,000), Canada (275,000), Brazil (140,000) and Rumania (120,000). The once flourishing Jewish communities in Germany and Poland have been reduced to about 30,000 in each country.

The pious Jew follows the Torah, the Talmud, and the Prayer Book. The Torah consists of the first five books of the Bible (Genesis, Exodus, Leviticus, Numbers, and Deuteronomy). The Talmud provides the rabbinical commentary on the Torah. Strictly speaking an orthodox Jew must keep the 613 rules of Halaka but many of these are obsolete laws involving agriculture or property.

Observance of the Sabbath is basic to Jewish life. From sunset Friday to sunset Saturday the devout Jew leaves the things of the secular world and enters a world of prayer and family celebrations. Orthodox Jews will not travel, cook, write, use electrical appliances, buy or sell, light fires, or smoke on the Sabbath. The Sabbath begins when the mother lights the candles at the festive table 20 minutes before sunset and the father says the prayer over the wine.

Throughout the year Judaism marks the seasons and the religious events of her history with festivals. There is Passover in spring, Shavuous in summer, and Sukos in the fall. The minor feast of Hanaka has assumed increasing importance in recent years as a sort of Jewish counterpart of Christmas. Even Jews who seldom attend a synagogue or temple during the year will try to observe the High Holy Days in the fall. Ten days after Rosh Hashanna, the Jewish New Year, comes Yom Kippur or the Day of Atonement. Many Jews observe a 24-hour fast from food and drink and spend all day in the synagogue. This is the day on which man makes peace with his God.

Traditional Jews follow a regimen of daily prayers. During morning prayer he wears a shawl called a tallis and a head covering which is usually a skull cap called a yarmulka. He affixes phylacteries or tefillin to his forehead and left arm. These are black leather boxes containing small scrolls.

Orthodox and Conservative Jews observe dietary laws which continually remind them of the covenant between God and Israel. These laws demand that a Jew will eat no flesh cut from a living creature, will drink no blood, will not mix milk and meat at the same meal, will not eat certain fats such as suet. Certain foods such as ham, pork, lobster and shrimp are forbidden. Animals must be slaughtered in a ritual way in order to qualify as kosher.

The infant male is circumcised eight days after birth. Of course, circumcision has recently become a common practice among Gentiles as well. The young Jew of 13 becomes a full member of the congregation at his bar mitzvah. After years of study under a rabbi he reads the scriptures in Hebrew and perhaps delivers a short sermon. A similar rite called the bas mitzvah has been introduced into many congregations for girls of 12½ years.

Women are excused in Judaism from prescribed daily prayers and attendance at the synagogue since their tasks are seen to be primarily in the home. In Orthodox synagogues men and women sit in separate sections.

The Torah allows polygamy but this has not been allowed in Judaism for 1,000 years. Bride and groom in a Jewish wedding are married under a canopy, receive seven blessings, and break a wine glass. Married couples in the Orthodox branch follow a sexual code which traditionally forbids marital relations during the menstrual period and for seven days thereafter. Judaism upholds the permanence of the marriage bond; the Jewish divorce rate is low but the religion allows numerous grounds for divorce.

Traditionally the dead are buried as soon as possible in a shroud and wooden coffin. Embalming is forbidden unless required by law. The mourners recite the Kaddish at the fresh grave and during the 11 months of mourning.

Almost all Jews believe in an after life but Judaism discourages speculation on the nature of the immortality of the soul. Judaism rejects the concept of original sin and the Christian idea of salvation. It also rejects the idea of eternal punishment or hell.

Because of the influence of the Enlightenment and the liberation of the Jews from the restrictions of the ghetto, many Jews in the early 19th century were shedding Judaism and becoming Christians or agnostics. The Reform movement in Germany sought to adapt Judaism to modern life by denying the normative value of many laws and traditions. The Reform leaders preferred a religion of ethics to one of laws. They changed the liturgical language from Hebrew to the vernacular, introduced organ music, allowed men and women to sit together, abandoned the dietary laws and prescribed daily prayers. Instead of a personal Messiah the Reform Jews spoke about a Messianic age for mankind. Isaac Mayer Wise became the leading Reform spokesman in the United States; Cincinnati became the center of Reform Judaism. Contemporary Reform has reintroduced some Hebrew and some of the older traditions.

To certain Jews uneasy with the radical nature of Reform the abandonment of traditional elements had gone too far. They formed the Conservative movement which seeks to occupy a middle ground between Orthodoxy and Reform. Conservatives keep the dietary laws and Hebrew liturgy but allow mixed seating and some vernacular. Conservatism owes a deep debt to Solomon Schechter who came to the United States from Cambridge University to head the Jewish Theological Seminary (founded in 1886). About 600 Jewish congregations can be identified as Conservative which is approximately the strength of Reform Judaism.

Each of the three branches of Judaism in the U.S. has its own affiliated congregations, seminaries, rabbinical organizations, day schools, lay organizations, publications, etc. About one third of U.S. Jews are Orthodox, one half of Jews in Israel, and most Jews elsewhere. Of 6,000 synagogues in Israel only nine are not Orthodox.

Within Orthodoxy various sects interpret the Torah and Talmud in their own ways. For example, the Hasidim movement began in the Polish ghettos by Baal Shem (1700-1760) and combines Judaism with the magic and forklore of the Cabala. The Cabala is the expression of Jewish mysticism which corresponds to Gnosticism in Christianity; it concerns itself with numerology and angelology which hold little interest for most Jews. The Hasidim attach themselves to a Rebbe or wonder worker and remain suspicious of secular education. Yet the movement has had a considerable influence on Martin Buber. The Hasidim can be identified by their long earlocks, fur hats and beards. They live in certain neighborhoods in Brooklyn and other cities.

Recent years have seen a blossoming of Jewish grade and high schools in this country. In 1945 there were only 49 such schools but by 1968 the number had risen to 339. American Jewry has founded only two institutions of higher education outside of rabbinical seminaries. These are the Yeshiva University in New York City which includes the Albert Einstein College of Medicine and the Brandeis University in Waltham, Massachusetts. The Hillel foundations serve Jewish students and scholars on many campuses.

The number of Jewish organizations devoted to charity, culture, Zionism and other causes runs into the hundreds. Twelve Jews founded the B'nai B'rith mutual aid society in 1843 which supports Hillel groups and the Anti-Defamation League. Others established the Young Men's Hebrew Association, Jewish counterpart of the YMCA. All three of the major Jewish denominations support these organizations. At least 200 periodicals are published in the United States in English, Yiddish, and Hebrew.

Judaism is a family-centered religion but the synagogue or temple also serves the community. Each synagogue is an independent body although it may belong to larger associations. The congregation hires and fires the rabbi and sets the pattern of religious observances.

At least ten male Jews are needed to offer public worship; even nine rabbis could not offer such worship. The service consists of prayers, the chanting of psalms, and the reading of the Torah. A rabbi (literally a teacher) has no powers which any Jewish male does not have; his role in worship can be assumed by any man in the congregation. Of course, a rabbi is trained in rabbinical school and is expected to strive for holiness and scholarship but he receives no special spiritual authority as does, say, a Catholic or Eastern Orthodox priest. The rabbi preaches and teaches, marries and grants divorces, conducts funerals and other ceremonies.

In a thousand ways American Jews have enriched the nation's culture. For example the field of music includes George Gershwin, Nathan Milstein, Mischa Elman, Benny Goodman, Jascha Heifetz, Leonard Bernstein, Jerome Kern, Irving Berlin, Richard Rodgers, Arthur Rubenstein, Yehidi Menuhin, and Aaron Copland.

Survival in the ghettos and in times of trouble demanded a self defense of humor. Perhaps this partially explains the number of Jewish comedians: Jack Benny, Jerry Lewis, Eddie Cantor, Alan King, Ed Wynn, Milton Berle, the Marx Brothers, Danny Kaye, Shelley Berman, Charlie Chaplin, George Burns, Art Buchwald, Sam Levinson, Myron Cohen.

The supreme court of the United States has been served by Louis D. Brandeis, Benjamin Cardozo, Felix Frankfurter, Abe

Fortas and Arthur Goldberg. Jews have been governors, senators, congressmen. The names of Lehman, Javits, Ribicoff come to mind. Barry Goldwater, whose grandfather was a Jewish peddler, is an Episcopalian.

Americans sew dresses on a machine invented by Singer. Their children are protected from the ravages of polio by a vaccine bearing the name Salk. They read the Jewish-owned *New York Times.* They enjoy the plays of Arthur Miller.

Despite the prosperity of American Jews and the lessening of anti-Semitism in this country Judaism faces serious problems. The survival of Judaism in Soviet Russia is a matter of deep concern. Only 100 synagogues remain open to serve the millions of Russian Jews; the government forbids the religious education of children in the faith and harrasses the Jews in many ways. The state of Israel lives in a state of constant tension with her Arab neighbors who are armed by the Communists.

The threat of assimilation in the United States grows as anti-Semitism declines because the outside pressure on the Jewish community eases. Far more Jews become Christians or abandon all religion each year than the 2,500 converts who adopt Judaism. (Some recent converts to Judaism have been Marilyn Monroe, Sammy Davis, Jr., and Elizabeth Taylor.)

Most of the children of Jewish-Gentile marriages lose all contact with their Jewish heritage and such intermarriages are on the increase. No large-scale immigration of Jews can be expected, Judaism receives few converts, Jewish families are small, and many Jews shed their faith as they merge into the society. In 1937 the Jewish percentage of the U.S. population was 3.7; by 1980 it is expected to drop to only 2 percent. Almost 1,000 rabbinical posts are vacant.

Yet for the first time in almost 1900 years the Jews govern a nation of their own and have demonstrated their determination to defend it to the death. European Jews, those who survived the Nazi era, have a chance to rebuild their communities. American Jews make an enormous contribution to almost every area of society. Jews worry about assimilation, the survival of the state of Israel, persecution, latent anti-Semitism but the ancient faith remains.

Further Reading

Epstein, Isidore, *Judaism, a Historical Presentation* (New York, Pelikan, 1959).

Steinberg, Milton, *Basic Judaism* (New York, Harcourt, Brace, and World, 1947).

Trapp, Leo, *Eternal Faith, Eternal People* (Englewood Cliffs, N.J., Prentice-Hall, 1962).

Wouk, Herman *This is My God* (Garden City, N.Y., Doubleday, 1959).

Yaffe, James, *The American Jews* (New York, Random House, 1968).

Chapter XXIII

THE MUSLIMS

Youngest of World's Major Religions
Claims 450 Million Followers

MOST Americans go through life without ever meeting a Muslim although the religion of the Muslims—Islam—rivals Christianty in size and influence on the world scene. In the Arab countries North Africa, Pakistan, and Indonesia the estimated 450 million Muslims constitute the dominant faith and way of life.

This religion started in Arabia in the seventh century when a religious genius known as Mohammed proclaimed that God (Allah) is one and that he (Mohammed) is his prophet. Influenced by Judaism and Christianity, Mohammed acknowledged that Abraham, Moses, and Jesus were also prophets but that Mohammed was the final revelator of God's will.

Mohammed (probably born in A.D. 570) lived in Mecca which was a trading center also known for its religious shrine, the Kaaba. This was a huge cube-shaped structure full of idols and a black meteorite. Some Jews and a few Christians lived in Mecca but most of the people were polytheists.

Mohammed worked as a shepherd, camel driver, and merchant and finally married a widow some 15 years his elder. He cultivated a deep interest in religion and meditation but despised the idolatry of most of his fellow Meccans. As he later recounted the Angel Gabriel appeared to him during one of his periods of meditation and began to dictate the words of what became the Muslim Bible, the Koran. These revelations from the angel and from Allah continued for 20 years.

At first Mohammed's converts consisted of his wife and a few friends who formed what was almost a secret society in Mecca. As their views became known the townspeople who profited from the pagan pilgrimages turned against them. Mohammed fled to the city of Yathrib (renamed Medina) in 622 which became the year 1 of the Islamic calendar.

Far more successful in winning converts in Medina Mohammed led his forces in an attack on Mecca and entered his hometown in triumph in 630. He destroyed the idols in the Kaaba but retained the black stone as an object of veneration and promised the city fathers to continue the pilgrimages. Before his death in 632 the prophet had unified most of central and southern Arabia. In a few decades his followers, sometimes through the Holy War or Jihad, had won over most of the Middle East and North Africa. The Muslims swept into Spain, Portugal, and France but were defeated by the Franks at the battle of Tours in 732. Almost all the Christian communities of Africa disappeared in the Muslim advance.

Islam means "to submit" to the will of God; Muslims object to being identified as Mohammedans since they insist they follow God (Allah) rather than any man. Mohammed is revered as the greatest prophet but in no sense a divine person or messiah. He never distinguished himself as a miracle-worker or ascetic.

Muslims believe that God's final word to mankind is given in the 200,000-word Koran. The book is mainly a series of maxims grouped in 114 chapters or *suras*. It expresses the simple theology of Islam that God is one and that Mohammed is His prophet. The anthropomorphic character of Islam startles some Christian observers. For example, the afterlife is described in very human terms. Hell is described in terms of intense heat, scalding water, and hot winds. But the faithful Muslims can anticipate a heaven of gardens, wine, and abundant sexual opportunities.

Islam rejects polytheism as well as the Christian doctrine of the Trinity. The religion honors Jesus as one of the messengers of Allah but in no sense a divine person. Islam pays particular respect to Mary as the Mother of Jesus; she is mentioned 34 times in the Koran and is honored above Mohammed's favorite wife and his daughter Fatima. Mohammed taught that Mary and her mother Anne were the only women not touched by the power of Satan.

The religious life of the Muslim demands daily prayers, recited at daybreak, noon, midafternoon, sunset, and early evening. The strict fast of Ramadan is imposed on all believers except the sick, aged, very young, and pregnant women. During this lunar month Muslims must not eat, drink, take medicine, or engage in sexual intercourse between sunrise and sunset. Each Muslim is expected to make at least one pilgrimage to Mecca during his lifetime. All pilgrims wear the identical seamless white robe; they walk seven times around the Kaaba, run seven times between two hills in Mecca, and make a journey to the Mount of Mercy about 25 miles away. Unbelievers are forbidden to enter either Mecca or Medina. Other religious requirements of Islam include the declaration of faith (the shahada) and almsgiving.

Islamic culture flourished in the 9th, 10th, and 11th centuries when the Muslims invented algebra, pioneered in medicine, and made important contributions in art, poetry, and philosophy. The schisms and sects within Islam weakened its impact but the imposition of colonial rule did more to limit its influence. In recent years foreign rule has ended and Islam is strong in more than a score of independent African and Asian nations.

Islam has won notable success in winning adherents in black Africa. In contrast to Christian missionaries the Muslims offer a simply theology, easy initiation, no objection to polygamy. Islam has no sacraments or prescribed ritual, no images. Although the Muslims once prospered as slave traders they do not bear the colonial stigma which handicaps many Christian missionaries in Africa and Asia.

Islamic society is strongly patriarchal. The role of women has been far more subservient than in Judaism or Christianity. Traditionally the Muslims have kept their women in seclusion and heavily veiled; this custom is still strictly observed in a country such as Pakistan but is ignored in modern Turkey. The Arabs of Mohammed's day practiced unlimited polygamy. The prophet revealed: "Of women who seem good in your eyes, marry but two, or three, or four; and if ye still fear ye shall not act equitably, then one only." The devout Muslim will never have more than four legal wives at one time although divorce is a simple procedure. Economic reasons and the rise of women's rights movements have discouraged polygamy in most Islamic societies. Mohammed himself hed 14 wives and three concubines.

Like Christianity Islam has not escaped fragmentation. Besides the majority Sunnites there are the Shias who predominate in Persia and have constituencies in India and Indonesia. The Kharijites form a Puritan elite and the Wahhabites seek to reform Islam from the taint of liberal tendencies.

The Arab-Israeli war has intensified hatreds between these two Semitic people but both share a number of beliefs and customs. For example, Muslims honor the Old Testament prophets, circumcise boys, forbid pork, worship one God. Muslims, despite the memories of the Crusades, display less animosity toward Christians. "Christianity and Islam have no animosity. We both aim to serve God and should cooperate in the fight against Communist atheists," declares Sheikh Siraj of the Moslem World League.

The Declaration on the Relationship of the Church to Non-Christian Religious of Vatican II looks on the Muslims with esteem:

"They adore one God, living and enduring, merciful and all-powerful, Maker of heaven and earth and Speaker to men. They strive to submit wholeheartedly even to His inscrutable decrees, just as did Abraham, with whom the Islamic faith is pleased to associate itself. Though they do not acknowledge Jesus as God, they revere Him as a prophet. They also honor Mary, His virgin mother; at times they call on her too with devotion. In addition they await the day of judgment when God will give each man his due after raising him up. Consequently they prize the moral life, and give worship to God especially through prayer, almsgiving, and fasting.

"Although in the course of the centuries many quarrels and

hostilities have arisen between Christians and Muslims, this most sacred Synod urges all to forget the past and to strive sincerely for mutual understanding. On behalf of all mankind, let them make common cause of safeguarding and fostering social justice, moral values, peace, and freedom."

Not more than 20,000 Muslims are reported in the 15 to 20 Muslim centers in the United States. The Arab countries built an Islamic Center in Washington, D.C. in 1953 which includes a mosque, library, and classrooms. Small communities of Muslims live in New York, Chicago, Philadelphia, Pittsburgh, San Francisco, Los Angeles, Sacramento, and Toledo. Better known to most Americans are the Black Muslims.

The Black Muslims

Although Islam has always emphasized the equality of all races, the hybrid form of Islam led by Elijah Muhammed frankly preaches black supremacy. His followers belong to what they call the Nation of Islam but they are popularly known as Black Muslims.

They are anti-white, anti-Christian, and anti-Jewish. Elijah Muhammad declares: "Christianity is a religion organized and backed by the devils for the purpose of making slaves of black mankind." He works for racial separation and attacks any Negro leaders or organizations who seek integration.

No one knows for sure how many Black Muslims are affiliated with the 47 Temples of Islam around the country. The number certainly exceeds 10,000. The Black Muslims have won most of their converts in Northern ghettoes. There they find recent immigrants from the rural South who find nothing but misery and frustration in the inner city. Without education or marketable skills they have no hopes of improving their lot by moving away. They expect to live and die in the ghetto.

The Nation of Islam offers them an escape and a sense of pride of race. The colored races will soon take control of the world, promises Elijah Muhammad. The black man must abandon Christianity and return to Islam which is said to be the proper religion for all but the "white devils."

Using the tithes of the faithful, Elijah Muhammad has started to build an economic empire. He sees this as a way to win the material resources necessary for separation from the larger white society. Recently the sect bought a 1,430 acre farm in Albany, Ga. and a 1,000 acre one in Cassopolis, Mich. The Black Muslims operate restaurants, grocery stores, dry cleaning plants, a printing plant, bakeries, and warehouses. They have announced a goal of controlling 2 million acres within 10 to 15 years.

A mysterious peddler-preacher, who claimed to have come from Arabia, started the movement in Detroit in the early 1930's. Known as Prophet W. D. Fard, he drew on such sources as the Bible, the Koran, Freemasonry, and the literature of Jehovah's Witnesses. He attracted the allegiance of several thousand Negroes before his disappearance in 1934. Today Black Muslims consider him to be God or Allah incarnate.

With Fard out of the picture control of the tiny cult passed to his lieutenant Elijah Muhammad, born Elijah Poole to a Baptist preacher and his wife in Georgia. Of limited education he worked at odd jobs during these Depression years and joined Fard's cult. His first step was to move headquarters from Detroit to Chicago.

Muhammad's followers scarcely numbered more than a few hundred until after World War II. He himself was jailed from 1942 to 1946 on charges of sedition and inciting his people to resist the draft. Out of prison he purchased a former synagogue on the city's South Side and expanded his missionary work.

Other temples or mosques were opened in Detroit, Milwaukee, and Washington, D.C. He set up the University of Islam in Chicago which now enrolls about 350 children in grades 1 through 12. His newspaper, *Muhammad Speaks,* is sold on street corners in the black neighborhoods and claims a circulation of 385,000.

Publicity in national magazines brought the movement to public attention as did the notoriety attached to the life and death of Malcolm X. He was a former convict and dope addict who joined the Black Muslims and became the popular minister of the New York City Temple. Malcolm X left the Elijah Muhammad organization in 1964 to launch his own black movement but he was assassinated on Feb. 21, 1965 as he was about to address a rally of 400 followers in a Harlem ballroom. Three men who were identified as Black Muslims were convicted of the slaying.

Even though the Black Muslims make a special effort to win converts in prisons and pool halls they expect all members to adhere to a strict moral code. Many applicants fail to qualify or backslide after they have joined. The code forbids liquor and tobacco, extramarital sex relations, drugs, dancing, sports, gambling, motion pictures. Black Muslims may not eat pork or other specified foods, straighten their hair, use more than a minimum of cosmetics, act in a boisterous or loud manner. They are urged to eat only one meal a day; chubby Muslims are reprimanded until they diet off excess pounds. Members have been suspended for varying periods for dozing during Temple meetings, fraternizing with Christians, flirting with women, or eating forbidden food.

The sexual standards of the Nation of Islam are exceptionally high for people living in this type of environment. The Muslims insist that their women wear modest clothing which covers their legs and arms. Fornication or adultery is cause for immediate dismissal. Women hold no positions of authority in the Nation and are outnumbered by the men, but they are held in great respect.

Black Muslims do not vote in local or national elections but black politicians are forced to recognize their influence in the black community. Elijah Muhammad's weekly newspaper column is carried by a number of Negro newspapers not affiliated with the sect. Muslim rallies draw thousands of blacks who do not belong to the movement.

Elijah Muhammad retains full control of the Nation of Islam although each Temple is under the direction of a minister. Malcolm X posed the only threat to his power. Muhammad lives in the Hyde Park area of Chicago but also spends time at his home in Phoenix, Ariz. His wife, six sons, and two daughters are all involved in the movement.

The form of Islam propagated by the Black Muslims bears little resemblance to orthodox Islam. Elijah Muhammad's peculiar racial doctrines find no parallel in worldwide Islam. The Black Muslims ignore such prescriptions as the Ramadan fast. They deny that a white man can embrace Islam even though the Arabs are Caucasians.

Some of the cult's doctrines bear a close affinity to those of Jehovah's Witnesses. Man has no soul and is not immortal; only Allah is immortal. There is no heaven or hell. After the coming of the battle of Armageddon, expected in the 1970s, the black man will assume his rightful control of this planet.

One of the basic myths of the Black Muslims is that the white man was not created by Allah but was the invention of a black genius called Yakub. When Yakub accomplished this mutation through scientific techniques he was cast out of paradise for his crime. This was about 6000 years ago. Yakub is also known as Adam, the father of the Caucasians.

In contrast to the white man, a late arrival on the world scene, the black man has been on this earth since the creation 66 trillion years ago. The white interlopers enslaved the black men, deprived them of their cultural heritage, and imposed an inferior and foreign religion: Christianity. Allah appeared in human form in the person of W. D. Fard and appointed the Hon. Elijah Muhammad to restore the black man to his true place and bring him back to his ancestral religion.

The white man even took away the black man's name and substituted a slave name. Each convert to the Black Muslims gets a new designation. He keeps his proper name and uses X for his surname. If there are more than one with his proper name he becomes 2X or 3X.

Black Muslims must attend Temple services two or more times a week. Everyone is thoroughly searched before admittance to any Temple. Any contraband such as guns, knives, liquor or cigarettes must be checked at the door. Men and women sit in separate sections during the meeting.

At the start of the service the minister gives an Arabic greeting which is returned by the congregation. He may then spend a few minutes in Arabic language instruction. Hopefully all members will learn to read the Koran in its original language.

The main feature of the Temple service is the address by the minister which lasts two hours or more. He recapitulates the teachings of the Hon. Elijah Muhammad. Every half hour the two guards posted at the front of the hall are ceremoniously changed.

Several organizations operate within each of the Temples. The Fruits of Islam is a paramilitary group which drills, maintains order at meetings, guards Elijah Muhammad or other officers. They do not carry weapons but specialize in karate and other methods of offense and self-defense. Women belong to the Moslem Girls' Training and the General Civilization Class.

High point of the year is Saviour's Day on Feb. 26, Fard's birthday anniversary. This holds the same place as Christmas in a Christian church. Black Muslims exchange cards and gifts and attend special services in the Temple.

Orthodox Muslims are divided over whether the Nation of Islam deserves the name Islamic. Elijah Muhammad was allowed to make a pilgrimage to Mecca and many Muslims believe that if the man says he is a Muslim he must be taken at his word. The relatively few American Muslims and the Islamic Center in Washington generally give the Black Muslims a wide berth.

Many of the slogans of the black militants have resounded in Black Muslim Temples for decades. The militants and the Muslims have much in common but the exacting moral standards of the Black Muslims discourage conversions from the ranks of the militants and revolutionaries.

Further Reading

The Muslims
Andrae, Tor, *Mohammed: The Man and His Faith* (London, Allen and Unwin, 1936).
Brockelmann, Carl, *History of the Islamic Peoples* (New York, Putnam, 1947).
Cragg, Kenneth, *The Call of the Minaret* (New York, Oxford University Press, 1964).

The Black Muslims
Essien-Udom, *Black Nationalism* (Chicago, University of Chicago Press, 1962).

Lincoln, C. Eric, *The Black Muslims in America* (Boston, Beacon, 1961).

Lomax, Louis E., *When the Word is Given* (New York, World, 1963).

Chapter XXIV

THE BAHA'IS

The Flavor Is Islamic, the Clothing Western

DOMINATING the Lake Michigan shoreline in suburban Wilmette, Illinois, is one of the most unusual religious structures in the United States. This is the domed, gleaming white Baha'i Temple. It is also the spiritual center for the estimated 25,000 American members of this faith—a tiny fraction of the 2 million Baha'is in 311 countries and territories around the world.

Baha'i stands in about the same relationship to Islam as Mormonism does to traditional Christianity. As the Mormons demand acceptance of Joseph Smith, Jr., as a modern prophet, so the Baha'is revere a pair of nineteenth century Persian prophets as Manifestations of God for this age. The 100 volumes written by one of these prophets—Baha'u'llah—receive the same veneration from Baha'is as does Smith's *Book of Mormon* from the Mormons.

At first glance the Baha'i faith offers a religious platform which might well be endorsed by a Unitarian or liberal Protestant. The Baha'is advocate the fostering of the unfettered search for truth, world concord as the fruit of world religion, abolition of prejudice and superstition, harmonious cooperation between science and religion, the equality of men and women, universal compulsory education, elimination of the extremes of poverty and wealth, adoption of an auxiliary universal language, an international tribunal to settle disputes, and the reduction of armaments and attainment of world peace. The theme of unity dominates Baha'i teaching; the followers of Baha'u'llah seek to erase differences of nationality, race, religion, and social class.

Baha'is do not deny the truth of other religions. A Baha'i author writes: "The Baha'i faith does not deny the older religions; it fulfills them." It is a textbook example of religious syncretism.

Baha'i started as another splinter sect in Islam and although clothed in Western vocabulary for missionary purposes, it retains a distinctively Islamic flavor. Acceptance of the Baha'i faith involves not only endorsement of the foregoing platform but of two Persian prophets and submission to a highly centralized religious authority with headquarters in Haifa.

Baha'i teaches that every few hundred years God "manifests" Himself through a prophet; the first of these prophets was Adam; later manifestations of God were Abraham, Moses, Krishna, Buddha, Zoroaster, Jesus, and Mohammed. Each "manifestation" presented as much divine truth as the people of that era could accept; each is supposed to have revealed the same message which later religious spokesmen have corrupted.

A former head of the Baha'i faith explained its basic belief in these words: "The fundamental principle enunciated by Baha'u'llah, the followers of His Faith firmly believe, is that religious truth is not absolute but relative, that Divine revelation is a continuous and progressive process, that all the great religions of the world are divine in origin, that their basic principles are in complete harmony, that their aims and purposes are one and the same, that their teachings are but facets of one truth, that their functions are complementary, that they differ only in the nonessential aspects of their doctrines, and that their missions represent successive stages in the spiritual evolution of human society." (*The Faith of Baha'u'llah*, by Shoghi Effendi.)

To understand the origin of Baha'ism one must take a look at Islam. Somewhat like Christianity, Islam has suffered schisms and heresies; rival sects within Islam have arisen and presented themselves as the authentic interpretation of the faith. One large group of Moslems broke with the others in believing that the earthly head of Islam had to be a descendant of Mohammed's son-in-law. These descendants were called Imams and eventually one of these Imams would be proclaimed as the Mahdi who would be accepted as the world leader of the faithful. The Mahdi would ascend the throne of Persia, conquer the world, and establish universal justice. Eleven Imams died as martyrs but the twelfth disappeared in the year 873 and is thought by the Shi'ites to be alive somewhere in the world; he is the Hidden Imam and someday he will reveal himself. Those who held to this belief were known as Shi'ites and they form the majority of the people of Iran, once known as Persia.

Within the Shi'ite community in Persia a man by the name of Shaykh Ahmad Al-Ahsa'i founded a new sect. He taught that the Imams were divine beings, that someone on earth is always in direct contact with the Imams, and that there is no bodily resurrection. His disciples were known as Shaykhis. The founder of this sect died in 1826.

In 1844 another Persian, Ali-Muhammed, offered the claim that he alone had access to the Hidden Imam. He took the name "the Bab" which means the Gate and was able to win over most of the members of the Shaykhis sect. He wote the Bayan which presented the prescriptions of the Babi religion.

The Babis propagated their new faith throughout Persia and aroused the wrath of the Moslem authorities and the government. Some of their statements gave the impression that they planned to overthrow the government and set up a theocracy. The Shah banished the Bab to a remote part of the country but violence continued to flare up between Moslems and Babis. Finally on July 9, 1850, the government executed the 30-year-old Bab by firing squad.

The religious system proclaimed by the Bab posed a direct threat to orthodox Islam. The Bab planned to establish a Babi state from which non-Babis would be generally excluded and whose property would be confiscated. He abrogated the traditional Moslem regulations about uncleanness. Babis worshipped three times a day instead of five times as did their Moslem neighbors; they modified other Islamic practices of prayer and fasting. The men shaved their beards and the Babi women discarded their veils. The Babis were forbidden to travel abroad and attempted to destroy all non-Babi books.

Before his death the Bab appointed Mirza Yahya Subh-i-Ezel to succeed him as head of the Babi community. The Bab indicated that the next manifestation would appear between 1511 and 2001 years after his own coming.

Two years after the execution a couple of mentally-unbalanced Babis tried to revenge the act by attempting to assassinate the Shah. The government then launched an organized massacre which eventually took the lives of thousands of Persian Babis including most of the sect's leaders.

The new Babi leader, Mirza Yahya Subh-i-Ezel, who was barely 21, fled to Baghdad and was joined by his older half brother, Mirza Husayn-'Ali. At the request of the Persian government the Turks deported the two brothers to Constantinople and then to Adrianople in 1863.

Here the older brother advanced the claim that he was a new manifestation of God; he called upon his half-brother and the other Babis to acknowledge his leadership. The older brother assumed a new name: Glory of God — Baha'u'llah.

His action precipitated schisms in the disorganized Babi communities but before long he had won most of the remnant of Babis to his cause. The transition of authority from younger to older brother was not without assassinations, libels, and bitter hatreds. But the younger brother gradually saw his support melt away. At least 16 of his followers were murdered by Baha'is. Mirza Yahya Subh-i-Ezel never did capitulate to his brother and a handful of Babis still follow the original Babi religion.

The Turks, wearying of the brothers' feuding, sent the younger brother to Cyprus and Baha'u'llah to Akka in Palestine. In Akka Baha'u'llah fashioned his new religion. Some elements of Babism were retained while others were dismissed as being suitable only for an earlier dispensation. The Bab now holds the role of a sort of John the Baptist to Baha'u'llah in modern Baha'ism.

Baha'u'llah sent letters to the civil and religious leaders of the world announcing his mission and inviting their acceptance of his credentials. These went to Napoleon III, William I, Alexander II, Queen Victoria, Francis Joseph, the sultan of Turkey, the Shah of Iran, and Pius IX. The Pope did not reply.

During 40 years of residence in this Turkish penal colony, Baha'u'llah wrote the books which have become the basic scriptures of Baha'ism. (Other scriptures include the writings of the Bab, Abdul-Baha, and the commentaries by Shoghi Effendi.) Of these the best known is the *Al-Kitab Al-Aqdas,* which was composed around 1875.

Oddly enough the *Aqdas* has not been translated from Arabic into an English translation acceptable to Baha'is. Baha'-u'-llah's son and successor declared in his will that all believers must turn "unto the Most Holy Book (the *Al-Kitab Al Aqdas*) and all that is not expressly recorded therein must be referred to the Universal House of Justice." Yet the English-speaking Baha'is have no authorized version to which to turn.

One explanation for the neglect in translating the *Aqdas* may lie in the embarrassing statements in the Most Holy Book which do not jibe with Westernized Baha'ism. The Most Holy Book clearly teaches polygamy and male superiority; contemporary Baha'is instead proclaim monogamy and the equality of the sexes. Recently the Royal Asiatic Society published a translation of the *Aqdas* from the Arabic by the noted Orientalists Earl E. Elder and William McE. Miller. It is now possible to compare Baha'u'llah's authentic doctrines with those proposed by Western adherents of the cult.

Bah'is acknowledge that Baha'u'llah married three wives who survived his death. Traditional Islam allowed a man to have four wives at any one time in addition to concubines. In the *Aqdas* Baha'u'llah wrote: "God has ordained marriage for you. Beware lest you go beyond two (wives) and whoever is satisfied with one of the handmaidens, his soul is at rest and so is hers, and one does no harm in taking a virgin into his services."

Baha'u'llah insisted that not only the bride and groom but their parents as well agree to the marriage in the interests of harmony. If trouble develops between a husband and wife he advised them to wait a year but then "after a year is completed and love's perfume is not diffused, then there is no harm in divorce." As in Islam a man may divorce his wife but not vice versa.

The *Aqdas* does not prohibit marriage within certain blood

relationships but declares: "The wives of your fathers are unlawful to you."

The crimes of murder and arson may be punished by death or by life imprisonment. Theft may be punished by banishment or prison; if the thief commits a third offense he may be branded.

Baha'is must not shave their heads but are expected to pare their nails and take a complete bath once a week. Every 19 years they are asked to renew the furnishings in their houses. Baha'u'llah told his disciples: "Wash your feet every day in summer, and in winter once every three days."

The founder of Baha'ism laid down specific rules for prayer worship. Though daily prayer is obligatory, the believer has a choice of three prayers. One is short and should be recited at noon; one is medium in length and should be repeated three times a day; the longest prayer need be said only every 24 hours. While praying the Baha'is engage in certain prostrations and postures similar to those of the Moslems.

The Baha'i faith employs no professional clergy. Public worship services consist of reading from the Baha'i scriptures as well as from the Bible, the *Koran*, the *Bhagavad-Gita*, and the sacred books of other world religions. The fast that corresponds to the Islamic Ramadan has been shortened and modified to 19 days each spring; on these days Baha'is abstain from all food and drink from sunrise to sunset.

Baha'is observe nine major feasts during the year: the Feast of Ridvan on April 21, the Declaration of the Bab on May 23, the Ascension of Baha'u'llah on May 29, the martyrdom of the Bab on July 9, the Birth of the Bab on October 20, the birth of Baha'u'llah on November 12, the Day of the Covenant on November 26, the Ascension of Abdul Baha on November 28 and the Feast of the New Year on March 21.

The numbers 9 and 19 hold a special mystical significance to Baha'is. Nine members are needed to form a local assembly, nine Baha'is make up the National Spiritual Assembly, nine members form the Universal House of Justice, Baha'i temples are nine-sided to represent the nine major world religions. Baha'is follow a calendar of 19 months of 19 days and meet for worship every 19 days.

Baha'is must abstain from alcohol and narcotics but are not forbidden to use tobacco. The religion prohibits "slavery, asceticism, mendicancy, and monasticism." The funeral service is simple and consists of readings from Baha'i scriptures; cremation or embalming are forbidden.

This religion denies the reality of evil, the devil, and hell. It affirms the existence of God as revealed by his various "manifestations" and the life of the soul after death. Baha'is believe in the possibility of communication with the spirits but do not encourage communication by means of seances and mediums.

When Baha'u'llah died in 1892 leadership of the sect was claimed by his eldest son, Abdul Baha (Servant of Baha). Another son rejected Abdul Baha's succession and won over almost all of Baha'u'llah's family; his followers were stigmatized as Covenant-breakers by the disciples of Abdul Baha who eventually gained the upper hand.

Abdul Baha was held prisoner for some years but was freed by the Young Turks in 1908. Between 1911 and 1913 he visited Egypt, England, France, Germany, and Austria-Hungary. In 1912 he came to the United States and broke ground for the temple in Wilmette. Unlike the Bab and Baha'u'llah he is not considered a "Manifestation of God." John Ferraby comments in *All Things Made New* that Abdul Baha was "more than a man. He was less than a Divine Manifestation." He is known as "The Mystery of God" to the devout. Abdul Baha lived in Haifa until his death in 1921.

His grandson, Shoghi Effendi, was studying at Oxford University when he assumed leadership of the religion. He had previously studied at a Jesuit school in Haifa and at the university in Beirut. Abdul Baha's relatives disputed the claims of Shoghi Effendi and tried to wrest control of the cult from him, but were defeated.

Shoghi Effendi cut the remaining bonds between Islam and Baha'ism and quit going to the mosque. He married Mary Maxwell, the daughter of a Montreal architect, and served as Guardian of the Faith until his death in 1957. He had no children. He continued to build the world Baha'i headquarters in

Haifa. This center now includes the tombs of the Bab and Abdul Baha on Mount Carmel, the archives, and administrative offices.

After the demise of Shoghi Effendi the affairs of the religion were guided by a group of 27 Baha'is known as the Hands of the Cause. In 1963 delegates of various Baha'i communities elected a nine-member Universal House of Justice. Four of these are Americans.

Most of the world's Baha'is live in Iran and India. The Baha'is claim 200,000 converts in India alone during the past decade.

In the United States Baha'is usually meet in private homes or rented quarters. The first American convert joined the faith in 1894 and by 1895 there were small groups in Chicago and Kenosha, Wis. Though still small in numbers, Baha'is are active missionaries. They sponsor World Religion Day on the third Sunday of January, insert advertisements in newspapers and magazines, donate Baha'i books to public libraries, sponsor study groups on college campuses, and operate summer schools in Maine, California, and Michigan. More than 400 American Baha'is are serving as Pioneers; these are unsalaried missionaries who are planting the Baha'i faith in foreign lands.

Special efforts have been directed at making converts in the South, especially among rural blacks. News reports indicated that some 9,000 such converts joined the Baha'i World Faith after a month-long campaign headquartered at Dillon, S.C., in early 1971.

Each year 100,000 people tour the temple in Wilmette and learn something about this religion from the guides. The first Baha'i temple was built in Russia early in this century. This temple was confiscated by the Soviets and turned into a museum; later it was damaged beyond repair by an earthquake and has been razed. Three other Baha'i temples have been completed in Frankfurt, Germany; Sydney, Australia; and Uganda in Africa. Almost 60 sites for future temples have been acquired. The next temple will be built in Panama.

The Wilmette temple was designed by a French Canadian architect, Louis Bourgeoise. Although Abdul Baha broke ground much earlier, the foundation was not dug until 1921. No work was undertaken for the next ten years and then the Depression and World War II slowed work. The Baha'is do not authorize indebtedness for temple building so they had to follow a pay as you go policy. The 1,200 seat temple cost an estimated $2,-600,000. It was dedicated in 1953 to the three unities: the unity of God, the unity of His prophets, and the unity of mankind. Only geometric designs, symbols of the world religions, quotations from the writings of Baha'u'llah, and Arabic inscriptions are allowed as decoration. Recently the first Baha'i humanitarian institution, a home for the aged, was opened near the temple.

Some well known Baha'i converts have included Queen Marie of Rumania, movie actress Carole Lombard, singer Vic Damone, jazz musician Dizzy Gillespie and painter Mark Tobey. Leo Tolstoy once commented: "The teachings of the Babis which come to us out of Islam have, through Baha'u'llah's teachings, been gradually developed, and now present us with the highest and purest form of religious teaching." The Baha'is refuse to furnish membership statistics to the *Yearbook of American Churches*. Young people may declare their intent to join the Baha'i Faith at the age of 15 but may not vote until they become 21. Children of members are not counted as part of the Baha'i community until they reach 15.

In accord with its basic principles the Baha'i World Faith fully supports the United Nations, the civil rights movement, and efforts to establish some auxiliary language, either an artificial language such as Esperanto or adoption of an existing language.

Baha'is are forbidden to belong to any political party, to vote in a primary election, or to accept any political office by vote of a political party. Shoghi Effendi warned his followers to "shun politics like the plague and be obedient to the government in power in the place where you reside."

Baha'ism has not escaped schism. When Shoghi Effendi died and left no line of succession, Charles Mason Remey, an American who lives in Florence, Italy, proclaimed himself the next Guardian of the Faith. He had been appointed by Shoghi Effendi as president of the Baha'i International Council. Remey and his few followers believe that there must always be a

Guardian of the Faith; this was also taught by the leaders of the faith for many decades. Most Baha'is rejected his claims but he attracted a few followers. Another splinter group is known as the New History Foundation with headquarters in New York City.

The slow growth of the religion in the United States does not seem to discourage Baha'is. They fully expect most of mankind to recognize the Manifestation of God called Baha'u'llah long before the end of the 1,000 years of his era. Devotees get a feeling of spiritual satisfaction in recognizing Baha'u'llah long before the rest of mankind.

Arnold Toynbee made reference to the Baha'i faith in his *A Study of History,* Vol. VII. He observed, "In a Hellenizing World early in the second century of the Christian Era the Christian Church loomed no larger, in the sight of an Hellenically educated dominant minority, than the Baha'is . . . were figuring in the sight of the corresponding class in a Westernizing World midway through the twentieth century."

Despite an attempt at Westernization, the Baha'i faith still smacks of Islamic mysticism and Oriental intrigue. Baha'u'llah's voluminous writings border on the incomprehensible to those who approach them for the first time. Yet the Baha'is have an imposing temple, dedicated devotees, an extensive literature, and a worldwide record of impressive growth. We may expect them to become better known on the American religious scene.

Further Reading

Baha'u'llah, *Al Kitab Al-Aqdas or The Most Holy Book* (London, Royal Asiatic Society, 1961).

Esslement, J. E., *Baha'u'llah and the New Era* (Wilmette, Ill., Baha'i Publishing Committee, 1962).

Richards, J. R., *Baha'ism* (London, S.P.C.K., 1965).

Chapter XXV

THE BUDDHISTS

Buddhism Embraced by 300 Million People but Few Americans

THE RELIGION which dominates the religious life of Asia, except for India, has attracted only about 100,000 followers in the United States. Most of the Buddhists in this country are Japanese-Americans although a few others have accepted Buddhism, especially in the form of Zen Buddhism.

In recent years all Americans have been hearing more about Buddhism because this is the major religion of Vietnam. When Buddhist leaders oppose or support the war or when Buddhist monks burn themselves in the streets the news makes headlines. Yet the Buddhists of Vietnam comprise only a tiny fraction of the estimated 300 million Buddhists. This religion has exerted a profound influence on every Oriental culture.

Buddhism began as a heresy within Hinduism in the fifth century before Christ. Hinduism taught the transmigration of souls; man is reincarnated in a series of lives. Many Hindu sects attempted to instruct devotees on how to escape this chain of incarnations. Originally Buddhism was one of these sects.

Buddhists venerate an Indian sage who showed the path to emancipation. He was known as Siddartha Gautama (born about 560 B.C.) or simply the Buddha which means the Enlightened One. He was born a member of the warrior caste and was apparently shielded from most of the harsher aspects of life as a young man. One legend tells that his father provided him with three palaces and 40,000 dancing girls for his pleasure.

He eventually married and had a son. But the Gautama renounced his family and began a search for the answer to the problem of suffering. His decision may have been brought about by contact for the first time with the facts of sickness, old age, and death. The search lasted five or six years. He tried Yoga and asceticism but these led to no satisfactory answers. One day while sitting under a Bo-tree the true path was revealed to him and he spent the rest of his life spreading this teaching.

Buddha proclaimed "Four Noble Truths." These are that existence involves suffering, suffering is caused by desire, the way to escape suffering and existence is to eliminate desire, and to eliminate desire man should follow the eightfold path. This eightfold path asked that man pursue right views, right intentions, right speech, right action, right livelihood, right effort, right mindfulness, and right concentration.

Essentially Buddhism offers a way by which man can escape suffering. This is accomplished by extinguishing the three main desires: for pleasure, for prosperity, and for continued existence. Buddhism neither affirms nor denies the existence of God but adopts an agnostic position.

This effort to escape suffering may take many lifetimes but finally a man should be able to achieve Nirvana which means the extinction of all desire, hatred, and ignorance. Buddha declared: "One thing only I teach. Sorrow, the cause of sorrow, the cessation of sorrow, and the path which leads to the cessation of sorrow."

Within the Buddhist world there developed two main schools: the Mahayana or Greater Vehicle of China, Japan, Korea and Vietnam and the Hinayana or Lesser Vehicle of Thailand, Burma, Ceylon, Cambodia, India, and Indonesia. In Tibet Buddhism blended with magic and demon worship in a form known as Lamaism. Since the Communist takeover of Tibet the Dalai Lama has lived in India and much of the property of the Tibetan monasteries has been expropriated.

Monasticism plays a part in almost all Buddhist sects. A man who enters a Buddhist monastery shaves his head, wears a yellow or orange robe, gets a new name, and agrees to follow the 220 rules of Buddhist monasticism. The monks beg for a living and carry with them only three robes, a needle, water strainer, begging bowl and razor. They may leave the order when they wish since they take no vows; older men often enter a monastery after raising a family. Buddhism also includes religious orders of nuns.

Japanese founded the first Buddhist church in the United States in 1905; in 1942 the *Buddhist Churches of America* was incorporated. A bishop heads the church which reports 50 ministers and 35 autonomous churches. These congregations hold weekly services and often sponsor Japanese language instruction. Members of the Buddhist Churches of America represent the Jodo Shinshu sect. Most of the adherents are found in California, Utah, Arizona, Washington, Oregon, and Hawaii. There are congregations in San Francisco, Los Angeles, and Tacoma made up of Buddhists who are not of Japanese ancestry. The church operates a home for the aged in Fresno, California.

Zen Buddhism, a monastic form of Buddhism originating in Japan, has attracted both Western intellectuals and hippies. A former Episcopalian minister, Alan Watts, has popularized this form of Buddhism in books and lectures. Many people study Zen more as a philosophy than a religion.

Communist takeovers in China, North Korea, and North Vietnam have hampered Buddhist activities but the displacement of Shinto as the state religion in Japan has given new life to Japanese Buddhism. The militant Buddhist sect known as Soka Gakkai claims 5 million families in Japan; in 1958 it numbered only 3,000 families. It says it wins 100,000 converts a month.

Further Reading

Gard, Richard A., *Buddhism* (New York, Braziller, 1961).
Humphreys, Christmas, *Buddhism* (London, Penguin, 1955).

Church Membership Statistics

Compiled for the *Yearbook of American Churches* for 1970, published by the National Council of Churches of Christ. Only denominations with an inclusive membership of 5,000 or more are listed.

Name of Religious Body	No. of Churches Reported	Inclusive Church Membership
Adventist Bodies:		
Advent Christian Church	405	29,838
Church of God (Abrahamic Faith)	122	6,600
Seventh-day Adventist Church	3,202	396,097
African Orthodox Church	24	6,000
American Rescue Workers	46	5,650
Apostolic Christian Churches of America	75	8,955
Apostolic Overcoming Holy Church of God	300	75,000
Armenian Apostolic Church of America	33	125,000
Armenian Church of of North America	59	300,000
Assemblies of God	8,570	626,660
Baptist Bodies:		
American Baptist Association	3,274	782,902
American Baptist Convention	5,968	1,454,965
Baptist General Conference	591	100,000
Baptist Missionary Association of America	1,550	200,000
Conservative Baptist Association of America	1,143	300,000
Duck River (and Kindred) Association of Baptists	81	8,492
Free Will Baptists	2,142	184,869
General Association of Regular Baptist Churches	1,100	154,767
General Baptists	834	65,000

National Baptist Convention of America	11,398	2,668,799
National Baptist Convention, U.S.A., Inc.	26,000	5,500,000
National Baptist Evangelical Life and Soul Saving Assembly of U.S.A.	264	57,674
National Primitive Baptist Convention	2,196	1,465,000
North American Baptist Association	1,450	174,000
North American Baptist General Conference	339	55,100
Primitive Baptists	1,000	72,000
Progressive National Baptists Convention	655	521,692
Separate Baptists in Christ	84	7,496
Seventh Day Baptist General Conference	65	5,623
Southern Baptist Convention	34,275	11,330,481
United Baptists	586	63,641
United Free Will Baptist Church	836	100,000
Bible Way Churches of Our Lord Jesus Christ World Wide, Inc.	347	26,010
Brethren:		
Brethren Church (Ashland, Ohio)	119	17,329
Brethren Churches, National Fellowship of	227	31,727
Church of the Brethren	1,054	187,957
Brethren in Christ (River Brethren)	156	8,806
Buddhist Churches of America	59	100,000
Christadelphians	850	15,800
Christian and Missionary Alliance	1,128	119,826
Christian Church (Disciples of Christ)	5,862	1,592,609
Christian Church of North America	108	8,000
Christian Congregation	257	45,995
Christian Union	130	5,821
Church of Christ (Holiness), U.S.A.	159	9,289
Church of Christ, Scientist	No statistics furnished	

Churches of God:

Church of God (Cleveland, Tenn.)	3,834	243,532
Church of God (Anderson, Ind.)	2,265	146,807
The (Original) Church of God, Inc.	75	18,000
The Church of God	1,925	74,171
The Church of God (Seventh Day), Denver, Colo.	56	5,500
Church of God by Faith	105	5,300
The Church of God of Prophecy	1,531	48,708
Churches of God in N.A. (General Eldership)	352	36,042
Church of God and Saints in Christ	217	38,127
Church of God in Christ	4,100	413,000
Church of Illumination	14	9,000
Church of Our Lord Jesus Christ of the Apostolic Faith, Inc.	155	45,000
Church of the Nazarene	4,674	364,789
Churches of Christ	18,000	2,400,000
Churches of Christ in Christian Union	242	7,930
Churches of God, Holiness	32	25,600
Church of the Living God	276	45,320
Congregational Christian Churches, National Association of	302	110,000
Conservative Congregational Christian Conference	92	15,127

Eastern Orthodox Churches:

Albanian Orthodox Archdiocese in America	12	17,000
American Carpatho-Russian Orthodox Greek Catholic Church	67	104,500
Antiochian Orthodox Archdiocese of Toledo	21	30,400
Antiochian Orthodox Christian Archdiocese of New York and All North America	84	100,000
Bulgarian Eastern Orthodox Church	23	86,000

Greek Orthodox Archdiocese of North and South America	470	1,875,000
Roumanian Orthodox Episcopate of America	44	50,000
Russian Orthodox Catholic Church in America, Patriarchal Exarchate	67	152,973
Russian Orthodox Church Outside Russia	81	55,000
Russian Orthodox Greek Catholic Church of America	300	1,000,000
Serbian Eastern Orthodox Church	52	65,000
Ukranian Orthodox Church of America, Ecumenical Patriarchal Exarchate	25	40,000
Ukranian Orthodox Church in America	107	87,475
Ethical Culture Movement	30	6,000
Evangelical Congregational Church	159	29,239
Evangelical Covenant Church of America	514	66,021
Evangelical Free Church of America	539	59,041
Free Christian Zion Church of Christ	742	22,260
Friends:		
Friends United Meeting	514	69,494
Ohio Yearly Meeting of Friends	88	7,429
Religious Society of Friends (General Conference)	315	31,461
Religious Society of Friends (Kansas Yearly Meeting)	89	8,227
Independent Fundamental Churches of America	921	121,485
Jehovah's Witnesses	5,341	333,672
Jewish Congregations	4,700	5,780,000
Latter-day Saints (Mormons):		
Church of Jesus Christ of Latter-day Saints	4,519	2,180,064
Reorganized Church of Jesus Christ of Latter Day Saints	1,016	149,708

Lutheran Bodies:

American Lutheran Church	4,880	2,576,105
Apostolic Lutheran Church of America	58	6,994
Church of the Lutheran Brethren of America	82	7,968
Evangelical Lutheran Synod	85	15,787
Lutheran Church in America	5,852	3,279,517
Lutheran Church–Missouri Synod	5,733	2,781,892
Synod of Evangelical Lutheran Churches	65	21,656
Wisconsin Evangelical Lutheran Synod	859	358,466

Mennonite Bodies:

General Conference Mennonite Church	181	36,337
Mennonite Brethren Churches	81	13,171
Mennonite Church	1,023	85,682
Old Order Amish Mennonite Church	280	22,000
Old Order (Wisler) Mennonite Church	35	5,421

Methodist Bodies:

African Methodist Episcopal Church	5,878	1,166,301
African Methodist Episcopal Zion Church	4,500	870,421
African Union First Colored Methodist Protestant Church, Inc.	40	10,500
Christian Methodist Episcopal Church	2,598	466,718
Congregational Methodist Church	223	14,274
Congregational Methodist Church of U.S.A.	100	7,500
Evangelical Methodist Church	150	9,311
Free Methodist Church of N.A.	1,126	63,611
Primitive Methodist Church, U.S.A.	86	11,945
Reformed Methodist Union Episcopal Church	33	11,000

Reformed Zion Union Apostolic Church	50	16,000
Union American Methodist Episcopal Church	256	27,560
United Methodist Church	41,901	10,990,720
Wesleyan Church	2,559	82,358

Moravian Bodies:

Moravian Church in America (Northern Province)	110	37,505
Moravian Church in America (Southern Province)	49	22,333
Unity of the Brethren	32	6,142
National David Spiritual Temple of Christ Church Union (Inc.) U.S.A.	66	40,815
New Apostolic Church of North America	189	20,913

Old Catholic Churches:

Christ Catholic Church of America and Europe	16	5,513
North American Old Roman Catholic Church	120	59,389
Open Bible Standard Churches, Inc.	260	27,000

Pentecostal Bodies:

Calvary Pentecostal Church, Inc.	22	8,000
International Pentecostal Assemblies	60	7,500
Pentecostal Assemblies of the World, Inc.	550	45,000
Pentecostal Church of God of America, Inc.	975	115,000
Pentecostal Free Will Baptist Church, Inc.	176	10,000
Pentecostal Holiness Church, Inc.	1,355	66,790
United Pentecostal Church, Inc.	2,500	225,000
Plymouth Brethren	665	33,250
Polish National Catholic Church	162	282,411

Presbyterian Bodies:

Associate Reformed Presbyterian Church	144	28,312
Cumberland Presbyterian Church	936	88,540
Evangelical Presbyterian Church	69	6,769
Orthodox Presbyterian Church	130	14,038
Presbyterian Church in the U.S.	3,960	961,767
Reformed Presbyterian Church	115	14,927
Reformed Presbyterian Church of N.A.	73	6,185
Second Cumberland Presbyterian Church	121	30,000
United Presbyterian Church in the U.S.A.	8,716	3,373,890
Protestant Episcopal Church	7,137	3,222,663

Reformed Bodies:

Christian Reformed Church	648	281,573
Hungarian Reformed Church in America	27	12,000
Reformed Church in America	939	383,166
Reformed Episcopal Church	75	7,085
Roman Catholic Church	23,781	47,873,228
Salvation Army	1,230	329,515
Spiritualists, International General Assembly	209	164,072
Triumph the Church and Kingdom of God in Christ	430	48,500
Unitarian Universalist Association	1,135	282,307
United Brethren in Christ	300	24,061
United Church of Christ	6,866	2,032,648
United Holy Church of America, Inc.	470	28,980
Volunteers of America	219	32,760

General Bibliography

Algermissen, Konrad, *Christian Denominations* (St. Louis, B. Herder, 1953).

————, *Christian Sects* (New York, Hawthorn, 1962).

Attwater, Donald, *The Christian Churches of the East*, 2 vols, rev. eds. (Milwaukee, Bruce, 1961, 1962).

Bouyer, Louis, *The Spirit and Forms of Protestantism* (Westminster, Md., Newman, 1956).

Braden, Charles S., *These Also Believe* (New York, Macmillan, 1953).

Brown, Robert McAfee, *The Spirit of Protestantism* (New York, Oxford University Press, 1961).

Campbell, Robert, *Spectrum of Protestant Beliefs* (Milwaukee, Bruce, 1968).

Clark, Elmer, *The Small Sects in America* (Nashville, Abingdon, 1949).

Daniel-Rops, H., *Our Brothers in Christ* (New York, E.P. Dutton, 1967).

Davies, Horton, *The Challenge of the Sects* (Philadelphia, Westminster, 1961).

Dirks, Lee E., *Religion in Action* (Silver Spring, Md., National Observer, 1965).

Dustan, J. Leslie, *Protestantism* (New York, Washington Square Press, 1962).

Ferm, Vergilius, *The American Church of the Protestant Heritage* (New York, Philosophical Library, 1953).

Gaustad, Edwin Scott, *Historical Atlas of Religion in America* (New York, Harper & Row, 1962).

————, *A Religious History of America* (New York, Harper & Row, 1964).

Hardon, John, *The Protestant Churches of America* (Westminster, Md., Newman, 1956).

————, *Christianity in Conflict* (Westminster, Md., Newman, 1959).

————, *Religions of the World* (Westminster, Md., Newman, 1963).

Hoekema, Anthony, *The Four Major Cults* (Grand Rapids, Mich. Eerdmans, 1963).

Janin, Raymond, *The Separated Eastern Churches* (St. Louis, B. Herder, 1933).

Landis, Benson Y., *Religion in the United States* (New York, Barnes and Noble, 1965).

Littell, Franklin Hamlin, *From State Church to Pluralism* (Garden City, N.Y., Doubleday, 1962).

Martin, Walter R., *The Kingdom of the Cults* (Grand Rapids, Mich., Zondervan, 1965).

Mayer, F.E., *The Religious Bodies of America* (St. Louis, Concordia, 1954).

Mead, Frank, *Handbook of Denominations in the United States,* 5th ed. (New York and Nashville, Abingdon-Cokesbury, 1970).

Neve, J.L., *Churches and Sects of Christendom* (Blair, Nebr., Lutheran Publishing House, 1952).

O'Brien, Thomas C., ed., *Corpus Dictionary of Western Churches* (Washington, D.C., Corpus Books, 1970).

Rosten, Leo, *A Guide to the Religions of America,* rev. ed. (New York, Simon & Schuster, 1963).

Spence, Hartzell, *The Story of America's Religions* (Nashville, Abingdon-Apex Books, 1962).

Sperry, Willard L., *Religion in America* (Boston, Beacon, 1963).

Tavard, George, *Protestantism* (New York, Hawthorn, 1959).

Van Baalen, Jan Karel, *The Chaos of Cults* (Grand Rapids, Mich., Eerdmans, 1962).

Van de Pol, W.H., *World Protestantism* (New York, Herder and Herder, 1964).

Weigel, Gustave, *Churches in North America* (Baltimore, Helicon, 1961).

Whalen, William J., *Minority Religions in America* (Staten Island, N.Y., Alba House, 1972).

Williams, J. Paul, *What Americans Believe and How They Worship* (New York, Harper, 1962).

Yearbook of American Churches (New York, National Council of the Churches of Christ in the U.S.A., published anually).

INDEX

Other Books from Our Sunday Visitor, Inc.

THE CATHOLIC RELIGION

By Most Reverend Bernard Stewart, Bishop of Sandhurst, Australia. 67 pages, *paper $1.25*.

An outline of Catholic doctrine from statements made by Pope Paul VI and by Vatican Council II concerning fundamental truths of the Catholic religion.

CATHOLIC ALMANAC

Compiled and written under the editorial supervision of Father Felician A. Foy, O.F.M., 704 pages, *paper $3.95, cloth $7.50*. Revised and updated annually.

The most complete one-volume encyclopedia of Catholic facts and information. It contains accurate facts and statistics on every aspect of Catholicism, easy to find authoritative information and comprehensive up to date articles. A must reference book.

PASTORAL LETTERS OF THE AMERICAN HIERARCHY, 1792-1970

Edited by Father Hugh J. Nolan, Ph.D. 785 pages, *cloth $15.00*.

"This is an indispensable source for any future history of the Church in the United States or of the American Hierarchy."—John Cardinal Krol, Archbishop of Philadelphia, Pennsylvania. The ultimate addition to any clerical or professional library. This volume encompasses over two centuries of American history and the prominent role played by the Catholic Church.

THE FAMILY OF NATIONS

Edited by Father James S. Rausch, 144 pages, *paper $1.25*.

A book dedicated to those whose lives are committed to building structures for peace. Eight distinguished scholars and government leaders representing a broad range of opinion in the United States address themselves to the burning issues of war and peace in our times. Authors include John Tracy Ellis, Hubert H. Humphrey, Arthur J. Goldberg, and Robert McAfee Brown.

JOURNEY INTO THE VOID

By Donam Hahn Wakefield, Ph.D. 64 pages, *paper $1.25*.

Compares the main tenets of Buddhism with those of Christianity and points out the similarities and differences. Discusses Buddha and Christ, the 'I' of Buddha, his teachings, varieties of Buddhism, particularly Zen.

ST. PAUL AND THE AMERICAN BILL OF RIGHTS

By Edwin E. Willis, 64 pages, *paper $1.00*.

A prominent legal scholar here argues that the founding fathers of this nation, learned in moral and religious philosophy and the Bible, were influenced by the writings of St. Paul, "the apostle of liberty," in framing the "Bill of Rights" for which they fought.

If your bookseller does not have these titles, you may order them by sending listed price (we pay postage and handling) to the Book Department at the address below. Enclose check or money order —do not send cash.

Write for free book list.

Our Sunday Visitor, Inc. / Noll Plaza / Huntington, Indiana 46750